WREDE
on
WRITING

Tips, Hints, and Opinions on Writing

PATRICIA C. WREDE

DIVERSIONBOOKS

Diversion Books
A Division of Diversion Publishing Corp.
443 Park Avenue South, Suite 1004
New York, New York 10016
www.DiversionBooks.com

For more information, email info@diversionbooks.com

First Diversion Books edition December 2013.

Print ISBN: 978-1-62681-222-2
eBook ISBN: 978-1-62681-221-5

CONTENTS

GETTING STARTED

What writers need to know before they start writing: questions of story creation (where do you get your ideas?), story development (getting an idea ready to start writing), and process (how the heck do I do this?!).

How to Be a Writer

Write.

No, really, that's it. It's kind of a definitional thing. In order to be a writer, you have to be someone who writes. Period. You don't have to follow a bunch of rules; you don't have to be educated; you don't have to be nice; you don't even have to be particularly professional in your attitudes (though if you aren't, you can expect to have a much harder time selling your stuff to an editor). You certainly don't have to be worthy. All you have to do is write.

On the flip side, if you aren't writing, you aren't a writer. Talking about writing is not writing. Reading how-to-write books is not writing. Research is not writing. Telling stories is not writing. Writers write. That's the definition.

Writers write. Which is plenty enough, believe me.

So You Want to Write a Book

It being the new year—and the first year of a new decade—I went poking around the web and noticed a bunch of websites for people's New Year's Resolutions. A little further investigation revealed that "write a book" is, in some form or another, on an awful lot of people's lists (it was one of the twenty most popular goals on one website I found).

Speaking as someone for whom "write a book" is more a necessity than anything else, I have to wonder whether any of those people really know what they're getting into. In my experience, most people don't actually want to *write* a book; what they want is to *have written* a book (preferably without spending much in the way of time or effort). Even the ones who really do want to write a book are probably underestimating just how long it's going to take and how sick of it they're going to get before they finish.

Be that as it may, a lot of folks are apparently going to take a crack at writing a book this year. I have not been asked for my advice on this, but I'm going to give it anyway. (What can I say? It's what I do.)

The first piece of advice is: Take each and every piece of writing advice you get with a large boulder of salt. This is especially true of those things that "everybody knows" you have to do to write, write well, get published, or be successful in whatever way you define it.

Because most writing advice isn't true for everyone, and a lot of it is extremely likely to be untrue for you.

For instance, the first thing nearly everybody looks for when they want to sit down and write a book is an idea. OK, yes, you do need an idea or two at some point in the process, and this is not an unreasonable place to begin. But not every writer starts with an idea, except in the broadest sense. Some start with a place they want to write about, or a character, or a story they want to tell, or a theme, or even a purpose like "I want to write a book that will inspire people!" Other people start by methodically trying to acquire the skills they are going to need in order to write—they take typing or creative writing classes, keep a practice journal, or read mountains of how-to-write books.

All these things work—for somebody. All these things also don't work—for other somebodies. The real trick is to figure out what works for you.

And while a certain amount of thought and introspection up front seems to help, ultimately the only way to find what works for you is to try out a bunch of different things and see what happens. It does make sense to start by trying the more commonly useful methods first, like outlining or keeping an ideas journal or doing daily practice writing.

Some things will work for you from the get-go. Some things will work for a while then stop, and when they do, it's OK to abandon them. (I kept an ideas file for about fifteen years, full of notes, brief descriptions, pictures or poetry that make my backbrain go *ping*, and a bunch of other stuff. I quit keeping it when I realized I hadn't looked at it for over five years.) Some things will work for you, but not the way you think they're supposed to. (I always outline. Always. And then I don't follow the outline. Always. I have to have it in order to see where I'm not going. Or something.) Some things won't work at all. (I've tried doing practice writing, and I just can't stick to it. My "practice writing" is my actual pages for the day.)

The most important thing, though, is to figure out how you write—whether you're a page-a-day-at-nine-a.m. slogger or a burst writer who can crank out ten thousand words in one marathon session at the computer but then has to sit around doing nothing for a week or two in order to recharge. Or there's the sort who sort of graze constantly, producing a paragraph here and a sentence there all through the day or week, feeling as if you aren't getting anything done until you get to Friday and notice that you have written an entire chapter when you "weren't working."

Where Do You Get Your Ideas

The single most common question people ask writers—especially science fiction/fantasy writers—is "Where do you get your ideas?" The assumption always seems to be that ideas are hard to come by.

But it's not really coming up with ideas that is hard. For instance, anyone can sit down and come up with a grocery list. The trouble is that "broccoli, milk, hamburger buns, toilet paper" is not normally perceived as story material. But as soon as you ditch that perception and start looking at the possibilities, it changes. So a normal grocery list doesn't seem much like story material. What sort of list could be story material? "Broccoli, vardun swela, skim milk, flies-in-amber, eggs." OK—what's vardun swela? Why are flies-in-amber on the list—is that some new weird food, or does it really mean amber with flies in it? Who (or what) is eating that amber and vardun-whatever-it-is: Is it company (long-term house guests, or dinner party?), or does this person have a housemate/significant other/family member/pet who isn't human, or is the list-writer the one who's not human and it's the company/SO/pet who needs the "special" (normal) food? How did the list-writer get into whatever situation requires buying this odd mix of foods? How important is it? Is he going to have a hard time finding vardun swela, or is it carried everywhere now? Is it an expensive import or the equivalent of cat food? Why does she want it? Who did this list, anyway?

And the next thing you know, you've got a story about a college boy at Roswell University whose dorm room is haunted by the ghost of an alien that won't leave until it gets a proper meal, or a harried woman planning her first dinner party with her daughter's prospective in-laws, who happen to be elves, or a future diplomat engaged in touchy negotiations with some aliens, who is trying to get his stomach used to their food (which tastes and smells like rotten eggs) before the big banquet tomorrow night, or whatever else strikes your fancy. From contemplating a grocery list.

The trick is teaching yourself to look at everyday things this way (it doesn't come naturally to everyone, not even to all writers). Creative brainstorming is one way of training it, and it's the most fun if you get a group together, though you can do it alone. You can pick a topic, or you can simply open a dictionary and pick two random words, or you can just have everyone in the room write down a one-sentence character description, a one-sentence description of an object, and an action on separate pieces of paper. Mix the words or sentences or topics in a bowl and draw two or three; then set a timer for ten minutes and begin writing a list of ideas and associations and possible plots.

What you're trying to do here is stir things up. If you focus too hard on "getting an idea," you probably won't come up with anything—like those times when somebody says "Where shall we go for dinner?" and you suddenly cannot for the life of you think of the name of a single restaurant, not even McDonald's. If you just look slantwise at normal, everyday things, it becomes a habit after a while, and pretty soon you have more ideas than you know what to do with.

Anything can be the start of a story if you look at it right—but you have to be looking at it, not at "I want a story."

Default Values

Nearly every writer has what I call a "default setting" for most of the basic pieces of writing. They tend, for instance, to automatically write in first- or third-person, or from multiple viewpoints. When they're thinking up stories or developing ideas, they gravitate toward the action/adventure plot, or toward one focusing on relationships, or toward something more character-centered where the main point is someone learning a lesson. They are inclined toward the same kinds of characters, settings, or genres.

Which is not necessarily a bad thing. Every writer has strengths and weaknesses, and there's a lot to be said for playing to your strengths.

After a while, though, doing the same thing over and over can get boring. Also, once you've polished those particular aspects of your writing to a high gleam, it can be more difficult to improve the things you aren't as good at doing, because you never give yourself the chance to practice them. So when you finally do try them out, your skill levels are so far behind your strengths that they make everything new you try look terrible compared to whatever you're used to doing.

Which is why I'm a big fan of knowing what your defaults

are. If you know them, you can change your automatic choices, consciously and deliberately. This means that if you don't like writing exercises (which I mostly don't), you can learn how to do new things while you're also writing pay copy. (This doesn't work for everyone; some people learn better and faster from exercises. They should use them. This is a big part of figuring out your process and your defaults—figuring out whether you get the most out of learning specific pieces and then putting them together later, or from just jumping into the deep end and trying to not drown.)

Career writers are constantly torn between playing to their strengths (which often means writing the same kind of story over and over) and developing their weak points so as to have a broader range of possibilities available. Different writers make different choices about how to deal with this. Some are perfectly happy to never stretch too far beyond their current basic strengths, and sometimes that works really well for them, especially if they've developed a large fan base that is perfectly happy to have the same thing over and over. Others start off that way, polishing their strong points for their first few books, and only then begin pushing themselves. Still others begin pushing all their limits as hard as possible right from the get-go, striving to get their skills up to some arbitrary level before they allow themselves to relax, and others only push in one area at a time.

Me, I'm a slogger, and I don't mean just the day-to-day grind. I don't normally tend to push every one of my limits to the absolute max all at once, but I do try to stretch in a new direction with every book.

My first novel defaulted to an awkward (in retrospect) multiple-viewpoint /omniscient format; for my second, I deliberately chose to write single viewpoint, tight third-person. My current default values are for plot-centered, tight third-person, single-viewpoint, stand-alone stories that take place over a relatively limited time period, usually a few days to a couple of months. So my most recent books were a character-centered, first-person, memoir-style trilogy that takes place over the course of years—thirteen years for book one, two more years for book two, and two to three years for book three.

That's an unusually large number of defaults for me to upset all at once, but the main default that I'm currently upsetting is my habit of only making one stretchy writing-technique change per book. I don't recommend swapping absolutely everything around the first time you decide to shake things up, unless you already know that you need to do that kind of thing. But for me, it was time for a major shake-up, and while I deliberately switched a lot of my defaults, not all of them were terribly stretchy, one at a time. I've done first-person before, in a couple of different flavors (letters, over-the-shoulder narrative), and I've written things that were longer and more character-focused. It's certainly been stretchy trying them all at once, which was part of the idea (the other part being that once I got the story idea for the trilogy, particularly the narrator's voice, I wouldn't have been happy telling it any other way.)

The Jigsaw Puzzle Analogy

I keep running across people who think that there is One Right Way to write a story and who tie themselves in knots trying to force themselves to write "the right way" when it doesn't suit their particular mental processes. Somewhere, somehow, they've gotten convinced (usually because some authority figure like an editor or author or teacher told them) that the only way to come up with a really good book or short story is to do X.

Usually, X is something like "start with your characters," or "do a scene-by-scene plot outline before you do anything else," or "lay out the entire background in grim detail before you even start thinking about plot or characters," but it can be just about anything so long as the author is convinced that it's necessary to do whatever-it-is in order to produce a "good book."

The effect can be an awful lot like tying both hands behind your back and then trying to swim the English Channel, especially if the particular X happens to be contrary to the author's way of working. Even if X is something that works for a particular writer most of the time, it can cause problems if the writer is suddenly faced with a story that needs some other process, because when people think that they must work in a particular way, they're likely to find themselves in a mental straightjacket that can be very difficult to get out of.

Writing a story is like putting a jigsaw puzzle together. Some people start by doing all the edges. Some people look for easy bits and pieces throughout. One of my sisters used to drive everybody else in the family crazy because she'd start at one edge of the puzzle and work her way methodically across to the other edge, and nobody does a jigsaw puzzle like that!

But it doesn't matter what order you put the pieces of a jigsaw puzzle together in. What matters is that they are all in the right places when you are finished. And it doesn't matter whether you start at the end of the story or the beginning, with the plot or the characters or the setting, whether you skip around and write scenes out of order or whether you begin at the beginning and work straight through to the end.

What matters is that when you are finished, you have a good story, however you managed to get there.

Cinderella at the Rock Concert

Writing a short story is not the same as writing a novel. Oh, you need similar skills—knowing how to write dialogue, for instance—but there are fundamental differences that blindside an awful lot of writers who think that because they've learned how to write one, writing the other will just be more of the same.

Basically, short stories require a tight focus and a single, central plot thread; in a novel, there is more room for digression and development of more than one thing. The same basic idea can often be developed as a short story by keeping the plot/ focus tight or as a novel by letting it hang loose.

Starting with a simple idea—"I'll do Cinderella set at a rock concert!"—a short story writer might lay out one scene to establish Cindy, her rotten roommates, and the coming concert;

another showing Cindy's godmother arriving with tickets; the concert scene itself; and, of course, the stunning conclusion when the rock star shows up at the dorm to ask Cindy out. Four scenes, four to five major characters, fairly straightforward progression from setup through finish. Tight focus on Cindy and her starstruck eagerness to go to the concert and the happy ending. Most of the plot-work is already done; it's the specific details that have to be worked out—the lightly sketched-in personalities of the roommates, the encounter with the rock star at the concert when the power cable goes out and Cindy is in the right place (and has the right knowledge) to help fix the problem, just how to work in that lost sneaker, and so on.

A novelist, with the same idea, elaborates on just about every piece. "OK, I need to start with Cindy and her rotten roommates...why are they rotten? Why don't they like her? I know! I'll give one of the roommates a jealous boyfriend...and I can do a whole mix-up where she dislikes Cindy because she thinks Cindy is trying to steal the boyfriend, when Cindy is just trying to convince him that he has no reason to be jealous. And I'll make the other roommate be into drugs...yeah, and so is one of the band members! Hey, I can put an undercover cop in with the roadies; that'll give me an excuse to show how you set up for a rock concert. And the real pusher can be the assistant science professor, who's supplementing his salary by mixing stuff in the science lab, and Cindy finds out when she and her godmother raid the lab for the mice on the night of the concert, only the cop thinks it's really Cindy, so she has to hide from him and the pusher, and that's why the rock star can't find her. And the jealous boyfriend and the other roommate can help the rock star uncover clues in order to make up for causing Cindy so much trouble..."

Characters and subplots and complications proliferate quickly, and they just won't all fit into five or ten thousand words, not if they're done right. And the minute the writer actually starts in on the first scene, the senior down the hall shows up, bringing in even more possibilities, and of course there's the suspicious science professor, who was the one who called in the cops in the first place (though of course she didn't know it was her assistant who was making the drugs—she thought it was a student…maybe she can end up paired off with the undercover roadie cop…), and Cindy's slightly dotty godmother, who breezes through on her way to Jamaica, and…

The focus in the novel is still on Cindy and her romance and/or development from shy, put-upon roommate to rock-star date, but all of the characters are more complex. Each character still feeds directly into the main plot thread—Cindy going to the rock concert unexpectedly, meeting the star, and disappearing so he has to hunt for her—but they each have their own more developed sub-story. It's not just a matter of padding or adding subplots—if you added the subplot about the druggie roomie and the pusher science assistant as an afterthought, you'd probably already have some other reason why Cindy disappeared after the rock concert, and the subplot would just be a sort of overlay instead of integral to the main story.

Because the author needs to get the subplots in and to follow each of them until it feeds into the main plot thread, the progress in the novel isn't nearly as straightforward as the four-to-five-scene short story version. In the novel, the roommate's boyfriend has to be established, and so does the other roommate's odd behavior, and Cindy's shyness, so that when the roomies conspire to keep Cindy from finding out that the concert is almost sold out (so that she won't rush out and get tickets until it's too late), the reader has some idea why they did it. The lab and the science assistant have to be established so that later on they can be revealed as the source of the drugs.

It's also, obviously, not a matter of stringing together a series of related short stories to get a novel. The structure is all wrong. A novel builds to a single big climax/finish; a string of short stories has multiple small finishes, one for each story. You can do a certain amount to fix this by providing some overarching problem to be solved and setting the stories up as stopping points along the way ("He looked for his son *here*, and solved this little problem, and then he went *there* to look for his son, and solved this other problem, and then he went…"), but it never seems to work quite as well.

Also, more stuff nearly always comes up as the book goes along. You make up some trivial detail in chapter one—that the roomie's favorite CD is an expensive collector's item, for instance—and it turns out to be a really important clue in chapter thirteen, which suddenly makes the whole plot go in a new direction (it's not drugs, after all; it's an international money laundering scheme, and Cindy's godmother from Jamaica is really a topflight investigator who's using Cindy to get to the rock concert because she thinks somebody there is involved, and now it's the rock star who's the main suspect...). Short stories are less prone to such major diversions because they're, well, short. Nor does a string of concatenated short stories give you room for such diversions because they each started out as complete in and of themselves.

The main problem I've seen people run into when they switch from writing short stuff to writing long stuff is the tendency to try to have everything clear in their heads before they start writing. You can do that with a short story, but almost nobody's brain is large enough to hold a whole novel in that much detail. Short stories are like driving two blocks to the cleaner's—you can see the whole two-block trip from your driveway before you start. Novels are like driving from Chicago to Denver—you can't see the whole trip's worth of road, but as long as you have a map, all you need to see is the next stretch of road that you're going to drive. And it's a lot more likely that you'll encounter unexpected road work and have to change routes between Chicago and Denver than it is on the two blocks to the cleaner's.

The Big Three

Years ago, when I was an unpublished wannabe, I was at a local science fiction convention trying to learn the True Secret of Writing from the professional writers in attendance. One of them (I think it may have been Gordy Dickson) threw out a piece of advice that has stood me in good stead for all the years and books since.

The advice was this: There are three things that any scene in a book or short story can do: (1) It can advance the plot, (2) It can explain the background or backstory, or (3) It can deepen the characterization. If a scene does none of these things, it isn't actually a scene and doesn't belong in this particular book. If it does only one of these things, the writer can probably improve it by figuring out how it can do another as well. (That is, if the scene only deepens the characterization, figuring out how it can also add backstory or advance the plot will likely make it a better scene). If the scene does two of the three things, then it is a good solid scene—still susceptible to improvement, but a keeper nonetheless. And a scene that does all three things is the gold at the end of the rainbow.

It's not hard to see why. What is a story? It's something happening (plot) to one or more people (characters) somewhere/ somewhen (background/setting/backstory).

Plot, characters, and background are the Big Three when it comes to writing. Different kinds of writing tilt in different directions—adventure fiction is usually heavy on plot and maybe background/setting, but often light on characterization; genre romance novels usually put characterization first, with plot and background trailing along behind—but characters, background, and plot are nearly always there in some form because they are the basic building blocks of stories.

Before the Beginning

Probably the most frequent question writers get is, "Where do you get your ideas?" Very few people ever ask, "What do you do with your ideas once you have them?"—though that seems to me to be the logical next step. It seems a good many people don't realize that there is a lot of development work to be done in between having an idea and actually writing a story.

A story idea can be anything—a scrap of dialogue, a scene,

a setting, a situation, a character or two, a plot—that the writer finds intriguing and wants to follow up. Step one is usually writing the idea down somewhere, which is why so many writing books advocate keeping a writing journal or an idea file. Step two is developing the idea, which means figuring out what all the missing components are.

And there's always something missing. Scraps of dialogue usually (but not always) come with characters attached, but often have no plot (or only hints of one) or setting. Settings and situations usually don't come with characters, and even a plot may only arrive with stick-figure sketches of people where the actual characters ought to be.

These things don't just magically show up when you sit down to write (well, unless you're one of the writers whose process involves surprising themselves, but if you are, you've probably figured that out already). For the rest of us, those missing bits have to be developed before the story is ready to write.

As with every aspect of writing, there are lots of different ways to go about this, from making formal outlines and summaries to taking long walks in the woods or using action figures to model bits of storyline. But if you step back a pace or two, there are two fundamental ways that story ideas develop: (1) From the inside out, and (2) From the outside in.

For writers who work from the inside out, the starting idea is like a seed. It needs to be planted and watered and allowed to grow before it's ready to make into a story. Again, this manifests in different ways, but the one thing that story-seed can't be is ignored.

Pondering and paying attention are the equivalent of feeding and watering and weeding. Idea-seeds are incomplete, but they usually contain a lot of hints and clues that can be developed. One method is to think about the general things that are missing—does this idea need plot, or does it need more characters? Another method is to be more specific about what one ponders: drawing up the main character's family tree, or working out the sequence of events that got the characters into this mess, or inventing the greeting customs of each of the cultures one has. The growth isn't necessarily straightforward, but it doesn't have to be. It just needs to grow enough for the writer to start writing (which is a different amount for every writer, and sometimes for every book).

For writers who work from the outside in, the starting idea is more like one of those seed-crystals they used to demonstrate crystal formation in my high school chemistry class—the one where you make a super-saturated solution of something like salt or sugar or alum and then lower one tiny grain of whatever-it-is into the goo, and a week later you come back and there's a perfectly faceted crystal the size of a golf ball that's grown from the stuff in the solution layering itself onto the outside of the seed crystal.

When a story idea grows this way, the writer looks around for other scraps and ideas and bits that fit the existing seed-crystal. Instead of looking at the setting and thinking, "What kind of people live here?", the writer looks at people and characters (in real life or other fiction) and thinks, "Would somebody like this work in that setting?" It's like holding auditions for a play; there are far more real and imaginary people than you need to have as characters in a book, so even if you reject the first ten or twenty, sooner or later the right one will come along and you have your lead. Instead of looking at a character-seed-crystal and thinking, "Where does this person live? Who are her friends? What does she want?", the writer thinks, "Would she live in this house? Would she befriend that person? Is this thing something she wants?"

Most of the writers I know use both methods, though they have individual biases in one direction or another. It ends up being something of a circular process for a lot of us—looking at the developing seed or seed-crystal to see what's missing, then looking around outside to see if anything fits, then looking at the inside to see if the newly added bit implies more interesting things, until the story has enough there that it's ready to write.

Choice Paralysis

Starting a completely new story is exciting. There aren't any constraints to worry about: no dangling plot threads that you have to tie up, no previously established background that you have to stay consistent with, no inconvenient mysteries or revelations that you're stuck with. It's a clean slate, full of fresh new possibilities.

At least, it is until you sit down and try to start writing. Faced with a clean sheet of paper, a blank word processor screen, or an empty file, a significant number of writers are immediately struck with choice paralysis.

Choice paralysis is the term I use for the inability to move forward because the author has: a) way too many possible options to choose from, and b) a deep and abiding fear that whatever they pick, there's a much better choice out there that they're missing. In extreme cases, the author is convinced that *not* choosing the "best" option will result in a substandard book or even in one that's a total, horrible disaster.

This isn't a problem for everyone, and the folks who don't suffer from it are often unsympathetic. "Just write it!" my extremely decisive mother used to say. "It's fiction; you're *supposed* to just make it up!"

The thing they don't always realize is that it's not a problem with making things up. It's a problem with making *too many* things up. It's usually worst during the story development stage and early chapters, when the writer starts with infinite possibilities and every single word that goes down on the page eliminates great swaths of them. "She"—eliminates an entire gender—half the human/elvish/dwarvish/animal race, and maybe more if you're dealing with aliens who have more than two sexes. "She sat"—eliminates, in addition, the possibility that "she" is a fish or some other creature that can't sit, as well as eliminating many, many other things she could have been doing: running, standing, swimming, fighting. "She sat in"—eliminates a whole lot of things that you have to sit on, rather than in: a rock, the floor, a table, the hood of a car.

Maybe it would be better if it was he *and not* she, thinks the paralyzed writer. *Maybe she should be fighting something—aren't I supposed to begin with action? Or thinking something. Or…maybe I should start with dialogue. Yeah, that's good; she can be talking to an elf… wait, I was going to make this a hard science fiction story, not fantasy. An alien? OK. So she's talking to an alien and says…*And the minute the first word goes down, the writer is back second-guessing. If she says, "I think the problem is a leak in your stardrive generator," the story is going one way; if she says, "I'm here to negotiate the terms of the peace treaty," the story is going a completely different direction, and what if the broken-generator story would be better than the diplomatic-mission story? Or the other way around?

At which point the writer needs to back up a couple of paces, take a deep breath, and remind himself of a couple of things: First, that no decision has to be final. If he starts writing the broken-generator story and it just doesn't work, he can go back and write the diplomatic-mission story. Or he can write a perfectly fine broken-generator story and then write a diplomatic-mission story in addition. Same for the starting point—if having the character in mid-conversation (or mid-fight or mid-contemplation) doesn't work out, the writer can go back and change things, adding more so that the story starts earlier or cutting paragraphs or scenes so that it starts later.

One can't keep the story plastic forever, true; eventually, one has to commit to a final draft and send it out. But by that time, there's usually enough material that one can tell what hangs together and what doesn't; one isn't stuck trying to predict whether this technique, scene, character, or plot twist will fit with an as-yet-unwritten mass of material that's probably going to change significantly from whatever vague ideas one has in one's head at the beginning.

The second thing to remember is that all those possible stories that one is pruning away with each additional word and phrase are not necessarily *better* than whatever one actually produces. They're just *different*. A brilliantly written broken-generator story is neither better nor worse than a brilliantly written diplomatic-mission story. They'll likely appeal to different readers, but that's not an indication of quality. And if you want to write both, there's nothing stopping you.

Once the initial panic has subsided, the next step is to make some decisions. They can be arbitrary; in fact, they probably will be at this stage. The point is to cut down on the number of choices the writer is facing. If you make a cold-blooded decision to write a fantasy, then when that voice starts whispering in your head that maybe a science fiction story would be better, you can tell yourself firmly that you are not writing that story today. You've already decided on a fantasy, and you're sticking to it.

What those decisions are doesn't really matter. I tend to begin by deciding a lot of the worldbuilding and backstory—knowing where my characters are and what they've done up to now gives me a handle on where they can go and what they can do next. Other writers find worldbuilding dull and dry or dislike being tied down too tightly in that area, so they start by making decisions about their plot or their characters. It really doesn't matter as long as you get to the point where you've decided enough things that any remaining decisions don't stall you dead in your tracks before you've written the third or fourth word of your first sentence.

Useful and Unuseful Lists

The other day I was browsing writing websites and came across one that made me blink. Every post for months had a title like "Seven Dialogue Mistakes," "Five Ways to a Great Scene," "Ten Resolutions for Career Writers," and "Twelve Dynamite Endings."

I get that a lot of people really, in their heart of hearts, want a paint-by-numbers approach to writing a great book. I also realize that a lot of people don't want to read more than one screen's worth of blog post. Lists of tips and tricks and common mistakes seem like a perfectly reasonable way to get at both things at the same time.

The trouble is that, in my experience, a short list of tips or mistakes just doesn't work very well when it comes to helping people improve their writing.

Writing a short story or a novel is complicated; every bit of it affects everything else. It's easy to focus on one particular aspect of writing, like dialogue or endings, and dash off a list of do's and don'ts. But in an actual story, it's not so simple. That number three "Don't" from the dialogue list, for instance, may be both thematically appropriate and more perfectly in character than any of the alternatives, not to mention being the ideal way of moving the plot along. Number ten, "Do make sure," from the characterization list may be impossible to make work, given the constraints of the style and setting.

But there are several sorts of lists that I find extremely useful. They just don't have anything much to do with writing technique.

The first set of lists is stuff I use during the first draft to save time. For instance, I have one possible-next-book that involves characters from several different imaginary countries/ backgrounds. I want their names to sound as if they come from different places with different languages and naming conventions, and I don't want any of them to be token representatives of their cultures. That means that eventually, when I'm making up secondary characters like the barman and the traveling salesman, I'm going to need more names that sound as if they came from the same places.

So I make a set of lists: six to ten male and female names that would come from each country, along with six to ten family/clan/house/tribe names for each country that mix and match well with the personal names I've picked. When I need the traveling salesman, all I have to do is decide which country he's from and pick from the list.

Or I make a list of place names so that when they pass by that small town, I can grab a name on the fly. I'll also make lists of things I've mentioned in passing, like local foods or animals I've invented, so that I can use them again if I need to (and so I can make sure that I didn't name the fish stew "kishta" and the tiger with antlers "kitsa"—far too confusing, not to mention the potential for tragically horrible typos.)

The other kind of lists I find useful are checklists of things to do during the first round of revisions. There's an ongoing, ever-changing list of all the phrases I tend to overuse, so I can do a search-and-destroy on them easily. There's a list of things to check for consistency and continuity. (I have a really bad habit of changing the spelling of a character's name by one letter somewhere in the middle of the story or calling someone "Anthony" for two chapters and then switching to "Andrew" because I couldn't be bothered to look up which male-name-beginning-with-A I'd used, and I was sure it was Andrew.)

In other words, all the lists I find useful have to do with the *content* of the story: names, places, descriptive phrases. That's what I need to keep track of when I'm writing, not the five dialogue mistakes that I may or may not be making in any given scene or the twelve dynamite endings that don't fit the story I'm trying to tell.

Old Ways of Looking at Plot

Most experienced writers know in their bones that plot operates in far more directions and on far more levels than most modern how-to-write books acknowledge. It's the folks who are just getting started who get bogged down in strict adherence to the basic skeleton or act structure—or worse yet, to one of the many and several "scene formulas" that purport to be the One True Way to produce a successful story. There is a lot more to plotting than producing chains of action-reaction or crisis-catastrophe-consequences scenes.

About ninety years ago, there was something of a fad for analyzing and classifying plots in various ways. Georges Polti came up with thirty-six dramatic situations in a stunningly boring book that, when referred to, is nearly always condensed down to a list that occupies about two pages. Sir Arthur Thomas Quiller-Couch classified plots according to seven types of conflict:

Man against Man, Man against Nature, Man against Himself, Man against Society, Man in the Middle, Man and Woman, Man versus God. Unaccountably, his list omits Man versus the IRS. And Robert Heinlein summed it up in three: Boy Meets Girl, The Little Tailor, and the Man-Who-Learns-Better.

Looked at a little more closely, these classifications are actually about different things. The thirty-six situations are about content, and fairly specific content at that. "Adultery" (Number 25—Two Adulterers Conspire Against a Deceived Spouse) is barely different from "Murderous Adultery" (Number 15—Two Adulterers Conspire To Murder the Betrayed Spouse). The "seven types of conflict" are about the sorts of obstacles the protagonist can face: other people who don't want him or her to succeed, natural disasters, the narrator's own internal prejudices or flaws, etc. And Heinlein's three basic plots, if one looks carefully, are the three things that result in change/growth in the main character. People change because they've established (or want to establish) a new relationship, because they have to grow in order to face an external problem that looks bigger than anything they ought to be able to cope with, and because they have to face themselves and their own wrong judgments and mistakes.

One of my favorite old how-to-write textbooks takes a completely different perspective on plot, classifying stories as Character Story, Complication Story, Thematic Story, and Atmosphere Story, plus the Multiphase Story (a combination of two or more of the other types). It's a very dense text, but as near as I can make out, the classification is based on where the plot's main focus of attention is and/or where its driving force comes from.

All of these things are important, but none of them say much about the movement of a plot. That's left for a different set of classifiers, who generally draw diagrams and graphs to represent tension over time, or complications, or the protagonist's situation (good or bad). The classic one that's still in use is the saw-toothed triangle, with the rising action, the climax, and the falling action, but there are others. One of the older texts I've been looking at separates plots into three types: a cup-shaped one it calls the Comic Plot Arc, which begins and ends with the character in a good situation, but which dips in the middle where the character is in trouble; a hill-shaped one it calls the Tragic Plot Arc, which begins and ends with the character in a bad situation, but which rises in the middle where it looks as if the character is going to make it out of the mess; and a flat line, which the book calls the Modern Story, in which the protagonist doesn't struggle against Fate but passively accepts whatever events come his or her way.

And then there are the folks who attempt to deal with nonlinear storytelling, using circles and spirals and chains of linked boxes and arrows to try to sort out and classify plots that don't move in strict chronological order.

All of these different ways of looking at plot are valid. All of them. Internalizing this is really useful; it means that when you are looking in despair at a plot whose action doesn't follow the classic saw-toothed triangle pattern, you can switch gears and see it as a spiral Man-Learns-Lesson pattern, or perhaps as a Character or Atmosphere story whose primary plot pattern isn't on the action level at all. When there's a problem, one doesn't have to look only at the movement of the story; one can look at the obstacles, or the focus, or the content, or the shape.

The thing I like about all this is the richness of all the different ways of looking at plot, what constitutes plot, and what's important about plot. It allows for much greater complexity than the basic plot skeleton and/or three-to-five-act structure that is the main substance of most modern how-to-write books. The basic skeleton and the act structure are, certainly, one set of plot fundamentals, but they're only one set, and fundamentals are supposed to be something that you learn in order to build on, not something that you learn and then stop because that's all you need to know.

The Hat Lecture

Back in the day, on Usenet, I had a little lecture that I posted periodically, whenever too many folks seemed to be bemoaning the horribleness of the submission process and losing sight of the actual job of submitting. (Make no mistake; the submission process is horrible and lengthy and depressing, but there really isn't much that can be done about it—certainly not by writers.)

Recently I went looking for it in order to link it to a post I was writing, and found, to my surprise, that either I've never posted it on the blog or else I hid it well enough that I couldn't find it in ten minutes of searching. So for those who haven't seen it, here is:

THE HAT LECTURE

Because writers are self-employed, they must wear many hats. There's the Creative Artiste's black beret, the Accountant's green eyeshade, the Editor's fedora, the Publicist's whatever's-current-in-headgear, and many others. This can create dangerous fashion difficulties for the novice writer, as many problems can be caused by wearing the wrong hat at the wrong time.

Putting on the Publicist Hat during revisions, for instance ("Baby! Every comma is golden! Let's do lunch…"), leads to lousy revising (or none at all) and an expanding waistline. Wearing the Accountant Hat when deciding where to send things out is often a bad idea as well ("This will cost $3.27 to mail, plus return postage; if I send it to one hundred places, that'll be more than $600! If I don't send it out at all, I can save $600!") And, of course, the perils of wearing the Editor Hat during the first draft are well-known.

But possibly the most common fashion error made by beginning writers is to choose the wrong hat for dealing with submissions and rejections. Many put on the Publicist Hat, trying to come up with brilliant new ways of getting their manuscript noticed, like mailing it in a pizza box. How original! (Seriously, don't bother. I've been hearing this one from editors for *at least* twenty years.) In addition to making editors grumpy (how would you like to be all ready for nice, hot pizza and then open the box to find nothing but *another* unsolicited manuscript?), it wastes valuable time and money that would be far better spent elsewhere.

Worse yet is putting on the Creative Artiste Hat. The Creative Artiste Hat is for coming up with ideas and doing first drafts, not for mailing stuff off (too boring) or dealing with rejection letters. Faced with a rejection letter (or sometimes even just with the possibility of getting a rejection), the Creative Artiste strikes poses and wails—"It's over, over, I tell you! I'm through with this writing stuff! I'm going to retire to a monastery in Tibet." Meanwhile, the manuscript sits on the author's desk, where nothing can happen to it, instead of in an editor's slush pile, where it will eventually get read and maybe bought.

What the writer needs to wear in order to deal with a rejected manuscript or a stack of query letters is the humble but vital Secretary Hat. Where the Publicist gets sidetracked trying to decide whether neon pink envelopes would be eye-catching enough for the query letters, the Secretary grabs a stack of plain Number 10 envelopes and starts stuffing and stamping. Where the Creative Artiste moans and wails over the latest rejection, the Secretary merely gives the classic overworked-secretary snarl because the rejection means packaging the thing up yet again, and in time to make the mail pickup.

The Secretary does not care what is in the manuscript nor what the rejection letter said. She does not go into a funk because the manuscript might not be perfect yet or into deep depression because it has been rejected for the five hundredth time. Her job is to type the cover letter, assemble the mailing, and make sure it gets in the mailbox in time for the five o'clock pickup, and she performs this job with efficiency (and only a little eye-rolling over the antics she anticipates from the Creative Artiste later on).

In other words, if it was good enough to send out to your first-choice Publisher A three or six or eight months ago, then it's good enough to send out to your second-choice Publisher B now that A has rejected it. So send it out again right away, BEFORE you start angsting over the rejection.

Where Do I Begin...

How do you decide where a story starts?

Stories, short or long, generally are not about characters who are happily living their normal lives. Something unusual is going on; something has upset the status quo, whether the status quo was a miserable life as a slave or a happy life as a king.

Stories therefore generally start in one of four places: just before, just at, or just after the point at which the status quo is upset, or else *in medias res*, smack in the middle of whatever is going on.

I have found that, since I am a natural novelist, starting *in medias res* for a short story is seldom a good idea for me. Usually it means that I'm *trying* to write a novel, but because I've artificially decided to write a short story, I'm leaving off the beginning and most of the middle of the book, and the end result is just not going to work as anything but an excerpted piece of a novel, no matter what I do. Starting in the middle of things works fine for some novels, and I've used it at least once (*The Seven Towers*, if you were wondering), and it works fine for other short story writers. Just not for my short stories.

"Just before" works well for fantasies and science fiction because in these stories, the "status quo" background is usually unfamiliar. "Once upon a time, there was a woodcutter who lived at the edge of a great forest with his three sons" is a just-before-things-change opening; it sets up the status quo. The change arrives with the sentence that begins, "One day, when he was out in the woods working…" Something happened that set the story going. The trick is to keep it *just* before the thing that changes everything happens—it is very easy to back off too far and provide too much introduction to the status quo. The current situation isn't the story; the story starts happening when things begin to change. And, of course, this sort of thing isn't limited to starting with a fairy-tale opening; "The woodcutter shouldered his ax and started off into the forest for another day's work" is also a just-before sort of opening; he's not doing anything he hasn't done a million times before.

"Just at" the point where something changes the status quo would be, "A poor woodcutter, hard at work in the woods, heard a cry for help. Running in the direction of the cry, he found a small man about to be eaten by a lion…" It is not usual for the woodcutter to rescue small wizards (for that's obviously who this is) from lions, and the woodcutter's reward, whatever it turns out to be, is going to form the basis of the rest of the story.

"Just after" would be, "The woodcutter set his ax beside the door, stared at it a moment, and went in. His three sons looked up; at the sight of his face, their expressions grew worried. 'Father, what has happened?' said the oldest. 'I met a man in the woods today,' the woodcutter replied. 'And he told me…'" This opening is useful when the original status quo is familiar and the thing that changes does not initially look very interesting or exciting at first glance. If your main character is a modern-day college student who has just graduated and is starting a new job, both the status quo and the thing that changes are familiar to most readers, and most writers will skip describing those and start with the main character's new experiences on the first day at work.

In medias res would be something like, "The woodcutter crouched behind the arras, watching the guards pace outside the king's treasure vault. Through the iron grate that covered the window, he could see the glitter of gold—and, more important, the shine of his magic ax. If he could just get his hands on it again…" This works really, really well for lots of people, but as I said, for me it's a bit dangerous to open a short story with it because (for me) it usually means the story really wants to be a novel. In addition, one needs to be careful not to disorient the reader too much. Also, I find it hard to fill in the background/ backstory in the limited wordage of a short story unless I'm doing something like a fairy tale, where the backstory is so familiar to readers that they can fill it in themselves. "Cinderella stood at the top of the stairs, looking down at the sea of wondering faces that filled the prince's ballroom" would make a perfectly good *in medias res* opening for a short story. On the plus side, the *in medias res* opening generally gets things going with a bang; it is often a very good opening for an action-adventure.

How you decide which one works best—well, you just have to look at the story and think about it for a while. There aren't rules for this sort of thing, unfortunately.

So the Next Thing that Happens Is...

There are two kinds of novel outlines writers do: the sort meant to sell a manuscript to a publisher, and the sort meant to help the writer write the book. This section is about the second kind.

The first and possibly most important thing to know about the planning-and-guidance sort of outline is this: It is entirely optional and may be subject to change at any time at the writer's whim. (Or, as my friend Lois Bujold puts it, "The writer should always reserve the right to have a better idea.")

Allow me to repeat: outlining is optional. It works for some writers but not for others, and for still others, it is actively harmful. If it helps you, do it; if you try it and find out that it doesn't help you, for goodness' sake, don't feel guilty because you "aren't doing it right." There is no One True Way. And if you fall into the last category, that of writers whose work is actively harmed by outlining, feel free to sneer openly at anyone who tries to tell you that you should do so, and to ignore anyone who demands that you outline.

Now that we have that settled…

When writers outline as a planning tool, all bets are off. There are no rules for doing this other than "if it helps you, do it that way." Some writers do detailed outlines in advance (sometimes the "outline" ends up being longer than the actual book because the writer includes all the background and backstory and worldbuilding details that never make it into the finished manuscript). Some write several chapters and only sit down to outline the rest of the book when they hit the "first veil"—that first sticky spot where things have to start invisibly coming together in the writer's head behind the scenes. Some do a sketchy outline as prewriting, then a more detailed one after they've written a chunk of the book. Still others don't outline until they have a first draft—they use outlining as a revision tool. Some do any and all of the above as the situation demands.

What a working/planning outline looks like also varies from writer to writer. Mine usually look a lot like my submission outlines, only longer—they're just narrative summaries of what I think is going to happen, set down as if I were telling the story to someone: "Kim finds out that Richard's looking for this set of magical doohickies. The doohickies have been split up; he's got one and thinks he knows where the next one is. They head to the country house…"

Some writers do a chapter breakdown; some do a scene-by-scene breakdown; some just do key points. Some use the sort of outline we all learned in school, with points I., A., 1., a. staggered with increasing indentations down the page. Some get specialized programs for writing (which can be fun if you can afford them and don't take them too seriously); some use spreadsheets; some use diagrams (like Nicky Browne's circle diagram or the "Big W" diagram, where you draw a big W on a brown paper bag and start with "status quo" at the top of the first leg, put the first big crisis at the first bottom point, the mid-book turning point at the top of the middle, the darkest moment at the second bottom point, the ultimate resolution at the top of the last leg, and then fill in steps up and down to get from each point to the next one). I like Post-It Notes and flow charts, which I later resolve into narrative summaries.

The point is, there isn't a wrong way to do this, because the purpose of this kind of outline is to help you write the story, and what kind of help you need depends on what kind of writer you are. I need something for my backbrain to rebel against, so my outlines seldom, if ever, bear any resemblance to the finished novel.

The Most Basic of Basics

One of the things that a great many people seem to know for sure is that they don't need any knowledge of the rules of grammar, punctuation, or syntax in order to write to a publishable standard. It is possible that I am overstating this; perhaps many of them merely know for sure that what they write is correct, or at least allowable. Whichever it is, it comes under the last part of that Twain quote: what these writers think they know for sure simply isn't so, and it's killing them…or at least, it's killing their stories.

A glance through the various websites that allow writers to upload their fiction without any prescreening requirements should be enough of a demonstration for anybody. I don't know what some of these people are thinking. It's obvious that they didn't even bother to run the spell-check before they put their stuff up for everybody to see. And I *really* don't understand those writers who blast any reviewer who dares to mention the fact that they obviously don't know what a run-on sentence is, or how to correctly punctuate dialogue, or the difference between "affect" and "effect." Are they trying to drive readers away?

But incomprehensible as this behavior is when I see it in amateur arenas, it pales beside the would-be professional writers who blithely send their un-proofread, un-reviewed, un-spell-checked work off to editors in hopes of selling it. What are they *thinking*? (Answer: they aren't.) This is like going to a job interview dressed in stained blue jeans, a muscle shirt, mismatched socks, and filthy old running shoes with the laces in knots. It doesn't matter what your credentials are, or how well you might actually be able to do the job; you aren't going to get in the door for the interview.

I have some sympathy for the writers who truly don't know any better. It is very hard to improve your skill set when you don't yet realize that it needs improving, and I've run into an unfortunately large number of younger writers who were never really taught grammar, punctuation, or syntax because their teachers were more concerned with encouraging them to be creative and get their stories down on paper. There's nothing wrong with encouraging creativity, but in the long run, you still have to know the rules. At a bare minimum, you have to know that there are rules and that you don't know what they are, or you will never realize that there are helpful things you still need to learn.

I have no sympathy at all for the prima donnas who do know their work is full of errors but who are convinced that it doesn't matter. "It's fiction," they say. "I don't have to follow any rules." (Wanna bet?) Or: "Oh, it's the copyeditor's job to fix all that." (It isn't.) Or: "Editors are used to seeing unpolished manuscripts." Well, yeah—editors see a lot of manuscripts full of sentence fragments, run-on sentences, misspelled words, and incorrect punctuation. They see them in the slush pile. And what they do with them is, they pick them up out of the slush pile and move them into the "rejections" pile as fast as they can possibly manage. It's an obvious and easy filter: if the writer didn't care enough about the work to clean up the grammar, spelling, and punctuation, the writer probably didn't care enough about it to do a decent job on the plot, characterization, or setting, either.

The real trouble, though, isn't with the inevitable editorial rejection. It comes earlier than that. The real trouble with ignoring the basic rules of English is that it limits a person's ability to write effectively.

A writer whose work is littered with sentence fragments and run-ons cannot make effective use of sentence fragments to increase tension or pacing or emphasis. He or she can't use a run-on sentence to give a breathless feel to a particular character's dialogue, because run-on sentences are all over the place already. In extreme cases, such writers aren't even aware enough of syntax and sentence structure to get adequate variation in their sentences, resulting in prose that just plods along, regardless of whatever exciting or emotional thing is happening.

It's the contrast from standard English that makes sentence fragments, run-on sentences, and other nongrammatical techniques work. If everything else is in standard English, dropping some unusual syntax, punctuation, or grammar into the text has an impact because of the change. The less often the writer does it, the bigger the impact.

Those problems are a severe handicap while writing. Even if the writer (or their tame English major best friend) goes over the story later on and fixes the punctuation, grammar, and spelling, the story won't be as effective as it could be. The writer has lost the chance to get the maximum possible impact from his or her writing because a bunch of really basic tools are missing from their basic toolbox, and some things are nearly impossible to retrofit during revisions. Besides, if the writer doesn't know what a run-on sentences is and that they need to avoid it most of the time unless they're looking for a particular effect, they aren't going to be able to get that effect any better during revision than they were during the writing phase.

Of course, if a writer doesn't care about doing the best work, or even about doing a good job, that "writer" doesn't have to know the basic rules of English (or whatever language they're using) and doesn't need to think about learning them. I don't really understand why such people want to write, though.

No Battle Plan

"No battle plan survives contact with the enemy."
—*Helmuth von Moltke*
"A writer should always reserve the right to have a better idea."—*Lois McMaster Bujold*

Prewriting notes—whether they're about plot, background, or characters—are the writer's battle plan and therefore exceedingly important. Lots has been written about this aspect of writing, but there are really only two things that are absolutely vital to remember:

1. Every writer handles prewriting differently, and
2. Nothing is ever written in stone until the book is actually in print.

If you look at those two things long enough, you start asking yourself, "Well, then, why bother planning at all if there's no right way to do it and if it's not going to stay the same anyway?" All I can say is that, of all the authors I know well enough to have some idea of how they work, only one or two do no preplanning at all, and even they at least think about their stories a little before they sit down and write. Empirical evidence indicates that for most writers, planning works.

There are actually a bunch of other things that you may find useful to remember about planning, but they're not things that everybody needs to remember. I really need to remember to spend enough time on the background and worldbuilding; I don't seem to be able to get started until I have a solid feel for the world and its culture and history, as well as the more immediate background of the characters (i.e., how they heck did they get into the situation they're in at the start of the story, and where do they think they're going from here?). It's a bit like looking at a chess problem—you know that there have been a bunch of moves made to get the pieces into this position, and before you decide what the next move is, you want to understand how they all got to this point.

But that's me. I know writers who really need most of those pre-book moves to be unknown or undecided. They tend to be folks who have trouble changing their minds about "what happened" once they've made it up, and they need to leave lots of room for the pre-book events to change, in case they get to the middle of the story and discover that they need the bad guy to have stolen the crown jewels ten years ago instead of having kidnapped the diplomat's daughter (or vice versa, or in addition to).

Exactly what you have to do for prewriting, and how much, depends on how you think and how you write. Some people can figure this out by thinking about what works for them with other things, like cooking or learning to ski or building a new house. For the rest of us, there's trial and error.

You might need to work out who the characters are (or could be) and what their agendas and plans are, while leaving the plot strictly alone. Or you might need to work out the worldbuilding first, or a lot of the key events in the plot. Or you might need to do a massive plot tree, where you sketch out as many different ways the plot *could* go as you can think of, starting with "hero runs away to sea; gets berth as cabin boy, or doesn't get berth, or is taken on as assistant by cook/sailmaker/?, or is mugged before he ever reaches docks…"

A couple of my friends do "zeroth drafts," or what one of them refers to as "pseudocode"—a 100- to 150-page "draft" of what will eventually become a four-hundred-page novel, which they later revise into a real first draft by adding scenes and incidents to explain plot twists or change the level of tension when it's been too high or too low for too long. Often, adding these scenes alters the whole course of the rest of the book, which brings me to that second point.

However carefully you plan during your prewriting, it is never sacred and unchangeable. This is obvious if you think about it a little. When you're prewriting, you're making stuff up—collecting materials (characters, plot turns, background), some of which you'll use in the actual story draft. When you're writing a zeroth or first draft, you're making stuff up—only this time, it's the specifics of exactly what was said, by whom, in what tone of voice, or exactly what was done, by whom, in what manner, and with what consequences. In other words, your brain is in making-stuff-up mode in both cases. So it's not surprising for a writer to suddenly have a cool, new idea in the middle of the draft that unfortunately means having to change the plot, characters, or background in major ways. In fact, it's more than unsurprising; it's downright common.

Unfortunately, there seem to be a fair few writers out there who were scarred by their middle-school writing classes and who think that once they have written an outline, they must stick to it. But if you've just had a really cool, new idea that is going to make the story you're writing even more interesting…why not use it? A more interesting, more effective, more surprising story is usually more desirable than the less interesting, less surprising, less effective one.

Whatever the writer decides during any stage of the writing process, including prewriting, is subject to change without notice at any subsequent stage, right up until the book is published. Of course, it gets harder and more expensive to make major changes when the book is in production, but it's still possible right up through the page proofs. If there's a particularly egregious error, you can sometimes even talk the publisher into fixing it for the paperback version (e-books, of course, are a whole lot easier to fix at pretty much every stage of the game).

This does not mean things have to change in mid-story in order for it to be any good, nor does it mean that what changes must be large and significant. It depends on the writer. If you're the sort who puts a lot of thought into your battle plan—that is, outline and prewriting—the new ideas that you have while working on the first draft or revisions may be small tweaks that leave the main plot/characters/background mostly intact. If you're the sort whose prewriting consists entirely of something like, "I think I'll write a book about a pirate," and then you make it up as you go along, it's much less likely that you'll come up with something that changes your prewriting (though it's possible, as when the book turns out to be about the pirate's robot servant or the noblewoman he captured, instead of about the pirate you started with). If you are somewhere in the middle—say, you do a sketchy outline that shows three or four major plot twists but isn't too specific about how you get from one to another—then you have the possibility of massive changes to your outline, but you also have the possibility that a few minor tweaks will keep the whole thing on course.

Plotting and Planning

Plotting a story is one of those writing things where not only does every writer work differently, but every book works differently too. Oh, there are patterns—I've talked before about my write-a-plan-and-then-toss-it method—but they never seem to work one hundred percent consistently for even one writer, let alone a sizeable number of them.

A lot of people have particular trouble with plot. I think there are a variety of reasons for that, but most of them start with the notion that there is One True Way to come up with and develop one. There also seems to be a serious lack of understanding of what a plot is, at least in some cases.

A setting is not a plot. An idea is not a plot, nor is a character (or set of characters). Matching up a character and a setting does not automatically produce a plot, though for some writers getting the matchup right is a first and necessary step that can trigger a cascade of useful ideas.

Yet time after time, when I ask a would-be writer what the plot is, I get a description of a character or a situation. These things can lead to plots, but that's not what they are.

A plot, by my definition, is a sequence of events, nearly always tied together by causality, that involve characters and take place in a setting. I prefer the sort that have a problem to solve and some sort of resolution or closure at the end.

This is why so many writing-advice types claim that in order to write a satisfactory plot, the writer must know how the story is going to end. But actually, one doesn't always need to know exactly how the characters will solve the central story-problem; for many writers, it is often enough just to know what the problem is, at least during the early chapters. However, if one doesn't have a resolution in mind, one does have to keep alert so as to avoid writing oneself into a corner.

How a particular writer goes about plotting a book depends on two things: first, what bits of story-idea they're starting with, and second, the writer's personal preferences—whether she is usually most interested in the spiritual journey of the characters, or in displaying their competence at puzzle-solving, for instance.

Stories can and do start with *any* of the usual story-bits— plot, theme, idea, setting, character, even bits of description or dialogue. Some of these require more development and decision-making than others; if the writer begins with a situation involving a couple of characters, it's usually easier to figure out what problems these people will be having than it is if one begins with a general theme. If one begins with an idea and setting, but no characters, it can take a while to figure out who the players will be, what they want and need, and how their wants and needs will drive the idea to a conclusion.

This is where the writer's personal preferences come in.

Some writers like to surprise themselves. For them, too much planning can kill a story stone dead. In extreme cases, all they can have to begin with are characters and a setting; they have to develop everything else as they write, including the central story-problem and especially the eventual resolution. (This working method sounds terribly, terribly tempting to those of us who need to do a certain amount of work before we ever sit down to type "Chapter One." Going straight to the fun stuff and letting the characters develop it all sounds SO much nicer than working up a plot outline. If it's not your method, though, it seldom is as easy as that.)

At the other extreme are the writers who need a detailed, step-by-step plan to follow—something that gives them a clear framework within which they can let their backbrain loose to be as wildly creative as it can within those strict limits. And strung out between those two extremes are the rest of us.

Personal preferences also influence where a writer goes to look for a plot. One of the most common ways is to examine the characters, looking at what each of them wants and needs, and at the internal and external obstacles preventing them from getting those things. Some writers make a list of things they want in the story, which can range from "bandit raid" to "heroine jilts hero at ball" to "use vines as metaphor" to "include family— little sister?" to "giant explosions!" Some look at what's going on in their story-world—the politics, the natural disasters, the culture clashes—find something they're interested in examining, and put together a plot by looking at ways of examining it.

All this sounds very general…and it is. There's really no way I can think of to explain plot construction that isn't either very general principles or else so tied to a specific story that it isn't likely to be helpful to anyone but the author of that story. It's always a balance between what the author finds interesting to write about and what is available from the story elements the author has. It's kind of hard to write a comedy of manners if your idea is to have your character alone on a desert island for ninety percent of the story.

Where One Writes

Writing is one of the few occupations that isn't tied to a particular place and time. It's something that you can do anywhere, anytime. So I used to find it odd to hear so many writers talk about their desks and offices, and I thought it was especially odd that some writers actually went out and rented office space. Why spend money when you didn't need to?

A lot of this bemusement was because I started writing my first (unfinished) novel when I was in seventh grade. Literally in seventh grade—during the class. Sister Mary Louise never quite caught me; it was occasionally obvious that I wasn't quite paying attention, but she never seemed to figure out why I wasn't paying attention.

Starting off that way was excellent practice for the writing I did in college—at the library, outside in the arboretum, in the cafeteria, in the dorm elevator, in class, even sometimes in my dorm room with my three roommates talking on the other side of the big room we shared. Which, in turn, was excellent practice for the writing I did when I got out of school and got my first job, which once again was mostly in the company cafeteria, in coffee shops, on the bus (though not often; it was too hard to decipher the results), in restaurants, and occasionally on the dining room table in my one-bedroom apartment.

In other words, I started out writing anywhere and everywhere that I could carry a notebook and pen, mostly regardless of other conditions. I'd learned to block everything out so that I could grab writing minutes whenever and wherever they happened to occur.

And then I got a house, and a computer, and set up an office to write in. It worked well for a long time, but gradually I came to realize some things:

1. Having an office is great because if you go there every day and write, your backbrain gets used to thinking, "We're at the computer in the office; must be time to write!," and you start getting more productive after a while.

2. Having an office is terrible because it trains your backbrain to only write when you're in your office, so you stop grabbing those minutes at the bus stop or the coffee shop or the dentist's waiting room, even if you have a cool, new iPad that you can take everywhere (with a nifty app that lets you scribble notes right on it, just the way you used to take your paper and pen). Also, your frontbrain starts using "I'm not in the office" as an excuse to not write. Like you need another excuse.

3. Having an office is really terrible because the minute you start doing things in it that aren't writing (like paying bills and answering e-mail and searching the web and playing FreeCell), your backbrain decides that maybe it's not such a great place to write after all, and now you don't have anywhere that your backbrain likes writing.

4. Fixing points two and three is really hard. Especially three. It takes time and energy and application.

Once I realized all that, I figured that despite how time, energy, and application are all in chronically short supply in my life, I had better get busy on fixing things so that I could maybe get back to number one again. I started off by getting back in the habit of hauling writing implements around with me wherever I go and using them, even if only for a few seconds. "Writing implements" used to mean paper and pen; now it means iPad or laptop, but it's the same principle. The laptop turns out to be a little clunky for grabbing quick minutes—mine's several years old and takes long enough to warm up and shut down that if I only have a sentence or so to grab and a minute to grab it with, it's not the right tool. So my iPad has become my implement-of-choice for wandering around.

The next thing I did was to start taking advantage of time chunks that were already built into my day. Three days a week, I go walking with my friend Beth, and afterward we stop for coffee. So now I haul the laptop along, and when she goes off to work, I stay in the coffee shop and get an hour or so of work done. For larger chunks of non-office writing time, the laptop is perfect; plus, I've gotten myself in the habit of dumping my writing session onto the flash drive I carry on my keychain, which (1) makes it easy to transfer to the desktop when I get home and (2) means I have my most recent data backed up and with me at all times.

And then I started making new chunks—nipping out to the library in the afternoon, stopping somewhere that has a bench and an electrical outlet on my way home from shopping. All of which got me to stop the "I can't write now; I'm not in the office" mentality.

Getting the office back to being a primary writing environment is going to be a lot harder because the e-mail isn't going to stop coming, the research and blogging have to be done, and there's no point in taking Civilization off the computer when I know perfectly well that if I do, I will just put it right back on the minute I get the urge.

So I have to come up with balancing writing in the office with all the other things I have to do there. I'm starting small—when I return from a laptop session at the coffee shop, I'm now in the habit of immediately transferring the files from the flash drive to the main hard drive and then opening the file to check over what I did. Usually that means I write a few lines more, which always makes me feel smug and virtuous (because I generally get my day's word count done at the coffee shop; those extra lines are gravy).

What's Missing

Recently I got into another one of those discussions with a would-be writer who was convinced that before he ever sat down to write, he had to have the perfect idea—one with depth and resonance, something he found personally meaningful and inspiring, and, above all else, something original. If it wasn't original, fresh, and new, it wasn't worth doing as far as he was concerned, and he was positive that an original idea was all he needed to achieve not merely publication but wildly successful publication.

I blinked at him a couple of times and then quoted Watt-Evans' Law of Literary Creation: *There is no idea so stupid or hackneyed that a sufficiently-talented writer can't get a good story out of it*, and Feist's Corollary: *There is no idea so brilliant or original that a sufficiently-untalented writer can't screw it up.*

In other words, it isn't the idea that has to be meaningful and full of depth and resonance; it's the finished story that needs those things. Of course, he didn't want to believe me, but it got me thinking.

How do I get from the stupid, hackneyed idea to a reasonably decent, interesting story?

Well, I start by looking at the parts of the story that aren't included in the idea. Ideas, by their nature, need to be developed and expanded in order to become stories. They aren't complete in themselves or they'd be the stories we make them into. So whatever the idea is that one starts with, it's missing something.

A lot of the ideas that get lumped into the "stupid or hackneyed or clichéd" category are plot ideas: the orphaned hero turns out to be the lost heir to the throne, for instance. What's missing is characters (by which I mean "specific people with names and individual personalities," rather than just roles like "orphaned hero" or "smart-mouthed sidekick") and setting. Some of the "hackneyed or clichéd" ideas are the characters who've been around the block too many times: the spunky young girl, the thief with a heart of gold, the mustache-twirling villain, the noble hero who's good at everything. What they're missing is plot and setting. And, of course, Generic Fantasy Setting #2,349 needs a plot and characters.

So I look at the cliché "orphaned hero is lost heir," and I think about just who that orphaned hero/heroine is. Somebody different, somebody unexpected. Maybe she's a Goth girl with no patience whatsoever for the rules of the court she's suddenly thrust into. Maybe he's an emo poet, or really, really, really wants to play major league football, and to heck with this being a king stuff. Maybe she's the absolutely perfect ideal the court has been hoping for…too perfect? How'd she get that way when she didn't know she was a princess? What's she really thinking underneath all that perfection?

Or I look at the cliché, and I think about where it could take place that would be interesting and different. Aliens. Insectoid aliens…maybe something like bees, where the new queen has to destroy all her competitors? Or merpeople—I could combine the "lost heir" with one of the selkie legends about the selkie maiden who was trapped by the fisherman and forced to live as his wife until she found the sealskin he stole from her. That's certainly one way for the True Heir to get lost.

Telling a familiar story from the point of view of a normally minor character often works well—the maid or valet, the coachman, the cook, the captain of the guard, all can bring a fresh perspective to a familiar tale…or sometimes spin off it sideways into stories of their own, for which the familiar "main" story ends up being no more than something happening in the background.

Ultimately, though, it comes down to execution. You can make anything sound horrible and clichéd and stupid in a summary, without even trying much. (*The Lord of The Rings* is about a short guy with hairy toes who throws a ring in a volcano.) And if you boil things down far enough, there aren't any original plots…that's why Heinlein could claim that all plots are variations or combinations of only three fundamental types. It's the final product—the total impression made by ninety-thousand-plus words of novel—that's going to be meaningful and inspiring and interesting and deep. Not the log line.

Working at What Isn't Working

When I wrote my first novel, I knew there was something wrong with the way I was telling it, but I couldn't quite put my finger on it. I had, at this point, never read any how-to-write books nor taken any writing classes beyond high school English, so I had no vocabulary for what the problem might be. However, I could see that it had something to do with the way my different characters saw various things. So I decided that in my next book, I would stick to just one character's head and see what happened.

What happened was one of the more difficult writing experiences in my career. Learning to write from a single character viewpoint, instead of the sloppy omniscient viewpoint I'd been using, was really hard. I kept running into things that would be SO much easier to explain if I just did a little bit from someone else's viewpoint...but I'm stubborn, and by the time I was five or six chapters in, it would have been obviously wrong to use anything but the tight third-person viewpoint I'd started with. So I stuck with it, and in the end I decided it was one of the more rewarding things I'd ever done, as well as the hardest.

Which is why I started deliberately choosing different things—different basic writing techniques—to work on in each book. For my first five or six books, it's easy to spot, because I was deliberately using different viewpoints and viewpoint structures (tight third person, first-person, alternating, multiple). After that, it gets harder to see from outside, and eventually I stopped trying to pick a specific technique for each book and just went to "do something stretchy" as a goal.

But the general idea has stood me very much in good stead and here's why: in writing, you yourself are the only person who can really push you to improve significantly. A good editor can help, but editors work on a book-by-book basis. Their job is to make your current book as good as it can possibly be...which is a subtly different thing from making you as good a writer as you can possibly be. There's a lot of overlap, especially early in your career, but ultimately, it's up to you to keep pushing.

Not-Writing

One of the most common questions I get, right up there with "Where do you get your ideas?" and "How can I get published?" is "How do you deal with writer's block?" Sometimes it gets asked plaintively; sometimes with a note of desperation. Once in a great while, it gets asked merely with a note of curiosity. In all cases, though, there is an underlying assumption that writer's block is something that all writers will face sooner or later, inevitably and inexorably, probably multiple times per story, and that it is a demon to be fought and defeated.

I have always had trouble answering this question, because it's based on conflating at least two different definitions of "writer's block." There is what I think of as "true writer's block," which is an actual inability to get bits of fiction on paper despite wanting to do so and which in my experience is quite rare; and there is not-writing, which is a choice and which is common as mud.

The people I know who've had real, true writer's block have almost all had some clear reason for it: side effect from a medication, an episode of depression, sleep deprivation, massive stress. The only way to clear it up is to deal with the outside reason, and that often takes years. Not-writing, on the other hand, can go on and off like flipping a light switch because it is fundamentally a choice.

I spend quite a lot of time not-writing. I have, on occasion, been told that I have writer's block when I haven't produced anything in a long time. I always find this a bit puzzling because I don't feel particularly blocked. I *could* sit down and write a new first chapter or a bunch of backstory for something or any number of bits and pieces that might eventually find their way into a story; I just don't see much point in doing so right then, for one reason or another.

Sometimes the reason is that I have more important things to do, like getting the plumber to stop the waterfall in the bathroom while I move all my paper books out from under the leak in the ceiling, or like being executor of my mother's estate. Sometimes the reason is that I am sick and tired of the thing I'm working on, but I know better than to start a shiny new project while I am in the miserable middle of an older one, so I choose not to write anything. Sometimes the reason is that it is a nice day, and I am going to take a book outside and sit under a tree and read. Sometimes the reason is that I need to mull over the things I already know need to happen in the current story so that I can figure out the exact right thing to be the next piece of it. Sometimes the reason is that I've taken a wrong turn somewhere, and I need to completely rethink my plot, starting two or six or fourteen chapters ago. And sometimes I simply have a profound disinclination to write.

I don't call any of those things "writer's block." I don't think they are deserving of the term, and I don't think I ought to be allowed the cop-out.

Writing is work. Work of any kind does, occasionally, get boring. Nobody I know likes being bored. It is human nature to try to avoid doing boring stuff. This is not "writer's block;" it's self-indulgence.

Yet somehow, writers have pulled off one of the greatest marketing coups ever: they have convinced everyone that if they are not-writing, they must have "writer's block" and are therefore to be offered tea and cookies and sympathy and support. If a bank teller or accountant tried to claim they couldn't work today because they had a paperwork block, everyone would laugh.

In a lot of ways, this is a great boon to writers. Much of the work we do doesn't look like work to non-writers, and there aren't a lot of non-writer folks around who understand the creative process. Telling these people, "I have writer's block; I'm going for a walk to see if that helps" gets them off your back instantly, when "I need to think; stop distracting me" doesn't, and "I'm going for a walk to ponder the next chapter" gets you a long list of errands to run "as long as you're out."

The trouble comes when writers start believing their own press. Having convinced everyone else that it is normal for a writer to "get writer's block" ten or fifteen times per novel (at least one of which lasts for three weeks or more), people start worrying if everything is going along smoothly without interruption or else they start labeling the slightest sticky bit as "writer's block" and panic because they're sure it'll be weeks or months before they write anything else ever again.

The truth is that a lot of the sticky spots have nothing

to do with being *able* to write something; they are, more often than not, about not knowing how to make what you write into the shining, perfect thing it is in your head. They are, in other words, about being a perfectionist. This is particularly common among beginners because no matter how much raw talent or imagination they have, they almost certainly haven't nailed down all the skills they need just yet. It is inevitable that they will periodically come to a scene or a line that they don't know how to handle, simply because this is the very first time they've tried to write a flashback or a love scene. It generally takes them longer to figure out what to do and how to do it because they haven't done anything remotely similar, and it is very, very easy to go from "I am not writing because I don't have the skills I need to do this scene/fix this plot point/see what the structure needs here" to "Ohmigosh, I have writer's block, and it will be months before I can write again."

That kind of "I have to stop for a while and figure out how to do this" stickiness comes around less frequently as one gains experience, but as long as a given writer keeps trying to stretch, they'll keep hitting spots like that. Again, it is easy to call that "writer's block," because writers and non-writers alike will accept that as a reason, and they probably won't try to give you advice about how to do whatever-it-is (which is generally about as useful as me trying to give advice to a brain surgeon in mid-operation would be). The trick is not to call it "writer's block" to oneself; instead, one goes off and studies how other authors get in and out of flashbacks, or the way they structure love scenes, or one does some practice scenes or exercises if one finds that sort of thing helpful.

Working at gaining the skills one needs in order to write the next bit is still working at writing, even if one is not making visible forward progress on the book. The same goes for stopping to iron out a troublesome plot twist or make up a consistent backstory or bit of worldbuilding that you suddenly need (and that has to fit seamlessly in with all the other backstories and worldbuilding that you have already done).

BASICS

Fundamentals, including essays on the importance of grammar, plot, characterization, setting, dialogue, and **Wrede's Lego Theory of Writing**.

Making Soup

One of the things I inherited from my mother was her collection of cookbooks.

It's quite a collection, too. When Mom ran out of space on the kitchen cookbook shelf, she just started putting them elsewhere. I've taken three large boxes and two paper bags full of cookbooks out of the house already, and I haven't touched the ones in the bedroom, the office, or the bookcase in the spare room. I'm afraid to even look in the attic.

My mother loved reading cookbooks and clipping recipes out of magazines. She had a real eye for good ones, and when she took soup to work for lunch, she always took extra to share. And someone always asked for the recipe. So she'd photocopy the recipe and hand it to them, along with a few tips: "I didn't have any navy beans, so I used pinto beans instead. And I had some extra tomato juice left from a different recipe, so I used it up in this; I'm not sure how much. And some vegetables that were starting to look a little wilted—spinach and cauliflower. Oh, and since it used ginger, I added a little nutmeg, too, because it goes well with cauliflower and ginger…"

Needless to say, nobody could make one of Mom's soups by following the recipe she gave them.

A lot of people who want to write, especially when they're just getting started, want a recipe to follow. "Take three characters, one evil overlord, and eighteen pages of backstory. Stir twelve times counterclockwise. Add two mysterious magical artifacts; mix until blended. Pour into large computer; bring to a slow boil. Add six cups of action, two cups of character development, and a dash of narrative transition. Reduce heat and simmer for six months. Strain to remove adjectives and adverbs."

But writing doesn't work like that, any more than making Mom's soups did. Both things are arts as well as crafts. Oh, you can turn out a passable soup by following the recipe exactly, but a good cook tastes and adjusts as she goes, and a great chef doesn't even have to start from a recipe. You do need the skills— chopping and mincing, simmering and sautéing—but the skills alone aren't enough (or else it would not be possible for me to produce something that is adequately nutritious but not at all tasty from the same recipe that was one of Mom's "no leftovers, ever" specialties).

I don't have Mom's gift for messing with recipes, though I can produce a decently edible meal at need. But I use the same tricks she did all the time…in my writing. "Three characters… hmm, I only have two; well, how about if I throw in a dragon? And I haven't used the wicked uncle in a while; better substitute him for the evil overlord before he goes stale. Mysterious magical artifacts, check…oh, and I have an ancient spell and a couple of standard plot twists sitting around; let's just throw those in and see what happens. Eighteen pages of backstory? Way too much—let's give it two pages; I can add more later if I need to. Bring to a boil…hmm, computer overheats easily, let's just simmer it for a good long while and see if that will do.

"Yes, this looks promising. Now, to add the action and character development—darn, I'm low on action. I can manage four cups; maybe I can fill in the other two with a bit more character development and some cool, new extra background and setting. Right, this is working—a bit thicker than the original recipe would have come out, but that's all to the good. Now simmer and…strain? Why would I want to do that?"

The recipe never comes out the same way twice, but it's always good enough for me, so I'm not complaining.

Point of View

The term "viewpoint" can mean either the person through whose eyes the story is told, as in "Who is the viewpoint character? Whose viewpoint is this from?", or it can mean the way the story is told, as in "Which viewpoint are you using—omniscient or first person?" I'm using it in the second sense today.

The types of viewpoint correlate roughly with the pronouns used in conjugating verbs: I did, you do, he does. There are, however, a number of variations on the most common types of viewpoint, and I'll try to summarize a few.

First-Person: "I did."

First-person viewpoint is the "I" viewpoint: "I hate pickled beets. I've always hated them. But Ma thinks they're good for what ails you, so whenever I'm sick, I get pickled beets." First-person viewpoint is narrated by the central viewpoint figure (who is not necessarily the main character or protagonist), who can describe his or her own actions, thoughts, and reactions but can only tell what he or she thinks other people are thinking. Because the narrator is usually telling the story after the fact, and because the whole story is in that narrator's voice, the author can make judgments and give the character's personal opinions of people and events far more freely than is possible in most of the third-person viewpoints.

A lot of people jump straight to first-person when they start writing because it looks easy. For quite a while, first-person was so overused by beginning writers that it got a really bad reputation as something only an amateur would try. There are still traces of that around, some places.

The thing that's most difficult for a lot of writers to grasp about first-person is that they are not the putative narrator. When I say, "I did this or that" in normal everyday life, I mean me, the person currently sitting here typing. But when my first-person narrator says, "I did that," the "I" *doesn't* mean me-who-is-typing. "I" means the character.

This is so obvious that to most folks, it goes without

saying. But if one doesn't say it or think it or pay attention to it, one is likely to find that habit takes over. All my life, "I" has meant me-who-is-typing, and that's a lot of habit to overcome. It's no wonder that a lot of first-person narrators sound (and think and act) a lot like their authors. (It is also no wonder that a lot of readers leap to the conclusion that anything written in first-person is autobiographical or at least reflects the writer's opinions and errors of knowledge, rather than the character's—but that's a rant for another time.) Picking a viewpoint character who has a strong voice of his or her own can help keep the character from sounding too much like the author because with a strong, idiosyncratic voice, it is easy to spot when the author starts to drift out of character.

"Plain" first-person is the most common type—something written as if the reader is riding along in the narrator's head or being told the story a few minutes after it happens, with the narrator's thoughts, knowledge, and reactions right there in the text. It looks something like this:

> I hate the prince's birthday. I've always hated it. Prince Conrad is a brat; he changes his mind twenty times and always has a batch of last-minute "requests" that make things hell for me and the other servants.
>
> At least this year all he wanted was cream cakes. Last year, it was fresh peaches—in the middle of winter!—and the year before that, it was some delicacy from the Far East that he'd read about in a book. Turned out to be a special kind of raw fish, and after all the trouble we went to to get hold of it, he took one bite and decided he didn't like it and pitched a tantrum. Brat is the only word for it.
>
> Cook had the cream cakes waiting on the big silver tray. Normally it takes two people to carry that tray, but we were shorthanded, what with Roger out sick, so I took it in myself. That was my first mistake; my second was stopping right in front of the door to steady the thing. And then Duke Gregory cannoned

into me from behind. Cream cakes all over everything, and him cursing and glaring and trying to pretend it hadn't been his fault.

"Damn it, watch where you're going!" he shouted. I, of course, was properly dignified despite the green icing in my hair, as a good footman should be— though I confess that the Duke made it hard to keep my temper. But "Sorry, sir," and "Very good, my lord," was all I replied. It's professional touches like that that are important when you work in a palace.

The butler told me later that that was when she got in, that Jililt woman who made all the trouble. I think I even remember seeing her on the far side of the hall—tall and blonde and not half-amused, if you know what I mean. I can't say for certain that it was her I noticed, though, because I was too busy mopping up cream cakes.

In a good first-person viewpoint, every sentence is in the "voice" of the narrator—you want to use his or her particular turns of phrase in the narration as well as the dialogue because the viewpoint character is the one telling the story. Everything comes through his or her personal filter; if your narrator dislikes dogs intensely, for instance, you can't ever describe a toy poodle as "cute" because your narrator wouldn't ever do that—the most he'd ever do is concede that maybe this little dog isn't quite as bad as most of them. The author can't provide information the viewpoint character doesn't know or show scenes the viewpoint character doesn't experience.

Many people like first-person because they think it provides a more in-depth identification between the reader and the narrator; some horror writers have deliberately chosen to write psychopathic serial killers in the first person in order to force more of an identification from the reader for an unsympathetic character. Some readers detest this form because they can't see any excuse for the main character writing all this stuff down (or remembering it, for that matter.) Other readers prefer it.

First-person has a couple of variations, including:

Epistolary first-person:

April 3

Dear Mother:

Well, the Prince's birthday has come and gone, and what a relief that is! It's always hectic beforehand, with him changing his mind every few days about what he wants served and how many people he wants to come and us trying to keep up. You earn your wages in this palace, let me tell you!

This year, he wanted cream cakes. I took the first tray out of the kitchen, and just outside the door, Duke Gregory backed into me. Of course the tray wobbled and the cakes went all over everything. The Duke looked pretty funny with green icing in his hair, though that didn't occur to me at the time. He was swearing and making a scene, probably because he knew it was his fault, and he didn't want to admit it. The Duke is like that. I remembered all your lessons and just said, "Sorry, my lord," and cleaned up the cream cakes. There was a blonde woman watching from the other side of the room, not half-amused, but I figured she was another one of the prince's last-minute guests.

This is an easy form for most people because everybody has some idea of how to write a personal letter. It is harder to get dialogue in, but the author can work in any number of personal opinions and speculations and quite a lot of background. A lot depends on the personal style of the viewpoint character/letter writer.

Journal style:

April 1

Prince's birthday tomorrow. I ache already from carting tables around; he decided this morning to add 150 people to the guest list. It's nearly midnight, and

I'll have to be up at six, so I write no more this evening.

April 2

The prince's birthday party was more eventful than I expected. Roger sprained an ankle, (memo: remember to check on when he'll be able to come back to work again) so we were shorthanded. Then the prince disrupted everything (as usual) by demanding cream cakes, which nobody had planned for. I suppose it's better than that weird fish thing he wanted three years ago—thank goodness I wasn't here then!

Got picked to take in the first tray of cream cakes—Cook really did a splendid job on them. Right outside the kitchen door, Duke Gregory bumped into me. Cream cakes everywhere. (Note: have maids rewax floor tomorrow.) Naturally the pompous old windbag blamed me, and I couldn't say a thing without making an even bigger scene than it was already and probably getting fired. Should have shoved one of those cream cakes right in his face. I was in disgrace for the rest of the evening.

Again, this is a fairly easy form for many people to begin with because most people have some idea of how to write a personal diary or journal. Sentence fragments and disconnected bits or parenthetical remarks are more acceptable because this is assumed to be private, informal writing—but this, too, depends on the style and personality of the journal writer, and too much can easily become irritating.

Stream-of-consciousness style:

I hate the prince's birthday what a brat like to tell him what I think of him changing his mind all the time treating us like slaves not servants ought to stage a revolt cream cakes are revolting I can't see why he'd want them I just want some time off no I have to carry that tray that takes two people usually am I a weight lifter or a footman they should pay extra for weights if I had extra pay I could get married maybe to someone like that cute blonde at the party but not her too snooty-looking and anyway she caused all that trouble I don't want a troublesome wife I have trouble enough I won't get extra pay now anyway after Duke Gregory spilled the whole tray did he look funny slipping and sliding with icing all down he blamed me and she got in and now I'll never get out…

The idea is to give the point-of-view (POV) character's thoughts directly, imitating the rather disjointed thought processes of a real-life interior monologue. This version left out the punctuation (how many people think in proper, organized sentences?), though it's perfectly acceptable to do something like:

I hate the prince's birthday. He's such a brat. I'd like to tell him what I think of him, changing his mind all the time and treating us like slaves instead of servants. I ought to stage a revolt…revolting is hard work…cream cakes are revolting, I can't see why he'd want them. I just want some time off, but noooo, I had to carry that tray that usually takes two people. Am I a weight lifter or a footman? They should pay extra for weight lifting. If I had extra pay, I could get married, maybe to someone like that cute blonde I saw at the party. Not to her, though—too snooty-looking and anyway, she caused all that trouble. I don't want a troublesome wife. I have trouble enough already. I won't get extra pay now, not after Duke Gregory spilled the tray of cream cakes. Boy, did he look funny slipping and sliding in the icing. It's not funny that he blamed me, though, and that was when that awful woman got in, and now I'll never get out…

The punctuation (and a little rephrasing) makes this more readable but less like true stream-of-consciousness; dividing it up into paragraphs would make it even more readable but even less stream-like, until you work your way back around to plain old first-person. Consequently, small blocks of this kind of intermediate POV get dropped into plain old first-person narratives sometimes, when the POV needs to think intensely about something.

In both varieties of stream-of-consciousness, there's no actual stage business or action, only what filters into the character's interior monologue ("I have to carry that tray"). There's also an illustration of the kind of mental connections people make in real life, as with moving from "staging a revolt" to "cream cakes are revolting," with the author making sure that the character's interior monologue doesn't wander off into mumbles about how revolting his muddy old shoes are, instead of circling back to the events of the story the author is interested in telling.

Stream-of-consciousness is a lot harder than it looks, and a lot of folks find it difficult to read. Consequently, you tend to see it either in experimental or literary fiction, or in short stories, or in short sections that are part of a longer work told in a more conventional POV (such as when a character has a decision to make or is pondering something). Interestingly, it also gets used sometimes in action sequences, where the author wants a sort of slow-motion or surreal feel to the fight or the fever dreams or the hero getting shot. Too much stream-of-consciousness in one place can destroy any tension the narrative has because of the way it meanders; this is part of what makes it hard to do in long sections.

Second-Person: "You did."

Second-person also assumes a single central narrator, but the narrator is being described by someone else, as "you." The author is still stuck with what the viewpoint character sees, hears, knows, and feels.

You enter the kitchen. Everything is laid out ready for the prince's birthday. The cook hands you a heavy tray of iced cream cakes, and you stagger out into the main room.

As you pause outside the kitchen door to get a better grip on the tray, someone bumps into you from behind, hard. You stagger, trying desperately to keep control of the tray, but it is no use. Cream cakes fly everywhere, smearing you and the bystanders and the floor with sticky green icing. You turn and see Duke Gregory wiping frosting from his face.

"Damn it, man, watch where you're going!" shouts the Duke.

Fury fills you; *he* bumped into *you*, after all! But you are only a footman, and he is a Duke. You swallow your anger and force yourself to reply, "Sorry, my lord," as you begin cleaning up.

Second-person fiction is uncommon and somewhat "gimmicky." It is difficult to pull off because it requires the reader to identify closely with the viewpoint "you" character, and unless the reader *does* identify very strongly, there is a good chance that at some point the author will say "You swallow your anger…" and the reader will respond internally, "The hell I do! I pick up a cream cake and shove it in the jerk's face!" and close the book in disgust.

Second-person viewpoint is nearly always told in present tense. It has a lot of the same limitations as first-person: the narrative really needs to sound like the viewpoint character, and the writer is limited to scene where the viewpoint character is present and information the viewpoint character sees and knows.

Third-Person: "He/she/it did."

Third-person viewpoint, taken as a whole, is probably the most commonly used viewpoint in fiction. There are seemingly an infinite number of ways to do it because third-person viewpoint has a very broad range, from what I call "tight third-person," where the writer not only sticks with a single character's point of view but also provides his or her thoughts and emotions (and only that one viewpoint character's thoughts and emotions), to the broad sweep of omniscient viewpoint that can dip into anyone's thoughts at any time or tell the reader things that are going on elsewhere, that happened in the past, or that will happen in the future.

The worst part of it is, neither the terminology nor the ways of dividing up the third-person viewpoint are standardized. Some references will tell you that there is only ever the omniscient narrator (but sometimes the narrator chooses to focus on only one character); others will split viewpoints up into dozens of fine distinctions, depending on whether the narrative voice matches the character's voice, how much of the character's thoughts are or aren't shown, whether the narrator is explicit, and a bunch of other criteria.

I personally find most of those fine distinctions to be pretty useless from a writer's perspective. Maybe they're helpful if you're analyzing stuff after it's written, but I've never found them to be much help while I'm writing. So I break the third-person viewpoint up into three general sub-categories and lump the rest of the distinctions under "voice," where I don't have to worry about them so much.

Tight third-person:

In tight third-person (also known as intimate third-person, third-person-personal, limited third-person, and third-person subjective), the writer sticks with a single viewpoint character, providing the viewpoint character's thoughts and emotions directly. Like first- and second-person, tight third sticks to a single viewpoint character and tells the story as he or she would experience it. The only way for the reader to find out the other characters' emotions is for the viewpoint character to guess or infer them from what those characters say and do. The narrative doesn't have to be in the character's "voice" the way it should be for a first-person viewpoint.

> *Gods, but I hate the prince's birthday,* Jon thought as he hurried toward the kitchen. *If the little twerp isn't adding forty more people to the guest list at the last minute,*

he's demanding fresh peaches out of season. I wonder what it is this year?

"Cream cakes," the cook informed him when he arrived. "This year, he wants cream cakes. They're all ready, on the tray by the door. Careful, it's heavy."

"Right." Even forewarned, lifting the tray was more of an effort than he expected. "I hope he eats himself sick."

The cook's laugh followed him out into the hall. He paused for a moment, getting the tray balanced just so, and someone bumped him heavily from behind.

Desperately Jon tried to recover, but despite his efforts, the tray teetered, showering cream cakes in all directions. There was an angry roar behind him, and he turned to find the portly Duke Gregory brushing green icing from his cloak and glaring daggers at him.

"Damn it, man! Look where you're going," the Duke said.

The injustice of it held Jon speechless just long enough for him to remember his duties. *Pompous braggart!* he thought angrily. *It was your fault, not mine!* But all he said aloud was, "Sorry, my lord." Then, as he began to clean up the mess, he noticed that the Duke was avoiding his eyes. *He knows,* Jon realized, *but he can't admit it without looking foolish.* Jon's stomach clenched, and he felt his lips twist in a bitter smile. When a Duke didn't want to look foolish, it usually meant that a servant got fired. It wasn't fair, but that was how things worked.

As he straightened, he saw an unfamiliar blonde woman on the far side of the room watching them. Their eyes met, and her lip curled disdainfully before she turned away. *Wonderful. Everyone in the kingdom is going to think I'm a klutz.*

Since tight third sticks with the inside of one person's head and nobody else's, other people's reactions must be given as observations or intuitions of the viewpoint character, some of which may be correct (*"He knows…but he can't admit it without looking foolish…"*) and some of which may not be (*"Everyone…is going to think I'm a klutz."*) Background has to be filled in through dialogue or action for the most part. You can't give information the viewpoint character doesn't know or show a scene where he's not present.

Tight third-person is the most common form of the third-person viewpoints. You can give the character's direct thoughts either as italics (*"Pompous braggart!"*), as normal text with a "speech tag" labeling it as a thought (*"He knows*, Jon realized…"), or as plain text that isn't labeled but that is clearly the thoughts of the viewpoint character ("It wasn't fair, but that was how things worked." [This last requires great care or you end up writing sloppy omniscient; see below.]) Normally you wouldn't use all three varieties this close together, though. You can also give the viewpoint character's internal physical sensations ("Jon's stomach clenched"), but it's harder to show external cues ("he felt his lips twist…").

Advantages are that it gives the reader an immediate strong identification and allows the author to get deeply into the thoughts and feelings of the viewpoint character, while allowing a bit more flexibility in narrative style (unlike first- and second-person viewpoints, the narrative doesn't have to sound like the viewpoint character, though it can if you want it to do so).

Camera-eye:

Camera-eye third-person is also known as third-person objective, observer-in-the-corner, third-person-impersonal, fly-on-the-wall, third-person indirect, and camera-on-the-shoulder. In camera-eye third, the narrator does not give the reader *anyone's* thoughts or emotions. The writer just describes expressions and actions, provides dialogue and tone of voice— the stuff that a camera or observer could see and nothing more. Sometimes the writer's "camera" sits on one particular viewpoint character's shoulder; sometimes it's further away or changes focus; but it always shows only what is happening from the outside.

"Got the cream cakes ready yet, Mrs. Fuster?" Jon asked. "Prince Conrad has been asking."

"I bet he has, the little pest," Mrs. Fuster said, her arm moving constantly as she stirred the contents of a large iron pot that hung over the kitchen fire. "It's a wonder he hasn't changed his mind *again* about what he wants for his birthday party. Watch that roast!" she called to a kitchen maid. "You'll have it burned in another minute, and you know what the prince will say about *that*! Yes, Jon, they're on the tray by the door."

Jon looked and groaned. "Why that one? It weighs twenty pounds if it weighs an ounce, even without anything on it!"

"It's all we had left. Get on with you."

Picking up the tray, Jon staggered out into the great hall. He was barely two steps in when a large, portly man in an ermine cloak backed into him. The tray teetered, sending cream cakes showering over the ermine cloak and skidding across the floor. "Duke Gregory!" Jon gasped.

"Damn it, man, watch where you're going!" Duke Gregory said. He brushed ineffectually at the green icing covering his cloak, his eyes carefully avoiding Jon's.

Jon's lips tightened to a thin line. After the briefest of hesitations, he said in a wooden tone, "Sorry, sir," and began cleaning up the mess.

Around them, the courtiers snickered and went back to their conversations. On the far side of the hall, a tall blonde woman eyed them a moment longer. Then her lip curled slightly and she turned away, scanning the crowd as if in search of something...or someone.

Because it's camera-eye third-person, i.e. we don't get to know anyone's thoughts or see or hear about anything that isn't actually happening in the scene, the backfill about the party being "hell on servants" has to be done by implication through a new dialogue section between two of the servants. No thoughts are shown, just actions and dialogue, and no interpretations or judgments are given. Only action, physical description, and dialogue is given. In a longer piece, "physical description" could easily include more description of the place (the hall, the kitchen), including sensory details like the smell of the stew. Camera-eye is more distancing than tight third, because you don't get to see individual characters' thoughts and feelings, but in compensation, the scope is greater—the author can show anything that is happening in the area, whether the main character notices it or not, and can point out that the main character isn't noticing it.

Camera-eye often gets used in multiple-viewpoint novels where the writer wants to give the reader a taste of what the villain is doing without actually going into the villain's head as a tight third POV character (and thus giving away the villain's whole plot). The villain's scenes get written in camera-eye, while all the hero's scenes are in tight third.

Omniscient:

In omniscient viewpoint, the narrator is an invisible character who knows everything that has ever happened or will ever happen and everything that anyone is thinking or feeling, and who can report as much or as little of this as seems appropriate. I've heard the term "limited omniscient" bandied around a couple of times, but it seems to mean contradictory things depending on who's using it, so I'm waiting until a consensus definition appears before I worry about using it.

Every year, the castle servants spent weeks preparing for Prince Conrad's birthday party. They cleaned, they decorated, and they prepared hundreds of special treats—only to have the prince change his mind at the last minute (sometimes three or four times) and call for some new and different delicacy. The sushi he'd demanded three years earlier had been a particularly memorable disaster, and the tale was still used by the senior servants to terrify newcomers to the palace staff.

This year, the last-minute addition to the menu was a tray of cream cakes with fluffy green frosting that had taken the cook two hours to get just right. Jon, the footman, took the heavy tray with a combination of appreciation and irritation then staggered directly out to the great hall. Unfortunately, he didn't see Duke Gregory backing away from Lady Dorington. The Duke didn't notice Jon, either; he was too busy trying to avoid hearing about Lady Dorington's latest illnesses, and in his haste and inattention, he collided with the overburdened footman.

Cream cakes slid and squashed, leaving green trails of icing behind them as they glided down the Duke's ermine cloak to the floor. "Damn it, man, look where you're going!" the Duke roared, trying to cover his embarrassment with a show of anger—he knew the accident had been his fault, but how could he admit it to a servant, and in front of so many other nobles? Jon, though internally seething with annoyance and frustration, responded with the bland, self-effacing control of the perfect footman and set about cleaning up the mess at once.

The minor accident had one further effect: while the crowd watched the two principles with varying degrees of amusement, a tall blonde woman slipped unnoticed into the hall. The woman, Jililt, glanced briefly at the disorder and turned away in disdain to pursue her own dark purposes.

Omniscient viewpoint doesn't always give the reader a clear character to identify with. It is thus more distancing than intimate third-person or camera-eye third and, partly for these reasons, is uncommon in modern fiction. Omniscient viewpoint is, generally speaking, the easiest viewpoint to do badly and the most difficult to do well for most authors. It's easy to do badly because it's easy to do accidentally—the minute a sentence like

"Meanwhile, back at the ranch..." or "If he had only known..." or "She didn't realize that her sister was a crook..." or "Like the rest of us, they got confused by..." goes into a scene, the viewpoint becomes slippery. However, it is *extremely* easy for someone who has been steeped in the "rules" to mistake perfectly fine omniscient for sloppy tight third-person and flag it as "bad writing" inappropriately.

Omniscient is hard for a lot of folks to get a handle on because it can look a bit like pretty much any of the other third-person viewpoints if the author tries hard enough. Also, lots of folks who write omniscient tend to go for an omniscient that slants a bit toward either camera-eye or tight third-person. Many people also confuse multiple viewpoint and omniscient viewpoint because in multiple viewpoint, you get to know the thoughts of more than one character. The difference is that in omniscient viewpoint, you can get the thoughts of more than one character in the same scene. In multiple viewpoint, each scene is limited to one viewpoint character, and that viewpoint character changes from scene to scene.

The above example is one variety of omniscient; there are others (such as that used in *Lonesome Dove* or John M. Ford's *Growing up Weightless*) that are easily mistaken for tight third if you miss the transition bits where the viewpoint is handed off from one character to another. The extreme flexibility of omniscient is one of the things that makes it so difficult to do effectively.

What Not to do: Really Bad Omniscient:

> *Prince Conrad's birthday is always hell on servants*, Jon thought as he hefted a tray of cream cakes. Of course, Jon had never liked being a servant. If he had had more resolution, he would have been a revolutionary, but he didn't. He was a footman. Mrs. Fuster agreed with him, though of course neither of them said anything aloud. They were right, though. The prince was a real brat. He always demanded something special at the last minute.

This year, it was the very tray of cream cakes that Jon was staggering through the crowd with. If Jon had only realized that, he'd have been more careful, though it still wouldn't have helped. Duke Gregory would have cannoned into him just the same, but Jon would have felt better about it afterward. The Duke was avoiding Lady Dorington, the biggest bore at court, and he didn't notice Jon until he had upset the cream cakes all over both of them.

"Damn it!" the Duke roared as cream cakes slid from the polished silver and smeared green icing softly across the back of his ermine cape. Everyone nearby laughed at him. They thought he was a pompous windbag and deserved to be covered in green icing. Jon thought so, too. "Watch where you're going!" *Damned careless servants these days, not like when I was a boy. He should have avoided me.*

It was his *fault, not mine!* Jon had never liked the Duke. *What a stuck up, pompous braggart.* "Sorry, sir," he said aloud, brushing ineffectively at the Duke's cloak. *Buffoons, the pair of them.* Jililt glided through the doorway on the other side of the room. *This may be easier than I thought.* She was disgusted with the whole business. Had she only known it, the little accident and the widening circles of attention it had attracted were the sole reason she had been able to slip into the hall unnoticed.

Problems with the above: The section starts off looking as if it's third-person intimate, then turns into omniscient in the second sentence. Narrator makes judgments about characters' actions and reactions ("They were right." and "If Jon had realized…he'd have been more careful.") which has the effect of trying to force the reader's reaction to what is going on instead of letting the reader decide for him or herself. Narrator also makes judgments about characters ("The prince was a real brat"), which looks like tight third or first-person.

The narrator makes obtrusive predictions ("it still wouldn't have helped…he'd have felt better about it afterward.") and inserts irrelevant information ("Everybody thought he was a pompous windbag…"). Jumping from head to head so abruptly makes things choppy and awkward; sometimes it is confusing as well (does Mrs. Fuster agree with Jon's revolutionary views or with his opinion of the prince's birthday? Is it Jilit or Jon who thinks "Buffoons"?). The reader has to keep switching between an intimate and a distant viewpoint or between different intimate viewpoints, with very little transition. And the "Had she only known…" construction and its variations are clumsy and dated. Omniscient also makes it much easier to "tell" what people are feeling ("she was disgusted") instead of "showing" it ("Her lip curled in disgust").

Multiple Viewpoint

Multiple viewpoint is not really the same kind of thing as first-second-third-person viewpoint. Multiple viewpoint refers to how *many* viewpoint characters there are (more than one), not to what POV the book is actually written in. In a multiple-viewpoint book, each scene or each chapter is from a single viewpoint, but the viewpoint character changes from scene to scene or chapter to chapter. A book can be either single viewpoint (one viewpoint character) or multiple viewpoint (many viewpoint characters), regardless of whether it is first-person, second-person, third-person, or some mixture.

Tight third-person is usually the viewpoint that is used for individual scenes in a multiple-viewpoint story or novel, though sometimes authors will use first-person or alternate between first and third. Multiple viewpoint is, therefore, really more of a structure than a different viewpoint. It's in here, in this place, because people get confused about it, because it's termed "multiple *viewpoint*," and because third-person is most common for the sections of a multiple-viewpoint piece.

Gods, but I hate the prince's birthday, Jon thought as he hurried toward the kitchen. *If the little twerp isn't adding forty more people to the guest list at the last minute, he's demanding fresh peaches out of season. I wonder what it is this year?*

"Cream cakes," the cook informed him when he arrived. "This year, he wants cream cakes. They're all ready, on the tray by the door. Careful, it's heavy."

"Right." Even forewarned, lifting the tray was more of an effort than he expected. "I hope he eats himself sick."

The cook's laugh followed him out into the hall. He paused for a moment, getting the tray balanced just so, and someone bumped him heavily from behind.

Duke Gregory saw Lady Dorington before she saw him. Instantly he ducked behind a pillar. The last thing he wanted was to spend half an hour hearing about the woman's latest imaginary illness. *Of all the bores at court, she's the greatest.* Cautiously he peered around the pillar to see where she was now.

She was coming in his direction. The Duke backed away, keeping his eyes on her, and bumped into someone. He turned to apologize and found himself facing a wide silver tray half full of little cakes with green frosting. Looking down, he realized what had happened to the other half of the cakes; his ermine cloak was streaked with green frosting, and when he took an involuntary step backward, something squished unpleasantly under his boot.

The apology died on his lips. "Damn it, man! Look where you're going," he burst out, knowing even as he spoke that it was unjust. The accident had been *his* fault, not the servant's, but it was too late to admit it now.

The footman who had been carrying the tray looked at the Duke and his lips thinned, but all he said was, "Yes, your grace."

The servant's reaction made the Duke feel even

guiltier about his unfortunate outburst. He'd have to see that the man got some compensation later; in fact, he'd speak to the steward at once…well, right after he got someone to take his cloak away to be cleaned.

The first half of the scene is tight third-person from Jon's viewpoint; the second is tight third-person from the Duke's viewpoint. Normally one would not switch viewpoints quite so quickly (the scenes would be longer), and the viewpoint characters would be central to the story being told. If this were the opening of a story about the development of an unlikely friendship between the Duke and the footman, both viewpoints would be very appropriate; if it were the opening of a story about the Duke's dealings with the prince, in which Jon plays no part, I would cut or rewrite the section that's told from Jon's viewpoint; if it were about a servant's-eye view of palace intrigue, I would probably rewrite or cut the Duke's viewpoint.

Multiple viewpoint is sometimes confused with omniscient viewpoint because in the course of the story, the reader sees into the thoughts and feelings of a number of different viewpoint characters. In both multiple viewpoint and omniscient viewpoint, the reader knows more about what is going on than any of the individual characters do. The difference is that in omniscient viewpoint, there is a single invisible narrator who knows what everyone is thinking and feeling, while in multiple viewpoint, there are a number of different narrators, each of whom knows only what he himself is thinking and feeling. Again, it is perfectly possible to use multiple first-person viewpoints or to use first-person in some scenes and third in others, so long as it is not confusing for the reader and so long as each type of viewpoint is maintained consistently within its scene. This is, however, not terribly easy to pull off.

Unfortunately for precise terminology, these categories (tight third-person, camera-eye, omniscient, and multiple viewpoint) do not have neat gaps in between—there's a fuzzy area between each pair, where stories seem to be too objective to be called "tight third" but are still providing the viewpoint character's thoughts, so they can't quite be "camera-eye," or where the narrator sticks with the same two characters' thoughts, so it doesn't really look like a truly omniscient viewpoint, but it's still not a single, tight third viewpoint character. This is of great interest to a lot of folks who like to analyze and categorize writing, but I don't think it matters nearly as much to writers.

What really matters to writers is that whatever the writer comes up with works. Usually this means that there's a certain amount of internal consistency—you don't start off in tight third and then switch to camera-eye or omniscient halfway through (unless there's a major section break to clue the reader in that the writer is doing this on purpose).

As I said, third-person viewpoint, taken as a whole, is probably the most popular viewpoint among writers of fiction. I think this is because of its flexibility—in tight third, writers can get almost as up close and personal with the viewpoint character as they can get in a first-person manuscript, or they can provide an illusion of objectivity by backing away into camera-eye or even omniscient. The writer can manipulate the focus and scope of a story by choosing which viewpoint to tell it from, making a sweeping epic feel more intimate and personal by sticking with a tight third-person viewpoint and a single-narrator structure, or opening up what would otherwise be a restricted, personal tale by using omniscient viewpoint to bring in broader social and political consequences that the obvious tight third viewpoint character wouldn't know about.

And you can even have it both ways (both intimate/ personal and with broader scope) by using a multiple-viewpoint character structure while telling each characters' scenes in tight third. (One can, of course, do the same thing with multiple first-person viewpoint characters, but it's a lot more difficult to pull it off because it's a lot easier for the reader to confuse three different "I" characters than three tight third viewpoint characters, each of whom has a different name.)

Of my three categories of third-person viewpoint, omniscient was historically the most popular, up into the early twentieth century. Somewhere since then, tight third has become the predominant type of third-person viewpoint. I found tight third hellishly difficult to learn to do, but once I learned how, it became my favorite.

The LEGO Theory Of Writing

The Lego Theory, Part One

Fiction is like Legos. It's built out of a series of different units, stuck together. Each new level of unit is built from a clump of previous units. The more units you have, the more complex effects you can achieve by moving them around, putting them in different configurations, and making different associations.

What units am I talking about? Starting small and working up: letters, words, phrases, clauses, sentences, paragraphs, scenes, chapters, sections, books, multi-book story arcs.

Most of the time, creative writing advice focuses on things that matter at the middle levels: stuff like plot and characterization and setting, which build up over the course of a scene or a chapter or a book. The assumption seems to be that everyone has already learned all they need to know about the words-to-paragraphs level of writing back in grade school, so that by the time people get to the point of trying to write a novel, they can jump right in learning about scenes and chapters and plot skeletons.

Now, what I learned from Sr. Agnes and Sr. Winifred back in grade school was essential and invaluable, and I got a long way on just those basic rules of grammar, syntax, spelling, and punctuation. Eventually, though, I came to a point where those basics weren't enough. I knew how to build letters into words and words into phrases and phrases into clauses, but I wanted more. I didn't just want to build large, square Lego houses. I wanted to build Lego dinosaurs and airplanes and astronauts. And to do that, I needed to understand more than just how to snap one block into the next. I needed to know how and why they fit together, starting from the smallest units.

Yes, from the smallest. Most people don't even think about letters; they're just sort of there. They string together to make words, but as long as you run the spell-check and aren't making up your own language, you're probably right.

Yet letters have the first key property of all these building blocks that's important to writers: sound. It's predefined, and the only way the writer can control it is by choosing words carefully, yet the sound of a word can be just as important as what it means. Words with guttural or harsh sounds give things an unpleasant feel; they're a good way to add a creepy undertone to a description or a conversation without being too obvious. More smooth, liquid sounds, like oo's and l's, tend to make things flow peacefully.

Sound provides all sorts of tools, from alliteration to puns to rhyme. Some people are extremely sensitive to the sound of words, even when they are reading silently; others only notice the sounds if someone is reading the story aloud. Writers who fall into the second category need to remember that there are plenty of sound-sensitive readers out there, and do occasional checks (reading aloud) to make sure they haven't chosen words that don't sound right for the situation or that don't fit together properly.

You have probably noticed that I'm talking mainly about the sounds of words, even though I'm supposed to be talking about letters. This is going to happen a lot in these sections because many of the key properties of a particular unit of fiction only become useful to writers at the next level up, when you start snapping the Lego pieces together. You can't change the sound a particular letter is supposed to make, or the standard spelling of a word, but you can choose words with an eye to their sound as well as their meanings.

Which brings us to words.

What you do with words: you build phrases, clauses, fragments, sentences, and scenes. Most people do this more or less instinctively once they've learned to talk, but the real nitty-gritty of how writing works starts with words, with how they work, with how they relate to each other, and, later on, with the different effects you can get because of the different properties they have.

The very first key property of words is one that most writers have heard over and over: specificity. Specific, concrete words nearly always have more impact and are more effective at conjuring up an image than abstract words or general words. A "flaming sunset" has more impact than a "beautiful sunset;" a "brown car" has less impact than "a brown Lexus" or even "a brown convertible;" "he went away quickly" is less evocative than "he fled." This doesn't mean a writer can/should *never* use abstract words like "beautiful" or generic ones like "car;" only that if you do, you should probably examine them to see whether the "low impact" effect is what you really want—and, if not, whether there's a less abstract, more specific word that will do the job instead.

The Lego Theory, Part Two

Words, being the smallest and most basic building blocks of fiction, have lots of useful and important properties. I've already talked about specificity and sound; the next really key thing a writer needs to know about words is that they have different significance, or strength.

I define strong words as "the ones people pay more attention to." They have more weight in the reader's mind and therefore make more of an impact. Since fiction is usually about making an impact on the reader, strength is probably the most important property any word, phrase, or sentence can have.

What makes strength really useful, though, is that it isn't an absolute property—it's affected by a whole lot of other things that come along as words get strung together in different ways to make larger and larger units. This means that a writer can adjust the impact that a word or phrase or sentence has by adjusting some of its other properties.

A word's basic strength begins with the first four basic parts of speech that we all learned (one hopes) in school: noun, verb, adjective, adverb. Think of them as different sizes and shapes and colors of Legos. Put the right ones together in the right order and you get a cool dinosaur; opt for ones that are the wrong size or shape and you end up with an awkward unidentifiable lump.

So, parts of speech. The strongest one—the largest Lego— is the verb. Verbs are where the action is in any given sentence. Even so-called "passive verbs" indicate that something exists or is ongoing. A verb on its own can be an entire sentence, and a command at that. You can tell a story with verbs alone: Look! Scream! Flee! Hide. Peek. Shoot. Duck. Explode. Cheer!

This is the reason so much writing advice puts so much emphasis on using dramatic, active verbs. Verbs are the strongest type of word, by nature, and using a vivid, specific, concrete one can double up that strength. By the same token, if the writer wants a word to have less impact (perhaps so that an upcoming plot twist will not be obvious, or because the writer wants more focus on some other part of a phrase or sentence, or just to give the reader a rest for a moment), choosing a verb that is abstract or general may be the way to go.

Next in terms of strength come nouns. Nouns and verbs are the basic bricks that everything else gets built with. Nouns aren't as strong as verbs because until they have a verb to go with them, they just sit there. On the other hand, the more precise, clear, and specific you can make your nouns, the stronger they become. A red flower by any other name could be a carnation or a rose or a trumpet flower, but a rose is a rose is a rose.

Adjectives and adverbs are the weakest of the four basic building blocks because they can't stand on their own. "Small cold blue" doesn't tell you anything until it has a noun like "elephant" or "shotgun" attached to it. In addition, some of the time the right noun or verb can eliminate the need for one or more adjectives/adverbs; if so, you're generally better off using that noun or verb because they're stronger to begin with.

Another difficulty with adjectives and adverbs is that the more of them you use, the weaker they become. This applies whether you're overloading just one noun or verb with four or five descriptors or whether you have a modest single descriptor for each and every noun or verb on a page.

Because of all this, and because too many writers overuse

them, adjectives and adverbs get a bad rap in a lot of writing advice. In its most exaggerated form, this becomes the "never use adverbs/adjectives" rule. But even if you are trying to pack your prose with as many dramatic, high-impact words as possible, ignoring adverbs and adjectives is not automatically your best choice. Yes, they are weaker than nouns or verbs, but the concrete/precision property still applies: the more precise and specific the adjective, the stronger it tends to be.

And if you have an adjective or adverb that makes its noun more concrete and precise in a way that can't be done with just a concrete noun, you have a winner. "Holy book" is a generic noun plus an adjective; "Bible," "Koran," or even "prayerbook" would be stronger in most cases. But "scarf" is a generic noun; "silk scarf" is more specific, and there isn't a noun that would do the job. Likewise, adjectives and adverbs that are unexpected are usually good things: "Wonderful," he said glumly.

So the best advice is, as always, not to just delete all the adverbs and adjectives indiscriminately but to think about the desired effect and whether the adverb/adjective is really necessary. "'I hate you,' she said angrily" doesn't really need the adverb because the angry tone is consistent with the dialogue; "she snarled" would be better, and it would be fine with just "she said." But "'I hate you,' she said cheerfully" isn't a sentence that can drop the adverb and still mean the same thing. Neither is "The band played badly."

Notice that a lot of what I'm talking about here is the way that words relate to each other. Because face it, the important thing about Legos is not the shape of each piece; it's how they fit together and what you can make with them. That really begins with the next level up from words: phrases. Which is what comes next.

The Lego Theory, Part Three

Every set of Legos has the basic square and rectangular blocks that you build most of your castles and dinosaurs and pirates with, and then there are a bunch of oddly shaped pieces that you use to make the fancy bits. Last time, I compared the basic Legos to the first four basic parts of speech—nouns, verbs, adjectives and adverbs.

With both Legos and words, you can get along reasonably well with just the basic parts, but as soon as you want to make something complicated, you really want those pieces that are triangular or round or trapezoidal or long and skinny to link things together or put the pointy tops on the towers or teeth or party hats. That's what the rest of the parts of speech do— the pronouns, prepositions, conjunctions, and interjections. None of them are particularly strong on their own, but they are invaluable once you start putting words together into phrases.

Phrases are the next level of English, up from "words," and this is the point where things begin to get interesting. Because as soon as you put two or more words together to make a phrase, they not only interact with each other, but they suddenly develop a couple of new properties that affect the impact they make.

The first of these is position or order. In English, and at the phrase level, the order that words go in doesn't have a lot of flexibility. You can say "the red flower" but not "red the flower" or "flower the red." If you move a preposition to a different position, you often change the meaning of the phrase; "of the African jungle" is not the same as "jungle of the African" or "African of the jungle."

Nevertheless, position in phrases is where the writer starts being able to control what is going on in his or her prose. Words are what they are; unless the writer goes to the same extreme as J.R.R. Tolkien and invents whole new languages, the only control the writer has is over which words he or she chooses to use. The order the words go in is something the writer *does* have control of, at least to an extent, and that control grows with every level from phrases on up. You may not be able to move prepositions or conjunctions around without changing the meaning, but you can choose between "bedknobs and broomsticks" and "broomsticks and bedknobs" or between "on his champagne-polished black boots" and "on his black, champagne-polished boots."

The reason you want to control position or word order is

that, as a general rule, the first element in a phrase or clause or sentence has the most impact and is the most memorable; the last element has second-most; and the ones in the middle have the least. "Bedknobs" has slightly more weight or strength than "broomsticks" in the phrase "bedknobs and broomsticks," for instance.

Position stacks on top of whatever strength the word has on its own. "Bedknobs" and "broomsticks" are both nouns, so they start off more or less equal in strength; it's only the relative position in the phrase that makes one a little stronger than the other. But the first word in "to boldly go" is a preposition, which is a relatively weak linking word; the fact that it comes first doesn't add much strength because it doesn't have much of a base to add onto. "Go," on the other hand, is a verb, the strongest part of speech, and it comes in the second strongest position, at the end of the phrase. Putting "go" in the middle (so as not to split the infinitive) weakens it significantly.

The second key property of phrases (as compared to words) is rhythm. Multi-syllable words can have rhythm because of the differing emphasis on the syllables; this is what makes some words fun to say (like "supercalifragilisticexpialidocious"), but it's built in and the writer can't do anything about it. As soon as there are multiple words, as in a phrase, the writer can control the rhythm by choosing words carefully and positioning them properly. By doing so, the writer can increase or decrease the natural strength and impact of any shorter unit that is part of a longer one (that is, you can use rhythm to put greater or lesser emphasis on a particular word in a phrase, or a particular phrase in a sentence, sentence in a paragraph, and on up).

Rhythm stacks with position and the other things that give a word strength. For example, with "bedknobs and broomsticks," the rhythm (DUH-da-da-DUH-da) is the same, whichever noun you put first. But "to boldly go" has a nice, regular rhythm—da-DUH-da-DUH—and ends on a strong beat. So the phrase has a verb, at the end, on a strong beat—three strengths all stacked together. "To go boldly," on the other hand, puts two strong beats together in the middle ("GO BOLDly"), interrupting the rhythm, and ends on a weak beat as well as with a weaker part of speech (the adverb). This is why "to boldly go" has so much more of a ring to it than "to go boldly" (for everyone except really strict grammarians, anyway). Poets do this kind of thing all the time, but it's useful in prose, too.

The Lego Theory, Part Four

Before I go on, I would like to remind everybody once again that the vast majority of authors do not consciously and deliberately micromanage their writing to wring every last bit of strength out of every word's position, rhythm, strength, and sound. Most of the time, we work by feel—this way feels better/stronger than that way. I personally find that it helps to know *why* things work, especially when one is struggling with those one or two places in a piece that just don't seem to be working, but I rarely do this kind of conscious analysis on my own stuff, and when I do, it's pretty much always in a revision pass.

Back to phrases.

I've already talked about position and rhythm. The third key property of phrases is length. Theoretically, you can string together as many nouns or verbs, or stuff in as many adverbs and adjectives, as you want in a phrase, but it doesn't take long to overload something this short. If you have to wade through six or seven adjectives/adverbs to get to the noun, you can lose track. On the other hand, you can manipulate how much impact a phrase has by making it longer (less) or shorter (more).

Length gets more important the further up the chain of units you go, in part because the amount of flexibility you have increases. A phrase can only get to five or six words before it starts to collapse under its own weight and becomes useless; two words is as short as you can get (I think; I'm not sure a single word counts as a "phrase," no matter how much information and context is packed into it). But sentences can be as short as one word or go on for hundreds of words, and so can paragraphs, allowing the writer a lot more room to create different effects by changing the length of a sentence or paragraph (more on that when we get there).

Next on the "properties" list comes contrast. At the phrase level, most of the contrast comes from word choices—putting a long word next to a short one or a color adjective next to one for smell or changing the rhythm in a longer phrase. But once again, the further up the levels you get, the more possibilities for contrast you have—not just word choice within phrases, but the contrast between two phrases, between phrases and sentences, between different kinds of sentences.

Many writers think of contrast (if they think of it at all) as a matter of *content*—the difference between action scenes and emotional ones, for instance. That's certainly one aspect of contrast, but it only becomes important when you get way up in the middle levels and start talking about types of scenes. Contrast can be really useful at much lower levels of structure. Think of that big red Lego dinosaur. Now picture it with just two of the red Legos replaced by pale pink ones. You can get this same effect in prose by suddenly changing one or more of the properties (rhythm or length, for instance) through a change in word choice.

Contrast loses most of its impact if there is too much of it, too often. Two pale pink Legos on a giant red dinosaur would stand out because of the contrast. If, however, the dinosaur is built of Legos that change color every two or three blocks, none of the colors would stand out much and instead you'd get a confetti effect. I'm not sure what you'd call this in prose, but it certainly happens now and again, and if for some reason the writer is actively trying to make contrast less important in a piece, using a confetti effect is at least as useful as trying to avoid any contrast at all (and possibly much easier to do).

Phrases and their properties are important because they are a big part of what creates complexity in clauses and sentences, and all of their properties—position/order, rhythm, length, and contrast—apply to every unit of English from phrases on up. In other words, just as the first word in a phrase is a little stronger because of its position, so is the first sentence in a paragraph, the first paragraph in a chapter or scene, the first chapter of a book (hence the whole concept of the "hook"). There's a rhythm within phrases, within sentences, within paragraphs. Shorter sentences and paragraphs have more impact than longer ones (if they aren't used so much that there's no contrast—see confetti effect, above). I'll talk about this more when I finally get to some of the things you can do with all this stuff.

The Lego Theory, Part Five

Clauses are the next step up from phrases, and they are intimately connected with sentences. They come in two varieties, independent and dependent, and the first sort *is* a sentence or could be if you punctuated it differently. "He ran, but she escaped" is a single sentence built out of two independent clauses with a comma and conjunction in the middle; "He ran. She escaped" is two sentences. Independent clauses are stronger than dependent clauses because they're whole.

The difference between a dependent clause and a sentence is that a dependent clause can't stand alone. Putting a period at the end of a dependent clause doesn't make it a sentence because it isn't finished. It needs an independent clause to prop it up and finish it off, the same way a string of adjectives needs a noun at the end in order to be more than a random collection of words. "The giant red cold blinking artificial" is just a collection of adjectives until you add "goldfish" to the end, whereupon it becomes a phrase. "When the volcano exploded" and "because he knew" are both dependent clauses; sticking them together doesn't make a sentence until you add an independent clause like "George ran" or "she would escape."

If you leave a dependent clause or a phrase lying around all by itself, like "if Helen had set off the bomb" or "to swallow unwary travelers," you have a sentence fragment. Sentence fragments aren't really a separate level; they're broken-off bits of other building blocks. Like half a Lego, fragments can still be useful to achieve certain effects, but you have to be careful where and how you use them because a broken-off bit of a block frequently isn't as strong as a whole one and doesn't look as nice.

With the sentence level come some more key properties

of prose, two of which are variation and complexity. Sentences can be simple and straightforward or run on for a page of complicated interlocking clauses. Starting from a single, short, simple independent clause like "George ran," you can pile on phrases and descriptors: up the road, away from the airport, after the bomber, into the glowing forest, next to the fairy hill. You can add a few dependent clauses or link your first independent clause to a second one to make a compound sentence. Or you can do all of those things at once: "When the volcano exploded, George ran quickly up the road and away from the airport, because he knew that if Helen had set off the bomb, she would escape into the glowing forest next to the fairy hill, where the giant red blinking artificial goldfish waited to swallow unwary travelers."

And you can vary all of the elements you use within a given sentence (that is, if it has multiple elements; it's kind of hard to get much internal variation out of a short, simple sentence like "George ran."). In the above example, there are short clauses ("because he knew") and longer ones ("George ran up the hill and away from the airport"), different types of phrases and clauses, and every part of speech from noun to conjunction (except for interjections). The rhythm changes, but not too often (and the pauses indicated by commas fall in places where there's a missing beat, for the most part).

Variation is immensely important for fiction because fiction is entertainment, and no matter what kind of entertainment you are looking at, if it gets boring, it has failed. If your writing is all the same at any level—if all the phrases are the same length, or all the sentences have the same rhythm or complexity, or all the words are one syllable—the reader starts to get used to it. If this goes on too long, the readers can get bored or irritated, which is why you want to vary different elements from time to time. On the other hand, too much variation has the same effect as trying to work in too much contrast—you get a hard-to-read confetti effect if you try too hard.

As you can see, the further up the levels you go, from words to phrases to clauses and sentences, the more options and properties you have to juggle and the more complex things can get. This continues up through paragraphs and scenes and chapters, which is one reason why juggling all this stuff to get to a more effective outcome gets harder and harder. You can micromanage every word and phrase and sentence in a poem (you pretty much have to micromanage everything in a haiku), but if you try to juggle all this stuff consciously at all possible levels of language in a one hundred thousand word novel, you will go crazy.

The Lego Theory, Part Six

There are two more properties of sentences that I want to mention, and the first of them is pattern. It's a little more complicated than some of the other properties because you can create a pattern out of any of the properties I've talked about so far, and not just one at a time, either. Even in a short, simple sentence like "he hunted," you have the alliterative pattern of the opening h's. More commonly, you see patterns of repetition made by using the same words or structure in the phrases and clauses that get put together to make a complex sentence: "He hunted them with sharpened forks, with crumbling sealing-wax, with enameled thimbles, and with opaque glassware" and "I told you in French; I told you in German; I told you in Japanese and Arabic and Thai."

Patterns—especially simple, repetitive patterns—give more emphasis and strength to whatever is included in the pattern. Setting up a pattern and then breaking it, partially breaking it, or extending it, can make a sentence work even better, especially if there's a subtle pattern underlying an obvious one. In "I told you…," I was deliberately setting up a repetitive structural pattern—"I told you X, I told you Y"—and then extending it with "I told you A and B and C." What I didn't realize until I got to this paragraph and looked back at it was that I *also* had a pattern of syllables going, from one-syllable "French" to two in "German" to three with "Japanese" and "Arabic."

And as soon as I realized that, I tried changing the last one to "Mandarin" to carry the syllable pattern one step further, but I didn't like it. I tried a couple of other languages…and then I realized that the problem was that following the pattern of syllables had set up a rhythm, and that the reason I wasn't happy was that all of my three-syllable language choices meant that I was ending the sentence on a weak beat. Going back to a one-syllable language brought the whole pattern back around to the beginning while also providing a more emphatic closure by ending on a strong beat.

In a story, which word I'd pick would depend on what came next. If it was "…And you didn't listen, not once!", I'd go with "Thai" because the stronger ending shuts off the list of languages in preparation for moving on to the next part of the complaint. If what came next was "I sent you notes, I sent you letters, I sent you articles and novellas and haiku," then I'd probably go with "Mandarin" at the end of the first sentence because I wouldn't want to shut off the pattern just yet.

Which brings me to the last property of sentences that I want to talk about: content. It's last because it's the thing most people think about first when it comes to writing sentences. After all, the whole point of a sentence is to get an idea or image across to the reader.

What people sometimes forget is that you can look at content in much the same way as any other property of a sentence: as a way of adjusting how much impact you want a sentence (or paragraph or scene or whatever from there on up) to have on the reader. People tend to react more strongly to sentences about exploding volcanoes than they do to sentences about doing the dishes. Yes, you can use other properties and word choices to make the exploding volcano feel less important and the dishes feel more important, but you have to work at it.

As you move further up the levels, into paragraphs and scenes, content (like variation and complexity and contrast) becomes more and more important because there are so many more ways to use it over a wider and wider range. The context— the wider content of the paragraph and the scene and the overall story—has a lot to do with whether the volcanic explosion is a sudden, high-impact shock, or whether it comes as almost a relief after a long, slow buildup of expectations, or whether it's just one more disaster in a string of disasters that's gone on so long it's become the norm.

The Lego Theory, Part Seven

As I said, paragraphs are where this analogy switches from looking at building blocks to looking at what you are building out of the building blocks. Consequently, the main properties of paragraphs aren't so much about the paragraphs as a unit; they're more about the way all the earlier blocks and bits of blocks fit together to get a particular effect.

Paragraphs are groups of sentences. That's the official definition I learned back in grade school—a paragraph consists of one or more sentences that deal with a single idea or topic. What I didn't find out until much, much later is that paragraphs can also be looked at as a way of breaking down a larger idea—a story, a scene, an essay topic—into smaller, more easily digestible chunks. In other words, you can look at them as the largest unit of grammar/syntax or as the smallest unit of story.

Either way you look at it, though, paragraphs are a collective, and so I call the first major property of paragraphs *relationship*. The sentences in a paragraph have to relate to each other in ways that aren't predefined by parts of speech or the rules of grammar and syntax. Paragraphs also have to relate to each other in some way, or the story or essay devolves into incoherence.

The tricky thing about paragraphs is that they don't have the same kind of structural, grammatical, or syntactical rules that you get with words, phrases, and sentences. This is especially true when it comes to fiction, and it means you don't have anything to fall back on when you're not sure which sentence should go where. It's pretty clear if you've gotten the subject and the verb in the wrong spots in a sentence, but sometimes the only way to figure out the order of the sentences in a paragraph is to move them around six or eight times to see what works better (and imagine what a pain that was prior to word processors!). Sometimes I end up moving a sentence up or down a couple of paragraphs because it relates better there than it does in the place where I originally thought it up.

The relationship between sentences within a paragraph is usually based on content—they're all about the same thing. The relationship between paragraphs usually has to do with moving the story smoothly forward—the way the action or the conversation or the description flows from one paragraph-sized unit to the next. If the relationship isn't clear and the topic of one paragraph doesn't move smoothly into the topic of the next, you probably need a transition to link the two (or at least clarify the relationship between the respective paragraphs). Also, it's worth mentioning that most paragraphs have to relate to both the previous paragraph and to the one that comes next (unless of course you're at a scene or chapter break. Even then, you usually want some kind of transition).

The second major property of paragraphs is…I dunno, I've already used "significance," so let's call this one "importance." Each paragraph is presumed to be about as important as every other paragraph in the story (if it isn't, why is it there?), and each paragraph theoretically has just as many sentences as it needs in order to get its idea across. Since importance is a property of paragraphs rather than sentences, it spreads out pretty evenly across all the sentences in the paragraph, whether it's a two-sentence paragraph or a ten-sentence paragraph. The sentences in a two-sentence paragraph thus end up feeling more important or more urgent than the sentences in the eight-sentence paragraph.

A one-sentence paragraph seems more important still.

Especially if it's short.

It grabs attention.

Hard.

At least, it does the first time you use the trick. After a while, though, the principles of contrast and variation come into play, and all those one-sentence, one-line, one-word attention-grabbers stop feeling important or urgent and start feeling gimmicky. "Fun with Dick and Jane" has almost nothing but one-line, one-sentence paragraphs, and I don't think anyone sees it as a great model for grabbing and holding the reader's attention.

The last thing I want to say about paragraphs is a reminder that they're at the top end of the chain of building blocks that runs from words to phrases to sentences. Consequently, all of the properties of those smaller blocks add up and apply to paragraphs. Paragraphs, though, are the point where things start to shift. Properties like complexity and variation and importance and content become more and more important from here on up, while properties like sound and rhythm and length become less so. A one-word paragraph commands attention. A one-word scene…I'm not sure that's even possible, and I'm quite sure I've never seen one, which tells you right there that even if it is possible, it's not really very useful for most writers.

The Lego Theory, Part the Last

This is the last of this series. Really. I mean it.

Part of why it's the last is that I'm up to scenes, and I'm not really sure I can take this analogy this far, let alone any farther. Paragraphs were OK, because they're the linking point between the basic blocks of language—words, phrases, sentences, paragraphs—and the things you can do by putting those blocks together in different ways—paragraphs, scenes, chapters, novels.

That means that from paragraphs on up, the writer needs to look at what he or she wants to build and make decisions based on the overall goal, then work backward to find the words and phrases and sentences with the properties he or she needs to get to that goal. You can't build a big red dinosaur if all you have are green and blue blocks. The way you fit the blocks together will be different if you want the dinosaur to be a raptor or a Tyrannosaurus rex, or if you want it to be standing upright instead of crouched.

In other words, you have to have some idea what you want to say and/or what you are trying to do.

This is why so much how-to-write advice starts from various theories of what a scene needs and how to get to it: critical elements, goals, disasters, conflict, tension, drama, theme. They're all trying to slap some structure or organization on the enormous number of possible things that writers can say and do in a scene. Everybody seems to take a different approach, which is fine, because with anything as complicated as a scene, there are probably as many different approaches as there are writers.

All that complexity means that I can't really sum up scenes in terms of a couple of properties because there are too many different things—*important* different things—you can do with scenes. The best rule of thumb for scenes I know is the one I talked about in *The Big Three*: that a scene that doesn't do one of three things (advance the plot, deepen the characterization, reveal background/backstory) doesn't belong in the story, that a scene that does only one or two of the three can usually be improved by adding the missing thing, and that a scene that does all three things is a keeper.

But it is equally useful to look at scenes through the lens of the old journalism concept of five w's and an h: who, what, when, where, why, and how. In fiction, some of those things are often not stated explicitly—the readers are often left to judge for themselves why the characters have behaved as they do, for instance, and the "how" is frequently left for the climax of the overall story.

Nevertheless, a scene involves characters (who), something happening (what and how), at a particular time (when) and place (where), for some reason (why). The fact that these things aren't laid out in so many words makes it even more important for the writer to know they are in there somewhere, or at least that the reader has enough information to figure them out.

That's about all I can think of to say about scenes that really applies to the category "scenes." Everything else I can think of has to do with specific subcategories: dialogue scenes, action scenes, contemplative scenes, reaction scenes, emotional scenes, which gets back to complexity and what you want to say and how the scene fits into the story as a whole. And since saying what you want to say is the goal of this whole series, I think that's a reasonable place to stop.

A Line Around the Outer Edge

"Outline—(1) A line showing the shape or boundary of
something; (2) A statement or summary of the chief facts
about something; (3) A sketch containing lines but no
shading"—*Oxford American Dictionary*

If you want to be a professional novelist, odds are that sooner or
later, you're going to write an outline. In fact, I would go so far
as to say that eventually you will *have* to write an outline, which is
an extremely rare sort of statement for me. But what I mean by
"have to write an outline" is not what most people think I mean.

This is because there are two types of outlines that are
commonly used by professional writers, and one of them
is entirely optional. The first, and the one that most writers
will have to do sooner or later, is the outline that's meant to
sell a book (which can be further subdivided into outlines of
unfinished manuscripts and outlines of finished manuscripts).
The second is the planning outline, which writers do for their
own guidance. It's totally optional; whether you use one of these
or not should depend on whether it helps your process or not.

An outline meant to sell a book fits under number two of
that opening definition: it's a statement or summary of the chief
facts about the book, with maybe a bit of number one, a verbal
line showing the shape of the book. If the book isn't finished,
the shape may be a bit vague and some of the facts may not
have been determined yet; if the book has been written through
at least a full first draft, the shape should be clear and the facts
solid. Otherwise, the outline for a book that hasn't been finished
yet and the outline for a book that has are usually quite similar
in form and general content—the main difference comes when
you sit down to write the one for the unfinished book and
realize just how much you still don't know about what's going
to happen.

Please note the emphasis on facts and shape. The two main
things an outline-to-sell needs to do are: (1) name the main
characters (not all the characters, not your favorite characters, but
the main characters, which even with an ensemble cast usually

means maybe three or four on the side of the protagonists and maybe two on the antagonist side. If you find yourself wanting to name more, you should stop and consider carefully whether you really need to name them. What's needed in a one hundred thousand word novel may not be in a five-page plot outline) and (2) summarize the major events and key plot points of the story.

A sales outline is not the place to play coy games about what happens or how major plot events occur if you know them. "Jack is imprisoned, but escapes the dungeon with help from a guard who changes sides" is acceptable, or even "Jack is imprisoned and escapes," if you're short on space. "Jack has many exciting adventures" is right out, unless there really are far too many to fit in five pages, in which case you give a couple of specific examples: "Jack is captured by pirates, marooned on a desert island, unjustly imprisoned and escapes, and has many other adventures before discovering that his real destiny is…"

There are also length restrictions on outlines you're sending to a publisher: five pages is the norm, but a few publishers request one-page or two-page outlines. If they specify, give them what they ask for. There really isn't a standard format for a selling outline, though some publishers will ask that specific points be covered. I just write a summary of the central plot, but some people prefer to do a chapter or section breakdown, or Dramatis Personae plus a paragraph of plot summary, or…well, there's lots of variety. Again, if the publisher says they want a particular format, do it that way. Rewriting five pages of outline shouldn't take *that* long, and you never know—looking at your story that way might tell you something interesting about it that you didn't know before.

There is no point in writing a "sales outline" for short fiction. Magazine and anthology editors don't want them; it takes more time to read an outline, send a form letter asking for the story, and then read a short story than it does to just read the short story in the first place.

When it comes to the second sort of outline, the one writers do for purposes of guidance and planning in actually writing the novel, all bets are off.

91

Lights, Camera...What?

Action scenes are the bread-and-butter of whole genres of fiction. As such, they're pretty important, and I was rather stunned to realize that I've said very little about writing them. I was even more stunned when I went to the bookcase that's full of how-to-write books—five shelves of them—and couldn't find even *one* that really talked about writing action scenes. (A couple of them pretended to, but what they were actually talking about usually turned out to be plot, or else conflict or suspense or drama within an action scene.)

I think part of the reason for this is that action scenes don't get much respect. They aren't very intellectual; they're lowest common denominator. Everybody knows what an action scene is, and everybody can spot a bad one at twenty paces. So they should be easy, right?

Yeah, right.

Another part of the problem is, I think, that as usual, "action" can mean more than one thing. There's the "action of the story," which usually means the events that make up the plot, even if those events are all conversations and social encounters, and there's "the story has no action," which usually means that the plot does not involve car chases, gun battles, or other physically demanding activities.

For purposes of this discussion, I am going to define action scenes as scenes of *physical* action: people attacking each other with fists or weapons, chase scenes, avalanches or trains barreling down toward people, escapes, and the like. Suspense alone is not enough; a ticking time bomb is not enough. A formal tea party can be filled with all sorts of emotional time bombs, generating plenty of suspense and tension, but it's not an action scene until the ninjas break in through the window to hold everyone hostage.

By that definition, the first key thing to remember about writing an action scene is that there is movement. People are *doing* something—running, fighting, sneaking, throwing, searching, blowing things up, whatever. Something physical (besides talking) is going on. In addition, whatever is happening often doesn't take much elapsed time (a fight scene is more likely to cover a minute or two than an hour). Action scenes generally move fast; more to the point, they read fast. If the action starts to drag or the scene feels like it's going on forever, something is wrong.

Note that this does not mean an action scene has to be short. As long as the tension and the pace remain high, an action scene can take pages or even chapters to cover a few minutes or an hour.

Action scenes are actually a subset of description, but instead of describing a static setting or backstory, the writer is describing movement…which means paying a lot of attention to verbs. Anyone who remembers "Schoolhouse Rock" should be unsurprised to hear this.

This leads me to one of the first big mistakes some people make with action scenes: dropping in some "action" to fill time or "liven up" a boring stretch of story. Action, like static description, needs a reason to be in the story. Readers will usually cut you some slack in this regard—they don't expect to find out why the ninjas are attacking the tea party right away. But random encounters seldom work well in fiction, so readers do expect there to be a reason for the ninja attack, they expect it to have something to do with the story, and they expect it to be explained eventually.

To put it another way, whatever action sequence the characters are engaged in needs two goals. The first one is the goal the writer has for the scene. It may be that the structure or pacing of the story requires some action at this point; it may be the way to reveal some plot-critical information or set up for a later revelation or plot twist; it may be a way to expose some aspect of the particular characters. Unless this goal is related to pacing or structure, it may not actually require an action scene to achieve, so the writer needs to at least consider the possibility that the most effective way of achieving his or her goal may be some other sort of scene entirely.

The second, and possibly more important, goal for an

action scene is the one the characters have. In fiction, characters usually act to achieve something, and it's usually plot-related in some way. The ninjas attack the tea party in order to kidnap the heroine; the bandits attack the caravan because they want the jade idol in the second wagon; the wolves attack the farm because they are starving, and they're starving because the recently arrived dragon has eaten all their usual prey. If none of the characters have a reason for doing whatever they're doing, the scene probably doesn't belong in this story.

So how *do* you build an action scene? There are a lot of things to consider. Some of them will be dictated by decisions the writer has made earlier in the story, and the first and most important of these is viewpoint, which frequently implies level.

Action can be "seen" by the reader from lots of different levels. A bird's-eye view is a big picture description that is most often employed when describing a full-scale battle (but it can work quite well for smaller fights). A general's view is closer in, but still fairly big picture, and allows for more surprises because the general can't see everything the way a bird could. A participant's view is restricted to his or her own experiences, but it can make the action feel more personal and involving. If the writer is telling a story in omniscient viewpoint, as a memoir written long after the fact, or in multiple tight third, he or she can think about which of these levels to employ and when, and how to mix them to get the best effect.

(Georgette Heyer's description of the Battle of Waterloo in her novel *An Infamous Army* is primarily an omniscient big picture description of the action, but she occasionally drops into a closer, more personal view of characters we've heard of or met earlier in the novel. The result is a masterpiece, which was actually used at Sandhurst Military Academy in England to teach the Battle of Waterloo. It is also an excellent example for writers to study.)

The first thing you do before writing an action scene (and here I mean action in the sense of a full-out *battle* scene) is to learn something about strategy and tactics. This means hitting the library; there are tons of good books on the subject.

However, when I hit the library back when, I read several books on strategy and tactics and emerged no wiser than before because even the basic ones were too advanced for my meager level of knowledge on the subject.

So I hit the children's section.

Seriously, if you really, truly don't understand basic terminology (which was at least half my problem with the adult-level "beginner" books), the children's section is the place to go. I think I worked my way down to middle-grade books before I found something comprehensible and then started working my way back up the age groups. It was exceedingly useful.

The second thing I did, which I also highly recommend if you can manage it, is to find someone who actually knows something about military strategy—a wargamer, a military history buff, someone who's actually been in the army or navy. Then you ask them to help you plan the battle and take copious notes on what sorts of questions they ask you because those are all the things you need to know in order to figure out what the battle is going to look like.

The very first thing my military consultant asked was, "What kind of terrain are they going to be fighting in?" And he didn't mean "plains" or "hills" or other general descriptors; he wanted a map showing the rivers, woods, hills, roads, and city walls in the immediate vicinity of the battle, along with basics like what the weather had been like and where the sun would rise and set.

The next thing he asked was, "What kind of forces does each side have?" This included numbers, equipment, and capabilities for every segment of the armies from cavalry and infantry to archers and magicians. This is moderately complex, even if the armies are all "regular" troops of the sort you'd find in real life, because you have to decide whether the army is balanced between infantry, ranged attackers, and cavalry, or whether it's predominately one kind of troops with few or none of the others. When you have multiple species involved—aliens, elves, dwarves—or futuristic technologies, it goes from moderately complex to insane.

Except for omniscient, memoir, or multiple tight third-person, the viewpoint the writer is using for the story pretty much determines the level from which the action is going to be described. A first-person narrator who is telling the story as it happens is not likely to know anything that is happening on the other side of a battle unless he's an observer with binoculars rather than a participant; the same goes for a single tight third-person viewpoint. The writer, however, quite often needs to know the whole big picture, whether we're talking about a full-scale battle, a smallish bandit attack, or a one-on-one duel.

Which brings us to my next point: planning. The larger the scale of the action, the more planning is a good idea for most writers. (Note that "most"; this is yet another area where personal process trumps how-to-write advice. Some people just can't plan ahead, because it wrecks their ability to continue on. These folks have to "plan" in retrospect, working out how the close-up scenes they've written can be retrofitted into a big picture that makes sense.)

Plans should be flexible. Action scenes are often most effective when the things that happen are as unexpected as they would be in a real battle or fight or chase, and a writer who has managed to surprise herself has a greater chance of surprising the reader than she otherwise would. I'm not talking about big surprises here, though that can happen; I'm talking about little things that may or may not change the outcome of the action: the horse that throws a shoe, the gun that jams, the opponent who drops his knife and bites…the things that come up without warning during the process of putting words down on the page. (If that's not how it works for you, don't worry about it. It's not something you can train or force; it's just how some—some, not all—writers' heads work.)

I've been talking here specifically about battles, but a lot of the principles apply to writing other types of major scenes and set pieces, whether we're talking about the king's coronation, the big heist, or the lifesaving operation at the end of the story.

At this point, it's time to really start talking about nuts and bolts.

What you need to know up front (unless you are a total

"surprise me" writer who can't know anything up front) is (1) what the setting is like, (2) who the actors are in the scene, (3) where each of them is at any given time and what each of them is doing, (4) what you (and they) expect to get out of this, and (5) how all this interacts with the larger picture, at least to some extent.

The setting determines what you (and your characters) have available to work with. If your action scene is a car chase through San Francisco, you have different options that you would if it's a chase on skis through the Alps; if it's a brawl in a bar, you have different options than if your characters are dueling with lightsabers on a spaceship.

Knowing who the actors are means knowing who all is present and watching as well as knowing which characters are actually going to be doing the punching, running, shooting, or whatever. It should be pretty obvious why you need to know who is supposed to be actively involved—which characters are acting determines what skills and weapons they'll use and, to a large extent, how they will approach what they're doing (as well as the details of what they'll do). It's not as obvious why you might need to know about the bystanders, but they, too, can have an effect on the action, so it's usually worthwhile deciding whether there are any around, what they are doing, and whether they will affect the main action.

Where each character is and what each character does during an action scene are inextricably intertwined. If A is sitting behind a desk and B is leaning against the wall by the fireplace, neither is in position to suddenly haul off and slug the other. On the other hand, B is perfectly placed to grab the antique sword hanging over the fireplace and charge…but if you don't know he's standing beside a fireplace, you aren't likely to think of the sword.

Choreographing an action scene can be done in a bunch of ways. You can get a bunch of friends together and actually role-play the whole thing (which I find a bit extreme, but which I know has been done to very good effect by a number of writers). Or you can act out the whole scene yourself, playing all the parts in turn (this is particularly helpful for writers who are strongly kinesthetic and need to feel the way the characters move and stand). You can get some action figures and play out the movement of the scene. Or you can diagram it on paper, like a series of football plays, with circles and crosses and little arrows to show who is supposed to be moving where, and maybe asterisks to show thrusts or punches and figure eights to show tripping over barrels, or whatever diagram codes you come up with. Storyboarding (drawing a series of sketches to illustrate the action) works well for some artistically inclined writers (and even for some who can only draw stick figures).

What your characters want out of the scene, and what you want out of it, determines where it's going. You need to know both; if your characters want to capture the traitor, but you need him to escape in order to move the plot to the next phase, then you arrange the choreography so the bad guy escapes, even though the good guys are trying really hard. If you need the traitor to be captured, you stack the deck in favor of the heroes.

The fifth thing the writer usually needs to know is what the big picture is and how all the local, character-on-character action fits in. If we're talking about a battle scene, the writer often plans out the overall battle first, then figures out which characters will be there and what will happen to them based on the ebb and flow of the larger battle (even though the reader may not find out how the larger battle went until a chapter or two after the big action scene). Sometimes, though, the writer knows he wants the hero run-down during an enemy cavalry charge, so the big battle has to be planned so that there is an enemy cavalry charge that makes tactical and strategic sense.

In other words, very little of this has to be done in any particular order (though it's a little hard to figure out what your characters are doing if you don't already know which of them are in the scene). And none of it is set in stone. If you get a better idea, jump on it, even if it means junking your last two hours of work.

Finally, if you look at your action plan, and it just looks too easy for one side or the other, there are two things to remember:

"No battle plan survives contact with the enemy," and Murphy's Law: anything that can go wrong, will. Murphy is a writer's best friend; bad luck and other people messing up (and consequently derailing the plan) are always more plausible in fiction than everything going right.

And a final reminder: some writers *can't* plan in advance; if you are one of them, you'll probably need to do at least some of this stuff in revision, retrofitting your battle to fit your action scene, for instance. If you *can't* plan without destroying your need to write, don't worry about it. But don't kid yourself, either; if it's just that you don't *want* to plan…tough. Nobody said this job was going to be easy.

Say That Again, Would You?

Dialogue is one of the bedrock necessities in about ninety-nine percent of fiction. Plays and screenplays are almost nothing but dialogue, and it's not unusual to see whole scenes or entire short stories that are told entirely in dialogue (sometimes without even speech tags to let the reader know who's talking). It's something that seems like it ought to come naturally—after all, everybody talks, right? Yet dialogue is a considerable problem for a lot of writers, and a tin ear for dialogue has brought more than one would-be novelist to disaster.

The first most important thing to remember about dialogue is that it is a model of speech not a transcription. The second most important thing to remember about dialogue is that it is communication between two or more characters. This means that it is almost always made up of short exchanges, back and forth. Unless one of your characters is giving a lecture, like the detective in a classic murder mystery doing his summing up, you should expect a page of dialogue to have paragraphs that are mainly one to three lines long. There's usually lots of white space as a result; in fact, one of the classic tests for whether the characters' speeches are running on too long is to print out a page and tape it to the wall, then walk across the room so that you can see the pattern of the paragraphs and how much white space there is on the page. These days, you can get the same effect by reducing the font size:

Above is an example. On the left is a page of descriptive paragraphs; on the right, a page of dialogue. Shrinking the font makes it instantly obvious which is which—and you can see immediately if your dialogue is bogging down in long speeches, and take steps to break it up.

The second classic trick for checking your dialogue is to read it out loud. This lets you know whether it sounds right in general; it also is an easy way to identify tongue-twister phrases that no one would actually ever say.

If you're having trouble figuring out how to do dialogue generally, try reading some plays or screenplays. Out loud, so you are seeing and hearing the words at the same time and can get a feel for how the words on the page work when spoken aloud and vice versa. If you really want a workout, get hold of the screenplay for any movie that has lots of dialogue, read it aloud, and then watch the movie while following along with the script. Even if you're not having trouble, paying a little extra attention to passages of dialogue in your favorite movies and novels will very likely give you some useful ideas.

The next thing to think about is the difference in the speech patterns of your various characters—the way each particular person phrases things, depending on their individual personalities and backgrounds. You can do this by consciously coming up with speech tics (like having a character who never uses contractions or who always ends their sentences with "yeah?"), which can be effective in small doses but which gets really annoying to read when every character in a story has one. Or you can come up with broader ways of distinguishing your characters' voices (Shakespeare had all his noblemen speak in unrhymed iambic pentameter and their servants and more ordinary people just any which way. The lyricist for *Man of La Mancha* gave Don Quixote complex sentences and syntax ["I am I, Don Quixote, the Lord of La Mancha; destroyer of evil am I!"] and his servant short, simple sentences and no words of more than two syllables ["I'm Sancho! Yes, I'm Sancho! I follow my master to the end!"]).

Or you can just look at different speech patterns in real life. Take the same sentence of dialogue/information and rephrase it in as many different ways as you can:

"I think you're making a mistake."

"That's wrong, dumbo."

"I believe, sir, that you are in error in this instance."

"Um, do you think...I mean, is that really the way you want to do that? Because it doesn't look quite right to me."

"That ain't no way to do that there thing."

"Kiddo, you got that upside down and backward."

"I'm afraid that's not going to work."

"A guy could have some problems doing things that way."

"You're screwing up again! Honestly, can't you do anything right?"

...and on, and on.

I was on my third book before I started trying to do this consciously, and my first few efforts were exaggerated (Telemain in *Talking to Dragons*, Amberglas in *The Seven Towers*) because it was the only way I could be sure I was keeping them consistent. More subtle variations took me longer to get the hang of. Most of the time now, speech patterns and character voices are automatic for me—I know when I've used a word or a turn of phrase that a particular character just wouldn't say, so I fix it immediately. But at the beginning, it required a lot more conscious attention. So don't worry if it takes a while.

But What Does It Look Like? (a bit about description)

Description is one of those love-it-or-hate-it things. Some readers want more, more, more; they want to see every button and bead on the dress, every scratch on the woodwork. Other people roll their eyes and complain about slowing down the story when they run across long passages of descriptive infodump. Still others want to have their cake and eat it, too—they want to know what everything looks like, but they don't want to stop and wade through two pages of scene setting every time the characters go somewhere new.

The writer can't please everyone, but there are a couple of different things one can try, depending on one's personal style and on the viewpoint of the story. You can, of course, go ahead and do the two-page descriptive infodump. If done well, this will please some readers enormously. Other readers will sniff and give the story a pass.

A related technique is to use *short* descriptive paragraphs every time a new character arrives or the POV character enters a new place: "Harvey looked at the cottage. The thatched roof was uneven and rotting; mice had clearly made homes in it. The door hung crookedly on rusty hinges, and the stone flags in front of it were cracked and half buried in mud. As he watched, a crow flew out of one of the empty windows. Sighing, he started toward the door."

This amounts to a mini infodump. It provides a description without stopping the story for long…but it does still stop the forward flow of the story, at least most of the time. If you're writing an omniscient viewpoint, the mini description often works fine. In tight third and first-person, it works best if your POV character is the sort to stop and take stock of every new place (and it helps if you intercut occasional character monologue/internal dialogue/reactions to remind us that this is the POV's description, such as: "The stone flag was cracked and half buried in mud; he would have to be careful not to trip when he got to it.")

A somewhat different approach is to give the description as part of the action, as the character experiences it through his senses: "Harvey started toward the cottage. His feet squished ankle-deep into the soft mud around it, and when he finally reached the stone flag that served as a doorstop, its two halves wobbled underfoot. The rusty door hinges had bent under the weight they held; it took all his strength and several minutes to wrestle the door open. Bits of half-rotted thatch dribbled onto his head as he worked, and his efforts startled a crow that had been hiding somewhere inside. As it flew out an empty window, cawing reproachfully, the door gave way at last. *Why me?* he thought, and went inside."

This gets in a lot of the same descriptive details as the mini infodump, but because Harvey is moving forward and doing things, the story doesn't stop while the reader gets the description. This technique works really well in both omniscient and tight third; in first-person, it depends on the POV narrator's voice. Again, it helps to intercut the occasional POV reaction or internal comment…but only occasionally. The more reaction you put in, the more psychological importance or weight the description has and the more convinced the reader will be that this place (or that rusty door hinge) is going to be vitally important somewhere. If it turns out not to be, it throws the reader off.

Sometimes, especially if there are several characters in a scene, you can give the basic setting in a line or so and then add details *both* in dialogue and as the characters act and experience the setting:

"As Harvey and Jane approached the ruined cottage, Jane shook her head. 'Looks creepy,' she said.

'It's just old,' Harvey told her in an unconvincing tone.

They started for the door, their feet sinking ankle-deep in the soft mud. 'Watch your step; the flagstone is cracked,' Harvey said.

Something rustled, and Jane jumped. 'What was that?'

'Mice in the thatch.' Harvey studied the door with misgiving. The hinges had rusted, and it hung crookedly. An experimental tug confirmed that it was jammed in place. 'Give me a hand with this.'"

In all cases, the thing to focus on are the details, the critical bits, the one or two things that make this cottage/castle/bar different from every other cottage/castle/bar or the one or two things that the POV character would especially notice. A bard, entering the bar, might well notice the worn carving of a harp on the end of the bar table, while a mercenary, entering the same bar, might be more taken with the oddly shaped sword hanging on the far wall. Neither one would be likely to comment on the wooden rafters or the beer kegs, unless there were something unusual about them. Of course, if you are writing in first-person and your narrator happens to be the oblivious sort who really doesn't notice anything...you're up a creek.

Also note that the more the description is sandwiched in among dialogue and character action, the longer the passage gets. For a short, not-terribly-important scene, you may want to use a mini infodump/summary in order to keep things short. And, as always, variation is good; if you always use the same techniques to provide descriptive details, sooner or later your readers will start noticing. Finally, using sensory cues other than visual ones (sounds, smells, textures/sensations/feeling, taste) can add a lot—things like the soft mud and the flagstone wobbling underfoot or the sounds of the mice and the crow.

Where Are We?

Every story, short or long, takes place somewhere. Every scene takes place somewhere. And every place has features about it that are unique, whether it is the collection of overly cute fairy-figurines on the mantelpiece in the parlor, the cracked and faded mural across the back wall of the bar, or the odd kink in the third-level corridor on the spaceship.

This is one of those too-obvious-to-mention things that a lot of writers seem to forget on occasion. In at least some cases, I think the cause is related to the intensely media-heavy world we live in—when you're used to seeing what everything looks like, all at once, the way you do in a movie, it can be difficult to slow down and describe things one at a time, the way you must when you're working with words and sentences and paragraphs. In other cases, I suspect the problem is that the author is so familiar with the setting that, for them, one word or a short phrase is enough to evoke it: "Chicago," "New York," "D.C." In still other cases, the author is so afraid of making a mistake that they leave out everything that is not absolutely essential, resulting in a story where they characters might as well be wandering around in a thick gray fog. And sometimes, the author wants to use a setting that is imaginary, or at least unfamiliar to them, but they're too busy or in too much of a hurry to do the work of making or looking it up in as much depth as they need.

Yet setting is something that affects nearly every aspect of a story, one way or another. Accurate portrayals of a real-life place will please or delight readers who are familiar with that place already, and often impress readers who haven't yet been there. The first time I saw the movie *The Sting* (set in Chicago in the 1930s), I was utterly delighted by the fact that periodically there would be this loud rumbling and all of the characters would have to stop talking for a minute. I'd never seen anything set in Chicago that included the effect of the El on conversation (the El = elevated trains—that's what made the rumbling). My first real job, the summer after high school, was a block from the El, and that's exactly what happened.

There are two parts to writing a setting, whether it's a real place or an imaginary one: (1) putting in the key things that make this place different from any other, and (2) not putting in anything that doesn't fit. This applies to both onstage and offstage settings. (By "offstage setting," I mean any places that affect the characters or story that aren't actually shown. For instance, if your story takes place in San Diego, but one of the characters grew up in Wisconsin, that character had better have seen snow and know about the wind chill factor. You don't have to mention those details specifically unless they're important to the story, but that Wisconsin-raised character had better not look ignorant or surprised if the subject of snow comes up.)

The key things that you put into your descriptions will differ from story to story. If a character works or shops in the Loop in downtown Chicago, the El and its effects are probably worth mentioning (especially if they're working in an older building without modern soundproofing). If they work four or five blocks from the train lines and shop in the suburban malls, not so much.

Not putting in stuff that doesn't fit is just as important, and this is where the writer has to really be aware of his or her assumptions. If all you know is the climate and geography of the mid-continental plains, and you're writing about mountains or the coast, or in some cases even forests, you want to do a bunch of research and maybe even get some things checked out by friends who live in places like the ones you're writing about. A San Diego native who does NOT have trouble adjusting to his first winter in Winnipeg isn't going to be any more believable than the Wisconsin guy who has never heard of wind chill.

And all of this is strongly affected by the viewpoint and viewpoint character you're using. An omniscient viewpoint can describe whatever the author wants, however he wants. In a tight third-person or first-person viewpoint, it will break the viewpoint if the author describes things the viewpoint character can't see, doesn't know, or doesn't care about. The Frontier Magic series I'm working on doesn't have a lot of physical description of places or people, and it drives some of my readers crazy. But the memoir form I'm using for those books isn't suited to much description, and Eff isn't the sort to describe things she's really familiar with (and the one time I did it, the editor very wisely cut that paragraph). The point is, I still have to know what all those things she doesn't describe actually look like so that when I get a chance to slip something in, I can slip in the right thing.

Three Kinds of Research

Every so often, somebody asks me if I do research for my stories. I suspect this is because I write fantasy, and there is a perception among non-fantasy writers and readers that fantasy can simply be made up straight out of one's head, without regard to tedious things like facts. This is, of course, nonsense.

There are three basic kinds of story research: specific, general, and accidental. I don't know any writers who don't do all of them, though I don't think anyone else breaks it down quite this way (or if they do, I haven't heard of them).

Accidental research is the kind of thing every writer does all the time, in the course of living. Some of it is common everyday life experience; some of it is stuff you stumble across when you're watching TV or talking to a friend; some of it is uncommon, unsought events that a writer stores up for later. It's the reason my writer friend who got caught in Hurricane Sandy spent her spare minutes scribbling notes (and when she didn't have a pen and paper, focusing on things and mentally chanting, "I have to remember this, I have to remember this."). It's the reason another friend, after crawling on hands and knees through a smoke-filled hallway to escape from a burning apartment, spent the next ten minutes cursing the fact that she hadn't grabbed her glasses before she left, because without them, she couldn't get a really clear view of the progress of the fire and, later, what the firefighters were doing so that she could remember it for later.

It's also the way the sky looks on a clear autumn day, the annoying jingly Christmas Muzak that's everywhere in December, the way the air smells near a freeway, the sounds the pots and pans make when someone's cooking in the kitchen, the way bare trees develop a green haze for a day or two in spring when the buds break just before the leaves come fully out. It's the way your best friend wrinkles his forehead when he's thinking or your sister flaps her hands (you can't call it waving) when she gets excited. It's all the little details that everyone glances at, but writers work at storing up and remembering for when they have to write that scene in the spring woods or on the summer beach or at the Grand Harvest Festival.

Accidental research is about paying attention to whatever is going on around you because everything is material, and you never know what you're going to need one of these days. It's not about going out hunting for experiences to have; that comes under general or specific research…and really, if you aren't paying attention to what's already happening around you, going out to experience something new isn't likely to be a lot of help.

General research, on the other hand, is about going looking for things you don't know that you need to know. When I decide to write a book set in another place or time, the first thing I do is read a bunch of books that I hope will give me a feel for that place and time—biographies, historical overviews, social histories, books about daily life. When I'm between books, I read random things that catch my eye—books about pirates, women mine owners, castle building, Roman engineering, British diplomacy in the 1800s.

Writers are intellectual pack rats; we store up interesting facts and curious stories from every source we can find, from Uncle Joe's terrible jokes to scholarly works on obscure subjects. Sooner or later, it all comes back out in the work.

Specific research is what you do in order to find out the things you know you need to know. If I'm writing a book set in London in 1816, I go looking for street maps of London in 1816 (or as near to then as I can get). If I have a character who speaks thieves cant, I reach for my copy of *The 1811 Dictionary of the Vulgar Tongue*. If my characters are mixing up a potion, I look through my various herbals in search of ingredients (1) that people of whatever time I'm writing about thought were associated with the things I want the potion to do and (2) that my modern herbals agree are harmless (I don't add mercury to anything, for instance, even though according to some of my sources, it was considered a good remedy for quite a few things in the 1600s).

Accidental research is continuous. General research is usually a prewriting activity—it happens between books or when you have settled on a type of book that hasn't been fleshed out yet and needs more real-life background before you can pick a direction to go. Several writers of my acquaintance allot particular amounts of time for pre-book research—two months, six months, a year or more, depending on the project and the particular writer's temperament.

General research shifts into specific research gradually, sometimes imperceptibly. By the time I'm through the opening chapters of a book, I'm usually not reading general background any longer; I'm looking for specific bits of information. When and where was the first railroad built in New England? How much did a pair of stockings cost in London in 1822? When did armies start using drum signals, and how old were drummers when they were recruited and trained?

Those sorts of questions go on all through writing a book, right up to the end and on into revisions. They start to taper off during the copyedit, which is when I go back to reading about typhus and geology and the history of coffee until the next book comes along and the whole cycle starts over again.

All Together at Once

Writing is difficult to talk about. I mean the real thing, the stuff that happens when you are sitting there with your paper and pen or at your computer and telling a story.

We talk about bits and pieces of writing all the time. We separate out plot, characterization, setting, and theme into neat little boxes so we can study each of them and try to figure out how they work and how to do them better. Then we slice it all in a different direction and look at action and description and dialogue as separate things. And this is a good thing. It's how we understand a lot of the world, from toasters to the Hubble telescope.

Too often, though, some folks forget that when it comes to actually writing, everything has to happen at once. During the brief period when I was teaching classes, I occasionally saw stories that looked as if the author had stuck together a string of writing exercises: here is the two-paragraph description of setting, followed by three paragraphs of description of the character, followed by a page of dialogue, followed by a long paragraph of the viewpoint character's internal musing. Each exercise was done well, but putting them together didn't make a story. Reading them was like riding a bicycle over a cobblestone road—ka-THUMP, ka-THUMP, ka-THUMP.

This is not to say that one thing can't take precedence over everything else. It only makes sense to play to your strengths—a writer who is really good at witty dialogue will tend to have lots of witty dialogue, and the characterization and theme and plot will probably happen mainly through exchanges of dialogue rather than through action or description. But if the only thing that gets down on paper is a lot of talking heads, what the writer has is a screenplay or a play script, not a novel. And turning it into a novel is going to take more than throwing in a few random lumps of description and narrative summary.

Part of the problem, I think, is that we get used to talking about the bits and pieces of writing. We become accustomed to looking at one thing at a time. When I go hunting for an example of good action, I don't pay much attention to how well setting or characterization or theme is woven into the passage because those things aren't what I'm interested in. If the passage does a lot of other stuff well (in addition to the action), I tend not to mention it, because what I'm talking about at the moment is the action part (or the dialogue, or the characterization, or whatever I'm ranting about that day), and the other stuff isn't relevant to the point I'm making. Experience also tells me that people get really confused really fast if I try to show them more than one unfamiliar thing going on at the same time; after a while, I just quit trying.

But that only works if, once folks have a handle on plot and description and dialogue, they learn how to put it all together at once. Most writers figure this out for themselves. For some, like the students I mentioned above, it takes a while, or someone has to point out that they need to do more than one thing at a time. How to do it...well, that varies. Some writers learn by trusting their instincts; some by consciously and deliberately imitating their favorite writers for a while. I learned a lot from actually analyzing some of my favorite writers—when I was getting started, I'd come to a bit where I knew what I wanted to do, but not how to make it all work at once, and I'd stop and spend hours combing my bookshelves, looking for an actual published writer who had done something similar, so I could figure out how they'd gotten everything in and made it work. Some writers learn during revision—they didn't get everything in the first time, but they can see what's missing and get it in during the second pass. Some use a layering technique, concentrating on one thing at a time and going over the scene multiple times to make sure they have everything there.

Eventually, most of us learn to do most of the stuff all at once, most of the time, without needing to concentrate on it all at once. But it doesn't start off that way for most writers, and I think it's worth pointing that out. It's not enough to know how to do dialogue and characterization and plot and action; one has to learn to do it all together at the same time.

Building a World

Worldbuilding in some sense is a requirement for all writers. The people and places in fiction may have analogs in real life, but a writer in the United States cannot depend on every reader (or even most readers) being familiar with the Lincoln Park area of Chicago or the lower east side of Manhattan, much less the streets of Bombay or London or Ladysmith. The writer therefore has to recreate the real place in her fiction, choosing key details that evoke or imply a raft of other things that add up to that particular place and culture.

For those of us who write fantasy and science fiction, worldbuilding is even more of a necessity. The places our stories occur often have no real-life analogs; you cannot travel to Edoras or Cair Paravel to check out the sights and sounds and smells. You cannot look up the fashions of the Galactic Empire or the social customs of the Kzinti or Klingons. The writer makes them up.

Thinking these things through is one of the more difficult bits of worldbuilding, in my experience, because I have to think about what things mean and how they work and all the larger implications of that, and I have to do it from the viewpoints of many characters, not just my own or my POV character. I find this particularly difficult because I tend to get a little over-focused sometimes, which makes it hard to see the big picture (much less notice how the effect of changing one or two specific details might propagate to other aspects of the big picture).

It's thinking through the implications of whatever bit of magic or technology you have stuck in your imaginary world. It's thinking about how real people would actually use this interesting new technology or spell (which is probably not going to be the way the inventor—or the writer—expected them to use it).

One of the first things you find out when you start paying serious attention to this is that every detail you invent implies other things, large and small. A codfish dinner served in a town far inland implies not only a fishing industry but fast and reliable transportation (or the fish would spoil before it got to the table). The existence of such fast and reliable transportation means news will move as quickly as the fish do, so if you want it to be three weeks before they find out about the magical thunderstorm on the south coast, you suddenly need to come up with a really good reason why they wouldn't hear about it a day later like everyone else.

Every time I make up a bit of scenery for an imaginary

world or a paragraph of history for a character's backstory, it implies a whole lot more than the few words that are on the page. Some of those things will be relevant to the story, if only in small ways; other things will not. But even the ones that don't get mentioned in the story are still there in the reader's mind.

If I mention a bird, for instance, it's a safe bet that this world includes feathers and eggs. The eggs may be mentioned as breakfast and the feathers as pillow stuffing, or they may not appear in the story at all, but they're part of the subconscious background that comes along with a bird. Similarly, if I mention feather pillows, the reader can safely assume that there is some source of feathers in this world, with birds as the most likely default (though in fantasy and science fiction, the existence of feathers may not imply the existence of birds, so readers tend to keep an open mind a bit longer than they otherwise might).

The existence of birds (and therefore feathers and eggs) is relatively trivial and unlikely to cause problems in most stories. But there are a lot of things, from magic and wands to anti-gravity to a character's wicked uncle, that have implications and potential ramifications far beyond whatever immediate point the author was making. And one of the easiest places to get into trouble with worldbuilding is to neglect to think through just what all those implications and ramifications are.

Back when I was still getting the hang of all this, I discovered that one of my biggest problems with making forward progress was that I'd forgotten to make up some aspect of my imaginary world that I suddenly needed. The heroine arrived in a new town, and I'd forgotten to make up the architecture; the city guard showed up, and I had no idea how they worked; a foreign diplomat arrived, and I had no idea what he considered a proper, respectful greeting and what he considered an insult.

So I started keeping track. Fast-forward ten years or so. I had a twenty-plus-page list of things to think about, and it was still growing. I mentioned this on an early online group I participated in, and people talked me into posting the list. One thing led to another, and my fantasy worldbuilding questions have been up on the Science Fiction and Fantasy Writers' of

America website for…I think it's getting on for fifteen years now.

Every so often, I get complaints about them. Interestingly, the complaints are always that I left something out, not that X or Y is not really important to worldbuilding. I always tell the complainers the same thing: The fantasy worldbuilding questions are *my* list of things I have a tendency to forget to think about. Stuff that I always remember to think about is not on *my* list. If they forget different things, they should make their own list of reminders.

But people persist in trying to make the questions into a prescription or a recipe. And of course, once again, there is no one recipe or set of rules that work for this aspect of writing, any more than any other. I know quite a few writers who do little or no worldbuilding in advance—they have the sort of brain that needs to not be tied down to a previous decision, and they also seem to have a gift for making everything tie together, even if it was made up on the fly.

Implications

Back in the day, I spent a couple of years as games master for what would now be called a role-playing game that I basically made up myself, based around the background I was using in my Lyra series. Paper-and-pencil gaming was fairly popular then, at least in my social circles, so there were quite a few other games, gamers, and games masters running around.

One evening, a bunch of us were at a party, and one of the other gamers was complaining bitterly about how cheap his games master was—his group would get almost killed fighting a dragon and then discover that its hoard consisted of a rusty dagger, six copper pieces, and a couple of tiny, badly flawed gems. He wanted to know why they never got any good spells or powerful weapons. Without even thinking about it, I shot back, "Because there is no spell or tool, no matter how cheesy or apparently useless, that the gamers cannot find some way of using to short-circuit the games master's most carefully worked-out plans. The only hope we have of keeping you guys under control is to limit your obvious firepower so that you have to work a little harder for it."

I learned a lot from being a games master, but that was possibly the most useful thing of all. It applies to writing in two ways: First, if your heroes get too powerful too fast, they'll overcome all their problems too easily. So you have to jack up the level of problem they're dealing with and the power level of the bad guys. Next thing you know, they've gone from needing to save the village to needing to save the universe, completely bypassing saving the kingdom, world, planetary system, and galaxy along the way (which can be really inconvenient if you end up writing a series because you could have gotten several more books out of saving all those other things along the way).

Second, anything a writer puts in a story has implications, and if you don't think about them at least a little bit, you can run yourself into believability problems. I recall one story I read in which, early in the story, it was established that (1) in this particular future, people had figured out how to manipulate gravity, and (2) they'd used this technology both to make their space stations comfortable and to make really deadly hand weapons.

So far, so good. But then in mid-book came the scene in which our heroes were waiting for the forklifts to unload their cargo, and I set the book down and didn't pick it up again for a long time. Because from the description, these were obviously normal twentieth-century mechanical forklifts, and if this society had whizzy gravity-control-based hand weapons, there didn't seem to be any reason why they wouldn't have applied that technology to unloading space ships.

This author was not a beginner nor was he terrible or careless. He was, I suspect, simply so wrapped up in his story that he didn't think through the implications of having gravity control. It happens to a lot of science fiction/fantasy writers because the things we come up with haven't been reality-tested. In real life, when someone comes up with a nifty new technology or gadget, there are billions of people to look at it and think, "How can I use this to make my life easier?" And it's fairly obvious from real-life experience that even the people who invent various new gadgets cannot always predict how people are going to use those gadgets in real life.

When I come up with a nifty cutting spell for my characters to use against the bad guys, there's nobody but me around to say, "How would that help me dissect animals in the lab?" or "That'll make butchering cows much easier!" or "What a great thing to use to cut the grass! Can I use it on trees, too?" If I don't think about the implications, nobody will. And when I'm focusing on getting my characters out of a sword fight and on to their next adventure, I'm not really thinking about cutting the grass or doing dissections or the hundreds of other places where a cutting spell might be useful in everyday life. I have to stop and think about the possibilities for a while (and even then, I probably won't come up with all, or even most, of the obvious ones).

And there isn't time to think about all the implications of each and every thing one puts into a book. When you're inventing a whole imaginary world, there's simply too much of it to catch everything. This is one of the reasons I prefer to do a large chunk of my worldbuilding in advance—because as long as I'm not head down in finishing the fight scene, I can take time to consider the implications of at least some of the things I'm putting into my imaginary world. I can, with luck, spot the things that could throw the world out of balance and put some limitations on them. I can talk about them with friends who will spot different problems from the ones I see, simply because they have different jobs, different life experience, a different point of view.

I'm never going to catch everything. Even the best writers occasionally miss things. And there are a lot more of my readers than there is of me; it is inevitable that some of them are going to spot places where some technology, spell, or ability that I've put into a book has important implications that I haven't thought of. All I can really do is stop and think…and try and make those people have to work a little harder.

Obsessive Overbuilding

There's a flip side to failing to think through the implications of your worldbuilding, and it is, of course, thinking too much about them. Some writers become obsessed with making even the tiniest, most obscure details of their imaginary world consistent with every other tiny, obscure detail. This is a great way to avoid getting actual writing done.

Overbuilding an imaginary world is a problem that is closely related to over-researching. They have similar pitfalls both before and during the writing process: there's the tendency to get so caught up in researching/inventing details that one keeps putting off the actual writing, then there's the tendency to try to pack all of the research/invention into the story (also known as "but I can't waste all that work!" and "I suffered for my art [doing all this research]; now, Dear Reader, it's your turn…").

It is, of course, a truism that the writer knows more about the world, its history, and the background and backstory of the characters than ever gets into the story. The thing that seldom comes up is the fact that when the writer knows it and how much the writer knows are things that vary from writer to writer and book to book. The most extreme examples at either end of the scale are those writers who sit down in front of a blank screen and make it all up as they go along, and those other writers like J.R.R. Tolkien, who spent somewhere between forty and sixty years developing the world of *The Lord of the Rings*.

In between are the rest of us, varying from one end of the scale to the other in terms of how much worldbuilding we need to do before, during, and after writing a story. Yes, after—it's not unusual for a book to require more worldbuilding to resolve plot and consistency problems discovered during the rewrite, and it is exceedingly common to need more worldbuilding when one is writing more than one book using the same setting. I made up steam dragons, daybats, spectral bears, and swarming weasels for *Thirteenth Child*, but I didn't nail down the entirety of the magical ecology of the Western plains and the Rocky Mountains. So there are a lot of new critters in *Across the Great*

Barrier that I didn't know existed until I needed to mention them, even though I'd already written an entire novel in that world. I still don't really know anything about the magical ecology of South Columbia, Aphrika, or the other continents. I know it's there, and that it's different from the ecology of the part of North Columbia I'm dealing with in the books, but I don't need to know the details unless and until they come up in the story.

On the other hand, I know way more about cinderdwellers and steam dragons than has made it into either of the books I've written so far. Some if it is written down; some isn't. This pattern holds for everything, from the politics and history of my world(s), to cultures and customs, to things about the family: some of it is written out, some of it is still just in my head. I also do not require myself to stick strictly to every worldbuilding decision I've made. There are always a few things that are non-negotiable, but most things, I'm not stuck with until I've used them in the story, and sometimes not even then.

I work this way because it suits the way my imagination handles things. I require a basic framework for my background, but it can't be too detailed. Without the basic framework, I go into choice paralysis—I could have any kind of setting, background, history, without limit, and my brain seizes up at the prospect. If the framework is too detailed, though—if I've made the mistake of trying to work out an entire imaginary encyclopedia of background—then I start feeling constrained and tied down. Too much detail, for me, makes it feel as if I were writing real-life mimetic fiction, without enough freedom to make up the stuff I want.

That closed-in feeling—the sense that you have to check every other noun against your encyclopedia to make sure you're being consistent with all that background that isn't even in the story—is the surest indication I know that the writer has produced more background in more detail than they really need in order to get on with the story. And that itchy point will be at a different level of background information for every writer. Some folks need a three-inch ring binder full of notes on everything from weather to favorite foods to different cultures;

others get twitchy if they have more than a few key facts tied down before they start writing.

The trouble is that the itch doesn't show up while you're doing the advance worldbuilding; it only shows up once you start to write, and by then it's almost too late. There are a few other signs of overbuilding a world; one of them is creating Tolkien-esque mountains of material that you find boring to read through. The whole point of writing down aspects of your worldbuilding, for a writer, is so you can write the book without forgetting key points or ending up with major inconsistencies. Enough worldbuilding equals however much YOU need to have in order for the book to be coherent, believable, and consistent. Whether your background notes are in the form of a glossary, an encyclopedia, a tiddlywiki, a stack of three-by-five cards, or a single handwritten page of bullet points—if they aren't useful and accessible to you while you are writing, there's not much point in having them.

Doing a lot of worldbuilding in advance is not a requirement for writing a fantasy/science fiction novel. It's one possible way of getting to the desired end, which is to have a believable portrayal of a world in your novel. Whichever way you work— doing it in advance or making it up as you go—if the result isn't coherent and consistent and believable without interrupting the story, you have a problem. Ultimately, the solution is yours to figure out, because your solution is going to have to work for your particular brain and writing process. It is, however, a good bet that if you have such a problem, the solution is unlikely to be "do more of whatever you were doing that got you into the problem."

If what you are doing isn't working, try something else.

From the Mailbag

Where do you start when you write a story? With characters, setting, conflict…?

It depends on the story. Sometimes it starts with characters, sometimes with setting, sometimes with plot, sometimes with a situation or an idea, sometimes with a theme…It really doesn't matter where the story starts as long as it has all the crucial bits in it when it's finished. I've started stories from an idea for a character, from a mental image that I wanted to explain, from a situation that I wanted to explain, from a title I wanted a story for, from a plot description, from playing a game…Even for the same author (me), stories don't all start in the same place.

Do you handwrite and then word process? Or just word process?

I've been touch-typing since I was sixteen; I type MUCH faster than I handwrite and with about the same facility (by which I mean, I don't think about what my fingers are doing when I type any more than I think about how to shape the letters when I handwrite—I just think what I want to say and write/type it). So I prefer to type straight into the computer when I can. If I can't for some reason, then I'll handwrite.

Do you always choose an audience before beginning to write?

Never. Unless you want to say that the audience is me. I write books I would like to read. Fortunately I have broad enough tastes that a lot of other people turn out to like the same sorts of things I like, so I can sell what I write and make a living at it. The only time I ever worried about "the audience" at all was when I was writing the Star Wars middle-school novelizations, and that was only because I was a little worried about whether my editor would make me simplify the vocabulary because of the grade level (he didn't).

If I wrote Easy Readers or chapter books, which are aimed at people who are just learning how to read, then I would have to think about the audience a bit before I sat down to write, because those types of books frequently have specific limitations in vocabulary and/or sentence structure. But for any other type of book—and here I'm including all genres and age ranges, from middle school on up to adult fiction—my philosophy is, write it first and then try to figure out who it's going to sell to. Because for me (and many, many of the other writers I know), worrying about the audience while writing is vastly counterproductive—not only does it slow down the writing process, it frequently ends up messing up the story because the writer starts second-guessing his or her ideas.

Hooking the Reader

Openings are important; nobody denies that. In my mother's collection of writing textbooks from the 1930s and 40s, there are chapters and sections on the importance of the opening, complete with admonitions to hook the reader. But something interesting happened along the way from then until now.

Back in those early how-to-write books, the opening, even of a short story, was considered to be the first manuscript page—basically two hundred fifty to three hundred words comprising several paragraphs and quite a few sentences. Over the years, that shrank from the first page to the first paragraph and then to the first sentence. "The opening is vitally important" became "The first sentence is vitally important." Sometime between then and now, the emphasis changed again, until these days you can hardly find a how-to-write book or blog that doesn't advocate writing a first-sentence "hook" that's dramatic, dynamic, and full of action.

When you stop to examine it, the assumption behind the "dramatic, dynamic, action-packed hook sentence" advice is that drama and action are the best way to grab the reader's attention. The trouble is that (1) there is no "the reader;" there are hundreds of thousands of individuals who don't all like to read exactly the same thing, and (2) a dramatic, action-packed opening may be inappropriate for a particular book (one that, say, is chiefly about a quiet romance between a shy scholar and his introverted next-door neighbor).

But even the book about the shy scholar needs a first line. So let's drop all the how-to advice for a minute and look at what a hook actually is.

A hook is an opening that makes the reader want to keep reading. Sometimes this can be as much as the first chapter, but these days when people refer to "the hook," they usually mean the first sentence, first paragraph, or the first couple of sentences/paragraphs (usually if the paragraphs are a series of snappy one-liners).

In order to make the reader want to keep reading, a hook has to do three things: (1) it has to catch the reader's attention; (2) it has to provide a reason for the reader to keep reading; and (3) it has to do both things in a way that is true to the story, characters, and plot that follow. Number three is not strictly a property of the hook but of the matchup between it and the story. If your opening sentence is "At full speed, the two trains bore down on each other, racing along the track toward their inevitable crash" and then you reveal some paragraphs later that these are a couple of model trains and the story is a sentimental tale of a small-town Christmas in 1940, you are likely to annoy your readers so much that not only will they skip the rest of this story, they won't pick up anything with your name on it ever again.

Drama and action tend to be eye-catching, which is why they're so often advocated as important in a hook, but there are a lot of other things that intrigue people. Gossip, for instance— why else are there all those magazines and papers full of stories about the relationships of people most of us have never even met? Mysteries, large and small—things that seem unexpected or out of place, yet there they are. Striking personalities, whether eccentric or merely emphatic. Sometimes a buildup of details will do it, or a sudden twist of prose.

Hooking the readers isn't about action. It's about telling them something interesting, something cool, something exciting. (Years ago, one of my writer friends hung a sign over his computer that said "Now I am going to tell you something cool" to remind himself.) And "exciting" is not synonymous with action. People get excited when their favorite singer releases a new album as well as when they're on the first downhill rush of the rollercoaster.

The thing to remember is that even the folks who advocate the *in medias res* action openings aren't advocating action because they think action is the only right way to open a story. They're advocating it because they think that action will catch the reader's attention and give him or her a reason to keep reading.

Too many writers hear all the emphasis on action and forget about the reason behind it; they end up with openings describing a car crash or a sword fight that isn't particularly interesting. They comply with the letter of the directions but not the spirit.

Part of why they do this is that their heart isn't in it in the first place. They don't want to open in the middle of a chase or a laser duel, but they think they have to. And while it is very true that sometimes a story will require the writer to write about things that he, personally, finds uninteresting, one doesn't want to be doing it in the first sentence. Because it is very, very difficult to take something that you yourself find boring and write it so that readers will find it compelling. In the middle of a book, one can manage it by embedding the boring bits in sections of stuff that one is interested in, but in the first line, there isn't anything else to surround it with. And unless the writer is very good and very advanced, it's going to show that he's not terribly interested in what's going on in the opening.

If you aren't excited and intrigued by your first couple of sentences—if what you're saying in them doesn't make you want to write more, just to find out what comes next—they aren't likely to grab your readers, either.

Obstacles

One of the truisms of writing is that a good plot must have conflict. And while this is, in fact, true, I've seen it misinterpreted so many times that I thought I'd talk about it a little.

The problem always seems to come in the definition of "conflict." We hear that word so often on the news that in many people's minds it seems to have become irretrievably associated with violent physical conflict between two or more people. And since there are a good many folks who don't want to write about violence or physical conflict, the near-universal insistence on conflict as a part of story can become an insurmountable obstacle.

But as I've said before, there are more kinds of conflict than the straightforward physical I-punch/stab/shoot-you, you-punch/stab/shoot-me sort. Emotional conflict is frequently far more powerful, story-wise, than physical conflict; social/political conflict can be just as gripping (and can also be far easier for a reader to identify with, as it's far more common in most people's daily lives than being punched, stabbed, or shot at).

More and more, though, I've come to believe that the thing some folks can't wrap their brains around isn't the definition or the possible types of conflict; it's the word itself. It just carries too much emotional freight. Also, it is inaccurate.

Stories do not require conflict in order to be effective. What they do require is struggle—steadily increasing effort on the part of the protagonist to overcome one or more obstacles, whether internal or external.

A two-block walk to the grocery store isn't a struggle for most people and therefore doesn't make for a terribly interesting story. Put some obstacles in the way—serious ones that the protagonist is going to have considerable trouble overcoming—and it becomes a lot more interesting.

And that's where the trouble begins. The first obstacle that occurs to most writers is usually another person—a gang of bullies after the protagonist's lunch money, a mugger in an alley, a robber holding the store clerk at gunpoint. If the author is really going for something big, they'll set the scene in a war zone somewhere, so that the two block walk becomes a matter of dodging bullets, mines, or bombs.

But that two-block walk can be just as dramatic (and perhaps even more powerful) if the obstacle the protagonist faces is not another person. You can make a perfectly good story out of an agoraphobe taking his first trip outside his home in ten years, or from the first post-accident walk by someone trying out her new artificial leg, or even from someone dreading they'll screw up on their first day at a desperately needed job working at the grocery store.

The key words are *obstacle* and *struggle*. An obstacle is something that the protagonist is going to have serious trouble getting past. Again, people are the most common, but there are plenty of others. An animal, a memory, an emotion, extreme weather, difficult terrain, physical incapacity…there are plenty of things to choose from.

The second point is that getting past the obstacle has to be difficult for the protagonist. Years ago, my then-husband and I went on vacation to the Canadian Rockies. Our second morning, we were hiking in the backwoods when we reached a rock face of maybe ten feet. My husband climbed it easily; I got stuck halfway and could not make further progress. My husband was five inches taller than I was; the handhold that he could reach to get past that point was a good four inches beyond my absolute farthest ability to stretch. What was barely an obstacle at all for him was an insurmountable block for me.

Which brings me to the next point: the reader has to understand just how difficult the obstacle is for the protagonist and why. This is, I think, one of the main reasons most people opt for physical violence/conflict as their struggle-of-choice— they don't have to worry about explaining why it's hard or dangerous for their protagonist. If I'd left out the next-to-last sentence in the paragraph above, everyone would have gone "Huh?" Because without knowing about the five-inch height differential, there seems to be no reason why I should have gotten stuck when he didn't. Unless the reader knows that the protagonist is an agoraphobe or a desperate new hire, the walk to the grocery store won't seem particularly tense to the reader even if the protagonist is flinching at every bush. The story might work anyway—giving people a mystery ("Why is this guy acting so scared?") can be as good as giving the protagonist an obstacle if the payoff is right—but the chances are a lot lower.

Character Motivation

People (and therefore characters) have reasons for everything they do. Sometimes those reasons are simple and obvious (the clerk at the Walgreens counter rings up your purchase because that's his job); other times, the reasons are complicated and unclear, with roots that reach far back into a person's past. One way or another, though, there's always a "because" in there somewhere—because she promised, because he likes working with his hands, because they enjoy a challenge, because he's afraid of pain/spiders/dogs/the dark, because she had a bad experience when she was eight, because, because, because.

The reasons people do things can be simple—because it's the only way to survive—or they can be complex—partly because she's ambitious, but partly because she likes the challenge, and partly because she really does want to help. They can be external—because that squeaky door hinge is going to drive her crazy if she doesn't oil it—or they can be internal—because he can't stand the thought of being betrayed again. They can be a desire to get or achieve something—because he wants that position, that ship, that girl; because she wants to become the best magician ever—or they can be a desire to avoid something—because she doesn't want to go to jail, because he doesn't want to feel pain, because they don't want the kingdom overrun. Motivations can be obvious—because the dragon is *right there*; run away!—or they can be obscure—because he reminds her of a second cousin she hasn't seen in thirty years and has never mentioned to her traveling companions.

It is, however, very important to remember that "because the plot says they have to" is not a motivation.

The plot is what the story looks like from the outside. The characters are inside the story; the plot may say they have to do X, but in order for that action to look and feel believable to readers, the characters have to have their own reasons for doing what they do. And those reasons have to be consistent with what the reader knows (or will learn) about the characters in the course of the book, or the reader very likely won't believe in the character (and by extension, the plot).

Not all reasons have to be spelled out extensively, any more than every action the character takes has to be described in grim detail. Yes, George got up, showered and shaved, combed his hair, dressed, and had breakfast; 99.9 percent of the time, the author doesn't need to mention that, much less go into detail about the position of the bed, the temperature of the shower, or the type of soap. About the same percentage of the time, the author doesn't need to mention why George does these things—habit, fastidiousness, childhood training—because neither the actions nor the reason behind them is particularly important to the story, the character, or the reader.

Generally speaking, the spear-carriers and walk-ons, the grocery store bagger, cab driver, palace guard, maid, messenger, who appear just long enough to bag the groceries, ferry the character from A to B, deliver the message—those characters don't need motives for their actions beyond "it's their job." Even the charmingly chatty cab driver seldom needs more than "because he likes talking to people" as his reason for going on for a couple of pages.

The more important a character is to the story, the more carefully the writer needs to look at his or her motivation to make sure it holds up—that it's believable emotionally and strong enough to explain why the character takes the actions he or she takes.

That doesn't mean the motivation always has to be complicated and deep. "Because I don't want the bad guys to kill me" is pretty simple and straightforward, for instance, and as long as the reader believes it, it can work well for everything from a straightforward action-adventure to a complex psychological thriller where nothing is quite what it seems and "the bad guys" keep changing from page to page. The reverse is also true—having a straightforward adventure plot doesn't mean that the characters' motives can't be complex.

What motivation does have to be is plausible. That means the reader has to believe that this particular character would do whatever-it-is in this particular situation, for this particular reason. Not that "a girl" or "an alien" or "an Australian" or "a soldier" or "a redneck" or any other generic type or category of person would do this—what has to be believable is that Blytzmi, the Rigelian pipefitter who was raised in an isolated space colony, would do this for these reasons. Or that Indria, the runaway princess-turned-mercenary who's spent three books now looking for revenge and who has no sense of humor whatsoever, would do it.

Because one of the other really important things to remember about motivation is that it is personal and individual. What works for one character won't necessarily work for another, no matter how similar they are or seem to be. Also, people change over time, and so do their reasons for doing things…even if what they're doing are the same things they've been doing for the last two hundred pages. What started off as just a job may become a patriotic duty or something done out of friendship rather than merely for money.

Finally, I want to add that as with many, many things in the writing process, figuring out the motivation of the characters is something that some writers do consciously, but other writers do intuitively. You may need to lay everything out clearly in your notes so that you can keep it obscure but consistent in your writing, or you may write by feel and only realize what your characters' real reasons are when you get to the climax or after. It really doesn't matter as long as the end product is a bunch of characters whom the readers will believe have their own individual reasons for whatever they're doing…whether the readers ever actually find out what they are or not.

Reactions

One of the things that bites even experienced writers from time to time is giving insufficient consideration to the ways their characters react to things.

In any given situation, whether it's a fistfight, an emotionally stressful conversation, or just a couple of people shooting the breeze after work at the coffee shop, each character will perceive what is happening differently, depending on that particular, individual character's personality and life experience. Even something as simple as the boss saying, "No, don't do that right now" may feel like a stinging reprimand to one character, an oblique warning to another character, and a friendly reminder to a third character, depending on each person's level of confidence/insecurity and his or her past history with that particular boss.

Each character in the scene will then have an internal, emotional reaction to what they think just happened, which will also vary depending on personality and life experience. Even if two characters both perceive the boss's remark as a stinging reprimand, one of them may feel bitterly put-upon by it or ashamed of his actions, while the other may feel an increased desire to prove herself.

The character's internal, emotional reaction will then be expressed in action, which will, again, be different for each of them. The character who feels put-upon may frown and turn away, or stiffen and go poker-faced, or smile and nod insincerely; in the longer term, he may decide to quit, or he may merely slow down and pay less attention to his duties.

In any viewpoint where the reader is seeing through the eyes of a character (first-person, second-person, tight third-person), the author can show the reader all three of that character's reactions—their perception, their internal emotions, and the actual physical body language and actions that result. For all the other characters, though, the author is limited to what the point-of-view character can see them do (i.e., the physical expression of the reaction). It is therefore all too easy to race past the "what the character thinks just happened" and "how the character feels about what just happened" parts and go straight to shrugging, smirking, eye-rolling, and hair-tossing without really considering whether this character would actually do any of those things in this particular situation or thinking about what they might do instead.

For example: start with a situation in which someone has just dropped a metaphorical bombshell in a room full of people:

this is the One Ring, Darth Vader is his father, that boy pulled the sword out of the stone. If the writer is in a hurry, and most of the characters aren't very plot-important, you get things like "A stunned silence fell" or "Everyone turned to look." And sometimes, that's exactly what you want because you want to keep the focus on the main character or the ring or the sword and not on all the different reactions.

If, however, there are six major characters present, their individual reactions are likely to be more important, so the writer needs to give a bit more thought to the matter. You usually don't want all the major characters to react to a revelation in exactly the same way, even if it is a huge revelation. Yes, they're all going to be astonished—but people will feel and express their astonishment in different ways, and many of them are going to have an additional reaction along with being astonished.

The oversensitive guy on the end is going to be astonished and resentful because he thinks he should have been told before everyone else. The woman next to him who hates surprises will be astonished and angry at being made to feel astonished. The guy beside her has been telling people forever that something like this was going to happen; he's as astonished as everyone else (because he didn't really expect this to happen now), but he's also going to gloat. His eight-year-old son who's been bored out of his mind by most of the meeting will be astonished and happy because something interesting is finally happening.

Unless the writer is using omniscient viewpoint, all of these internal reactions (except the point-of-view character's) are going to have to be conveyed to the reader through the various characters' physical actions and body language, and each character needs to react physically in a way consistent with who they are. That can mean fiddling with their glasses, or frowning thoughtfully, or chewing their lip, or having their eyes go wide—there are hundreds of small actions that can give the reader a hint of what the character is thinking and feeling. If a lot of characters are present, it is seldom necessary to provide clues to what each and every one of them is thinking; a few key reactions are all you need.

And of course, not every writer builds up to the physical reaction by starting with the characters perception and emotions. Early in a book, the writer may well be finding out what each character is like by assigning them different reactions and body language and then figuring out why each of them did that, while late in the book, the writer will probably know the characters well enough to know what they'd do without working laboriously through the whole process. Readers, though, only have the actions (and perhaps some thoughts from the POV character), and have to figure out what the characters are thinking and feeling from the way they behave. Hence the importance of making each character's reaction—both emotional and physical—characteristic and unique to them.

When Is It Over

When is the story over?

Really over, I mean, as in "this is the last paragraph, and what comes next is 'The End' at the bottom of the page." This is usually some way after the big climax in which the central story problem is solved (they kill the dragon/blow up the Death Star/arrest the murderer), but how long after?

The answer, as usual: it varies. To some extent, it depends on the length of the story—a five-page short story may be too long if there's more than half a page after the climax, but nearly every reader I know would feel that having only a page or two of wrap-up to a trilogy just wasn't enough. Similarly, if three pages out of the five are wrap-up, there's probably something wrong with the short story, while it may take five or ten chapters or more to do a proper job of wrapping up a complex trilogy.

The two obvious problems are stopping too soon and carrying on too long. On the whole, I tend to think that too little is better than too much. A reader who finishes a book wishing there'd been just a little bit more is a reader who is likely to come back for the next one; a reader who gives up with a bored sigh two pages before "The End" appears is a reader who is likely to avoid the next one like the plague. And it really hurts to discover that you have overshot the end of the story by two or six or ten chapters and that you must therefore cut all that material. For most of us, it's a lot easier and less painful to add a scene or a chapter than it is to cut one.

Nevertheless, most novels need a certain amount of post-climax wrap-up to be satisfying. A novel is a long haul, and many readers need to be eased out of it gently, so to speak. If it's a complex novel or a multi-book series, there are likely to be a bunch of subplots and loose ends that need wrapping up because they couldn't all be tied up neatly as part of the big climax. And since most novels follow the classic plot structure (a series of attempts by the protagonist to solve bigger and bigger problems, where each try ends with the protagonist in a worse situation than ever, until the very last one finally succeeds/ fails for good), they need something at the end to reassure the reader that this time the protagonist finally pulled it off, and there isn't some nasty surprise waiting to turn the "ending" into a cliffhanger.

And finally, this part of the story—the part between the climax/solution and "The End" on the last page—is about consequences. This is the part that leads a lot of writers astray, I think, because in a lot of books the consequence of the protagonist's actions is that he or she moves on to a new life (or returns to an improved version of the old one). This looks and feels like a beginning—and it is. But it's the beginning of a new and different and unrelated story. The writer is allowed to tell that story, of course, but in the next book. The bit that goes at the end of this book is the acknowledgement that things have changed.

For instance, one writer I know was working on an action-adventure of the sort in which the protagonist is a junior space officer, faces a crisis, succeeds while annoying the top brass, and is "rewarded" with the captaincy of the worst ship in the fleet and posted to the worst spot in the galaxy as a way of getting rid of him. Naturally, he goes on to shape up his new command, defeat new enemies (and make more political ones), and so on.

The problem was that this novel was approaching half a million words and the writer couldn't figure out how to cut it. But it didn't need cutting; it needed splitting into the several books that it actually was. The writer had run right through the ending of his first book (which occurred a quite reasonable hundred thousand words or so into the story) and on into the next. All he had to do was stop at the point where the hero was notified that he was being promoted and given a new ship, but before showing the rust-bucket full of misfits that was his new command.

Part of the difficulty here was that the writer was so caught up in the "show, don't tell" advice that he thought he had to show the new command, which led directly into the next story, leaving him no good break point. But the other part was that after spending one hundred thousand words and many hours working on making the characters "feel real" and planning all the hero's future adventures, the writer had made them too real in his own head. Real people's lives rarely divide themselves up into neat episodes, and their stories don't end until they're dead.

The second reason too many wrap-ups drag on is that the writer is trying to give attention to every single subplot and character individually, one scene or chapter per subplot. This is as unwise as it is unnecessary, especially in a book with lots of characters and subplots. A lot of long good-byes and subplot finishes don't make these things seem more important; they make the scenes feel thin. It's often more effective to pack two subplot resolutions and a couple what-these-characters-do-next into the same scene and then do some summarizing than to have four or five long scenes to show each character moving into his/her new life and another three or four to resolve subplots. Alternatively, a series of mini scenes—a two-to-three-paragraph look-in per character to hint at where they are now—can be very effective for a complicated, cast-of-thousands book or series, as long as they're mini scenes.

Finally, a lot of writers keep going in search of the boffo ending line, sometimes whole chapters past wherever the story should have cut off. Don't do this. Just don't. It never ends well.

NOT-SO-BASICS

More extensive discussion of particular tools and techniques, like flashbacks, transitions, structure, pacing.

Who's THAT?

So you have a bunch of characters, and you want your readers to get to know them. How do you do that?

Well, how do you get to know people in real life?

You find out about them based on what other people say about them ("He's a jerk!" Chris told her), based on how other people react to them (She scowled and stiffened as he came up), based on what you see them do (On his way out the door, he casually kicked the dog), based on what they say and how they say it ("Move," he snarled and shoved past her), and based on what you know (or think you know) about their past and their motives ("Don't mind him," Greg said. "He just found out that his daughter is in the hospital with rabies").

Your readers find out about your characters in the same way: they draw conclusions about them based on what your narrator says about them, what your characters say about each other, how they react to each other, how they behave, and what their motives seem to be.

The catch is that most people are more inclined to believe their own judgment about a character than they are to believe someone else's. Having your narrator tell me, "He was incurably honest, responsible, and a little vain" isn't terribly convincing. In fact, this kind of description always rolls right off the surface of my mind when I read it; I don't believe it (or ever register it, usually), until I see it in the character's actions—watch the guy turn in $5,000 in small bills that he found in a parking lot, see him drive fifty miles in a blizzard to make sure the report gets delivered on time, and observe the way he automatically checks himself out when he walks past a plate glass store window.

In other words, it's the old "show, don't tell" thing again. If your narrator tells me Joe is a great guy, but I watch him insult people, rob orphans, and cheat at solitaire all through the story, I'm not only going to believe Joe isn't so great; I'm also going to lose all trust in your narrator. (Sometimes you want that— that's why the concept of an "unreliable narrator" exists—but usually, you don't want the reader thinking your narrator is an idiot or a liar.)

One of the problems some folks run into is that showing the reader what a character is like takes a lot longer (and requires a lot more consistent attention) than doing a two-page infodump on the character's personality and background. If you think that your readers have to know everything about your hero (or villain or sidekick) the minute he or she walks onstage, the temptation to start with the infodump is likely to be well-nigh overwhelming...because that's pretty much the only way you can get all that stuff out there before your character actually starts doing things.

But most of the time, your readers don't need to know everything up front. *You* need to know a lot of it in order to keep the character's actions consistent, but the reader doesn't need to know that your character is grumpy in the first scene because he has serious issues with his ex, who called him right after breakfast about some other backstory, blah blah. All the reader needs to know in order to understand the scene is that the guy is grumpy today, and a couple of lines of dialogue will probably be enough to get that across. If the reason is actually plot-important, it'll come out later in the story, and it will probably be more believable, not less, for having done so.

Who Says?

I define "narrative voice" as "the way all the stuff that isn't dialogue sounds." Theoretically the writer has three basic options: (1) the narrative can be in the author's natural voice; (2) the narrative can be in the voice of the viewpoint character; (3) the narrative can be in the voice of an independent narrator who is not the author—essentially, in the voice of an imaginary character who isn't the viewpoint character (an example of this would be the Paarfi novels by Steven Brust).

If, however, the writer chooses to use a first-person viewpoint, options one and three disappear. All of the various styles of first-person viewpoint, whether they're memoir, diary, letters, or stream-of-consciousness, are told by the "I" character, so all of the narrative has to sound like that character. Word choice and grammar work similarly—if the first-person narrator knows nothing about trees, he'll say "I sat under a tree;" if he knows quite a bit, he might say "I sat under a white oak;" if he's a botanist, he'll say "I sat under a specimen of *quercus alba*." This is relatively obvious when the first-person narrator has a strong voice, especially if the character uses unique syntax, word choices, or grammar. It gets less obvious (and harder to do) the more the narrator sounds like the writer.

Where this really gets tricky is in the matter of dialogue. A first-person narrator will sound more or less the same in both their dialogue and in their narrative (though most people do have a slightly more formal writing style than they do speaking style, so there's some variation). The dialogue that is spoken by other characters—the non-viewpoint characters—has to sound like them rather than like the narrator, yet the first-person narrator's voice may creep into the way he or she reports the dialogue (unless he or she happens to be the sort of person who is obsessive about reporting exactly what everyone else says rather than telling it all the way he or she remembers it).

In third-person, the writer can choose any of the three options for voice. If the narrative is filtered through the eyes and mind of a tightly focused third-person viewpoint character, the effect will be almost the same as if the author were using a first-person viewpoint; if the narrative is in the voice of an imaginary character or in the author's voice, the dialogue and the narrative will contrast. How much they contrast is obviously a function of how different the voices of the characters are from the voice of the author or independent narrator.

Manipulating the narrative voice is usually a lot more subtle than, say, changing the tense or the viewpoint, but once you're aware of it, playing around with voice can be fun.

The Devil's In the Details

So pretend you've spent so much time on something that you've got gobs and gobs of backstory and little trivial details, like the main character is terminally left-handed, or her brother has to organize his pens in a very specific way, or their uncle won the very first US Open. These things have nothing to do with the plot but add humanizing quirks to the characters that would make them so much more interesting in real life. How do you find the balance of details without hitting overload?

I will begin by pointing out that this is a problem faced to a far greater degree by every writer who writes nonfiction, reasonably accurate and well-grounded historical fiction, alternate universe fiction, or even fiction with a modern setting that the writer expects many readers to be unfamiliar with. The real world is full of WAY too many interesting details for any writer to fit all of them into a book. Even the *Encyclopedia Britannica* gets edited.

To me, the problem doesn't seem to be the presence of all those interesting details; no, the real problem is the degree of attachment the writer feels to them, whether they've come from the writer's imagination or from tons of research. We joke about the writers who seem to be thinking, "I've suffered for my art by doing all this research; now I'm going to make the reader suffer, too," but really, writers are much more like geeks—"But this detail is SO COOL, how can I leave it out?" Too often, the end result is a lot of cool information that doesn't belong in the story—hence the oft-quoted advice to "murder your darlings."

Unfortunately, as with everything else in writing, there are no hard-and-fast rules for determining what the "right" level of detail is for backstory. It depends on the story, the writer, the style, the conceit of the book, and so on. If your style is modeled on Hemingway, you probably won't have as much description (and therefore you will include fewer details) than if your style is more like E.R. Eddison.

However (there's always a "however" when I'm doing one of these), there are a few things you can and should consider. First and foremost is the question, "How does this background detail affect the way the character acts or thinks?"

If your main character is terminally left-handed, that's going to affect how he or she does just about everything physical, even if it's only in small ways. Her left-handedness is going to affect nearly everything she does with her hands, from how she opens a door to smearing the ink when she's in a hurry writing a note. You don't just drop the information into the story in one place and forget about it; if it's a real detail (rather than mere window dressing), it will be an important consideration whenever you describe his or her actions all through the story.

The second question I'd suggest is, "How does this detail affect other characters?" If the brother organizes his pens in a certain way, it's going to make it easier or harder for his sister (or friends) to find something to write with when they need it in a hurry (and it'll give siblings and friends something to tease him about if they're so inclined). Again, it's something that will likely come up naturally in the course of the story rather than something you have to figure out how to include.

What this all adds up to is the question, "Is this detail important to the story?" "Important" does not mean it has to be a plot point. Really, "important" only means that you aren't cramming this thing into the story just because you know it. If nobody in the story is interested in golf or fame or family small-talk or sports history, there may be no reason for that US Open winner ever to come up. If one of those things does happen, then maybe that detail will come up, and the story will be richer for it…but if you manufacture such a conversation just to get that interesting detail in, it will very likely weaken the story.

Writers almost always know far more about their characters,

the backstory, and the setting than ever belongs in a book or story. If you are determined to make sure the reader knows everything, you can try offering your eventual publisher some appendices…but don't be surprised if they don't want them.

Fantasy versus Reality

Every so often, I get asked what the difference is between writing fantasy and writing realistic fiction. It's a pretty good question, though since I've never written anything that wasn't science fiction or fantasy, I'm not sure why anyone expects me to know. (Of course, I have opinions on just about everything, but that's another matter.)

There are actually several answers to this question, depending on what sort of fantasy one wants to write. In modern urban fantasy or magical realism, for instance, everything in the story except the magical/fantastical elements needs to be realistic because the story is taking place in a recognizable version of the real world where most of the background is the same as in real life. For most modern urban fantasy, the magical elements have to fit in the cracks as a secret that is unknown and unaccepted by the general public. For magical realism, the fantastical elements are simply assumed and generally accepted by the characters as how the real world works…but everything that's not fantastical has to be realistic (that's the "realism" part of this fantasy subtype).

In an alternate universe story, whether modern or historical, the writer has a lot more flexibility. The society can look very much like ours, only with an elf emancipation movement or forensic magicians. Alternatively, the setting can substitute magic for technology: flying carpets or dragons instead of airplanes, cooling spells instead of refrigerators, but a history that is more or less the same as in real life, resulting in a political and social landscape that is very similar to ours. On yet another hand, the writer can attempt a rigorous working-out of the political/historical effects of having working magic and/or magical creatures, depending on whatever departure point the writer decides to use for the historical discovery of reliable working magic. At the farthest end of the continuum are the stories in which nothing is the same except the geography, the assumption being that if magic worked, all of history would be completely different.

In a surreal or dreamscape fantasy, such as *Alice in Wonderland*, all bets are off, unless the writer decides otherwise. As long as what the writer is doing fits the "feel" of the story, mirrors and mice can recite poetry, chess pieces and playing cards can behave like people (rather strange people, but still people), cats can vanish and reappear at will. Very little resemblance to mimetic or realistic fiction is required.

The key element for all types of fantasy is internal consistency. If you say in chapter two that vampires cannot bear the smell of garlic, you'd better not send them out to dinner at a trendy Italian restaurant that serves roast garlic as an appetizer in chapter ten, and you'd really better not have them suddenly develop a garlic craving in chapter fifteen. Not without a lot of explanation, anyway. If you establish early on that wizards cannot work with fire in any form, you'd better not have your wizard hero throwing fireballs around later in the book, unless the whole point of the story has been for him to find out the secret of working with fire. In other words, in fantasy fiction, you get to make the rules for how the world works, but once you've made them, you have to follow them or you'll lose a large chunk of your readers.

External consistency is also important in fantasy, but for a different reason: most experienced fantasy readers will assume that any inconsistencies between the real world and the background in a piece of fantasy fiction are deliberate, conscious choices that the author has made and therefore clues both to the type of fantasy and to the way the author's particular fantasy world works. If the writer pays no attention at all to "real things" (like the way guns work or how far a horse can travel in a day), accidental mistakes can result in book-meets-wall moments.

Looking Backward I

There are two important things to know about flashbacks: *how* to do them, and *when* to do them. Both things can be trickier to figure out than they look.

First, a definition: as far as I'm concerned, flashbacks are a way of conveying some background/backstory information as if it were happening "now." The central story that is being told or the central problem to be resolved is in the story-present, and the flashback is usually just an illuminating scene or memory from the past. When an author is playing around with the temporal structure of a story—alternating chapters set in 2010 with chapters set in 1810, for instance—that, to me, falls under "structure," rather than "flashback." Feel free to disagree on this; the terminology of writing is not standardized.

Flashbacks are one of several storytelling techniques that periodically get overused and abused. It's easy to see why—they're a tremendously useful way of getting background/backstory across without using infodumps or as-you-know-Bob/maid-and-butler dialogue...especially when the writer has begun *in medias res* and needs to get the reader up to speed on why the hero is battling zombies in the first paragraph. They're also very handy when your viewpoint character is the only person who knows what happened twenty years ago but isn't the sort who would actually tell anyone this crucial piece of information...or when the twenty-year-old scene is far more dramatic and memorable seen than when summarized in dialogue. Mini flashbacks can be an absolutely terrific way of keeping the story moving while supplying important backstory.

On the other hand...well, one of the best examples of when not to use a flashback was a story opening I read a few years back which began with the main character walking through a deserted city, hearing distant noises. About two pages in, something triggered a flashback...of the events that happened fifteen minutes before the story opened, finally explaining all those distant noises. The author loved opening with the spooky deserted city (and it really was a great scene), but she lost most of her readers when they hit the flashback because the readers felt as if she was cheating by not simply starting the story fifteen minutes earlier.

Another example is the deservedly infamous and legendary manuscript that opened "Blood spurted!", which segued immediately into a two-page flashback, after which the reader discovers that the dramatic opening line happened because the protagonist had cut himself shaving. Basically, the closer you are to the start of the story, the harder you want to look at the flashback to see if you really need to do it that way.

How to do flashbacks is actually fairly straightforward. The first thing to remember is that one needs to ground the reader clearly in Who, Where, and When somewhere near the beginning of each scene. This applies to all scenes, but it's especially important for flashbacks because the reader generally expects the story to proceed linearly, so it's easier for him or her to get disoriented if that's not the case.

For flashbacks, it's often easiest to set up one or more of the Who, Where, and When parts in the present day scene:

…and she thought back to Paris, ten years before.

The Louvre was cool inside, even on a hot July day…

When you do flashbacks, you also have to remember to move the reader back to the present when the flashback scene is over—

…He walked out into the hot July sun, and she knew she'd never see him again.

Now there he was in Garden City, New Jersey, ten years older but as certain of himself as ever…

Using space breaks to separate "present" scenes from "flashback/past" scenes, as I did above, is a useful technique to use when (1) you are already using space breaks to establish scene boundaries elsewhere in the story, and (2) you're doing the flashback scene as a full-fledged scene rather than a summary paragraph or two. But you don't have to use space breaks to establish the boundaries (and if you're doing a mini flashback, you often don't want to); you can do it with tenses, too, even for long flashbacks.

Looking Backward II
or Some Tenses and How to Use Them

The second most common way of leading into and out of a flashback sequence is by shifting tenses. Most novels are told in what's called the "historic present," meaning that the "now" of the story is told in simple past tense (*He slept in the library all afternoon* rather than *He sleeps in the library all afternoon*).

This confuses a lot of people, so let me just repeat that: in most stories and novels, *"He slept in the library all afternoon"* is an action that is taking place in the present of the story, even though it is written in past tense. If you're following this convention, you only use present tense in dialogue: *"He sleeps in the library all afternoon, every afternoon,"* she said. *"I'm sure you can find him there if you look."*

You can tell a story in present tense (and there are considerably more of them told that way now than there used to be), but right now I'm talking about the most common convention.

When the "now" of the story is told in simple past tense, you need to use another tense to let the reader know that something happened earlier, in the story's past. The convention for this is to use the past perfect tense: *He had slept in the library all afternoon.* So *by the time dinner rolled around, he felt exhausted* is happening in story-present, but *even though he had slept in the library all afternoon* is story-past.

When you have a really short amount of story-past information to put in, you can usually just use past-perfect for all of it: *By the time dinner rolled around, he felt exhausted, even though he had slept in the library all afternoon. Griselda had woken him as the sun was setting, and he'd barely managed to get in a cup of coffee before coming down. One look at the dinner guests made him glad he'd had coffee;*

if he was going to be matching wits with Simon tonight, he needed to be alert. The nap in the library, Griselda waking him, and grabbing the coffee all happen in story-past and are presented as a mini flashback—the protagonist is currently coming down to dinner while remembering what he did this afternoon.

The trouble is that long stretches of past-perfect tense start reading very awkwardly, very quickly. The way most writers avoid this is by moving the "present" of the story backward in time using a sentence or two of past-perfect tense, then shifting to simple past tense for the rest of the scene until it's time to bring the "now" of the story back up to the point where the flashback started. This is a lot harder to explain than it is to do.

> By the time dinner rolled around, he felt exhausted, even though he had slept in the library all afternoon. Griselda had woken him as the sun was setting.
>
> "You missed tea," she told him. "Do you want to miss dinner, too?"
>
> He sat up and blinked at her. [...insert rest of scene...] "Coffee," he said. "I need coffee, now."
>
> Griselda had complained, but she'd gotten him a cup. He had gulped it down, heedless of the burn, and when he walked through the dining room door and saw Simon's grin, he was glad he'd taken the time. He needed to be alert to match wits with Simon.

Using the change in tense to move backward and then forward in time integrates the flashback a little more smoothly into the narrative than using space breaks (as I did in the previous section). The writer still has to be clear about who is the flashback viewpoint, where it is happening (since flashbacks frequently are not happening in the same place as current story action), and when it is happening (at least enough that the reader can tell which bits are story-present and which are story-past). In general, the longer the flashback is, the more transition you probably need between "now" and "then" and back to "now."

Oh, and notice that when I used the space break to delineate the flashback scene, I did not change to past-perfect tense anywhere. When you use the space break, the break itself is the signal that story-now is moving backward in time; you almost never need to also use past-perfect tense.

Meeting the Cast

How well does a writer need to know his or her characters?

There seem to be two sets of conventional wisdom about this. One holds that writing characters is rather like method acting—the writer has to become the character, so as to know them from the inside. The other is more mechanical and is typified by "character sheets"—pages-long lists of questions about each character's physical and mental attributes and backstory.

Each of these methods works sometimes, for some writers, and doesn't work other times, for other writers. Most writers lean one way or another, especially for their major characters, but I think both approaches can be useful. My major characters tend to walk into my head, so for them I'm more at the method-acting end of the scale, but I don't have to understand all my characters in depth all of the time.

For instance, I don't need to understand the inner soul of most of the walk-ons. The guard at the gate who says, "Welcome, heroes!" and opens the door does that because it's his job; he doesn't need any more motivation than that. Most of the time, these walk-on characters don't have more than a couple of lines of dialogue and don't even need names, let alone all the details from a six-page questionnaire.

Minor characters are usually more than anonymous faces in the crowd. They generally have more than two lines of dialogue in a book and often have several scenes or a recurring presence. I usually understand this kind of character "from the outside," the way I understand real, live people (which means, not very well). I can predict their actions, and sometimes I can say why they did X or Y instead of A or B, but sometimes I just know that that's what they'd do because they're like that. These are the characters where those questionnaires sometimes come in handy for me, though I don't need six pages or details about their childhood traumas.

The spear-carriers and minor characters have their own stories, but those are different stories from the one I'm telling. I don't have to know those stories in order to make those characters perform their roles in this one. In fact, getting too far into their heads can get in the way, rather like the method actor who was making a commercial for a fruit drink. He asked the director, "What is my motivation in this scene?", to which the director replied with a sigh, "George, you're a *banana*!"

Sometimes knowing more about the spear-carriers and walk-ons can make a story richer. The fascinating conversation with the cab driver is a classic example, both in fiction and in real life. It never really hurts to know more about your characters, so as long as what gets into the story is only as much as is needed. A three-page essay on the life history of every cab driver, city guard, and store clerk will slow most stories to a crawl, unless the whole point is to showcase all the interesting people with minimal attention to plot in the first place.

The central characters—the protagonist, antagonist, main and secondary characters—are the ones I want to have some sort of heart-level emotional understanding of. The questionnaires don't help me with this at all—if I know those characters well enough, I can answer the questionnaire without thinking; if I have to think to answer the questionnaire, all the answers are wrong in the end. I don't build my characters from childhood up, unless, like Eff in *Thirteenth Child*, they're starting off as a child on the first page and growing up as the book unfolds.

For me, it's kind of like writing real people. Some of them have very strong personal voices; given three different phrasings, I could easily pick out which one sounds like them and/or the thing they absolutely would not say, even though I've no idea what shaped those speech patterns and personal idioms or the reasons behind why they do and say certain things. Most real people don't start out your acquaintance by blurting out their entire past life, preferences, beliefs, fears, hopes, and idiosyncrasies. (And if they do, they're usually leaving out something important.) I learn about my friends gradually. I learn about my characters the same way. And the first thing I learn is usually something on the order of "Oh, she doesn't like fish," or "Huh, he doesn't drive," rather than anything traumatic or joyful out of their past history.

It's not nearly this clear-cut, of course; some minor characters I know inside and out from the moment they walk on, and once in a while a main character refuses to provide even a teeny tiny clue as to what's going on in his head, which is why he's been sitting in limbo for the past six or seven years—and why he'll probably end up a major secondary character rather than the protagonist when I do finally figure out where he fits.

Information and How to Dump It

Infodumps—those long passages of narrative summary that provide a huge wodge of background or plot development or characterization—have an undeservedly bad reputation among would-be writers. The allergy to infodumps is a bit of stylistic advice which is largely peddled to beginning writers, but which is not upheld by looking at real, live published fiction. Infodumps that are ineffective, boring, annoying, or unnecessary should be cut, obviously, but that is by no means the same thing as "all infodumps are horrible and a sign of bad writing." James White, for instance, used infodumps to great effect for decades in the Sector General books; ditto David Weber in his Honor Harrington series, Patrick O'Brian—the list goes on.

There are three basic approaches to fixing a story when someone has complained that it is infodumpy: (1) You can rewrite to remove the infodump, (2) you can rewrite to make the infodump work in the context of the story, or (3) you can ignore the advice and leave the story alone because you know your critiquer well enough to know that he or she has absorbed the "no infodumps rule" and is therefore not actually assessing whether your infodump really works in context.

Rewriting to remove the infodump is often appropriate if

the infodump is ineffective or boring. In quite a lot of cases, though, the problem is not that the infodump is the wrong technique to choose; it's that the particular author doesn't know how to write good infodumps or doesn't know how to make an infodump work in the context of the story and viewpoint he or she's chosen. Rewriting to remove the infodump will do nothing to solve this underlying problem, if it is present, since simply removing all infodumps provides no practice whatsoever in how to write effective infodumps, and odds are that sooner or later, the writer will need to write an effective infodump.

So the first question the writer needs to answer is: What is the most effective way to give the reader the information necessary to understand the story? Should I use an infodump or something else? This is generally a question of pacing rather than structure because traditional infodump mechanisms, like narrative summary or two-page blocks of lecture in dialogue, lay out information a lot faster and in a more condensed fashion than the slow revelation of needed details in a scene or during a conversation.

Assuming you decide that you need the infodump, the next question is how to make it work. One of the most effective ways to do this is to arrange things so that the infodump is of information that the reader already wants to know. This is one of the reasons why long prologues full of the background history of the world seldom work and are commonly cut by editors—when they pick up a book for the first time, most readers are more interested in the story or the characters than in all the cool history the author has worked out. It isn't until later, when the information becomes important to the characters and the story, that the reader wants to know more about the background.

Another technique is to lay out the story-problem as a central part of the infodump or (if the story-problem has already become obvious) give the infodump information in such a way that it clearly makes the story-problem worse. If, for instance, you have two characters at the top of a cliff preparing to go down and you need to infodump a bunch of geological and geographic information, you could probably get everything you needed into an infodump that described, in gory detail, just how high and pointy and hard to climb this cliff is (because of relevant geological facts) and just how many other people have died trying to climb down it (for various reasons). It's a matter of focus: the information you want to infodump is all still there, but the focus is on some plot point that increases the tension.

Some voices and stories lend themselves to effective infodumps more than others. James White makes extraordinarily effective use of the sessions in which his doctors are briefed on their new patients. He slides effortlessly from the setup conversation into two- or three-page narrative summaries of the important background information (which the reader already wants to know because of the hints in the setup conversation) and then back to his fully dramatized scene. A first-person narrator can get away with infodumping information a lot more easily than a third-person narrator. The trick here is to make the narrator sound as if he or she is musing on or analyzing or explaining to herself something that is important to him or her at the moment. A story that covers a lot of time—months or years—also often requires a good many chunks of narrative summary to fill in what happened. Memoir tends to have a lot more summary than dramatized scenes.

The Skeleton in the Closet

There are a couple of ways of looking at plot, ranging from the bird's-eye view at a macro level to the order of scenes and events and incidents within scenes. The one most people run across first—and one of the most useful ways of looking at it for many writers—is the macro level plot skeleton.

The basic plot skeleton works like this: your protagonist has a problem—solving the murder, stealing the Hope Diamond, restoring the true king to the throne, winning the love of a good man/woman, taking over the company. He tries to solve the problem: by interviewing people in search of clues, by studying the security precautions around the diamond, by recruiting an army, by sending flowers, by starting to buy up stock. These attempts doesn't work and may even make the situation worse: people lie, providing conflicting evidence; there's a new top-secret security precaution that the protagonist can't find out anything about; the usurper has a bigger and better-armed army; the potential love interest is allergic to flowers; the stock price rises so that the protagonist doesn't have enough money to get a significant number of shares. So the protagonist tries something else: studying the physical evidence, talking to the last thief who tried for the diamond, sneaking into the palace through a secret tunnel, asking the love interest to help with the Christmas toy donation program, undermining the Board of Directors' confidence in the CEO. Which does or doesn't work: the physical evidence combined with the interviews solves the murder; the attempt on the diamond fails and the protagonist is caught; the palace coup succeeds; impressed by the protagonist's dedication to kids, the love interest agrees to a date; the protagonist manages to get himself fired instead of the CEO.

The author continue this string of problem, attempted solution, worse problem until things are decisively settled one way or another: either the protagonist succeeds and the problem is solved, or (in a tragedy) the protagonist fails completely and perhaps dies.

You can start this string of events with anything. A character you find interesting—what does he or she want more than anything else in the world, and what's stopping him or her from getting it? What's he or she going to do to try to get it anyway? A place you find fascinating—what kinds of things happen in Hawaii and nowhere else? Who would be involved that you'd be interested in writing about? A situation or event—who was most strongly affected by the storming of the Bastille, and what happened to him or her afterward? A theme about which you care deeply—what people embody it, care about it, will explore it through their actions and problems?

But you can also dive right into a story without planning any of this out in advance. Plot complications and plot twists—

the problems and worse problems that are the "valleys" in the saw-toothed diagram that most people use to visualize a plot skeleton—can arise naturally from the characters' actions (and often work better from a story standpoint if they do). And of course as soon as the main character finds another problem or obstacle in his or her way, he or she will start trying to figure out how to overcome it. All the writer really needs to do is to remember to frustrate the character at some point (usually just before they think they're going to get what they want at last) in order to keep the story moving. (If this sort of thinking doesn't come naturally, you're probably better off doing at least some advance planning.)

If you're having trouble with plot, and this way of looking at the basic plot/structure of a story or novel isn't terribly helpful, then you probably need to look at plot from a different direction, or on a different level—scene by scene, maybe, instead of the whole story at once, or emphasizing causality or action/reaction instead of obstacles and strategies for overcoming them. I think, though, that it's still useful to start by looking at the basic plot skeleton because it is a macro-level view and most of the other ways of looking at plot have to somehow add up to the skeleton sooner or later.

A Few Words on Pacing and Structure

Pacing is how fast it feels like things happen. Not how fast things actually do happen or how many paragraphs or pages it takes to cover a particular incident; what it feels like to the reader. For example, three pages of dialogue often "read fast" and seem to the reader to go by in an instant, while two paragraphs of dense prose that require close attention often feel as if they take much longer than you'd expect from their word count or the amount of space they take up on a page.

Readers read stories in order to find out what happens. If they don't find out enough over the course of a page or a scene or a chapter, they perceive that part of the story as slow or dragging. The obvious thing to do to correct this is to cut part of that section so that instead of finding out two new things about the plot or character development in five pages, they find out the same two things in only two pages.

Sometimes, though, those two bits of information need to be spaced out over five pages for some reason. In this case, the correct cure for the too-slow pace is to add *more* material. The scene may stretch to six or seven pages, but if the reader is now finding out seven or eight different new things instead of only two, the longer scene will read faster than the original, shorter one did.

Similarly, if the pace is too fast—if too much new information is coming at the reader in too short a time frame— the obvious cure is to add some neutral material to spread things out and give the reader time to digest and remember the six important things the author had originally crammed into half a page. Other times, though, everything will flow better if the author *cuts* the too-fast section so that it only includes two important things and takes one paragraph.

In other words, the solution to pacing problems is often counterintuitive: sometimes the cure for a too-slow pace is to add more material and the cure for a too-fast one is to cut something.

Structure is the pattern of events; *where* in the story (e.g., beginning, middle, end) things happen. "Beginning-middle-end" is a story structure; so is "beginning of beginning, middle of beginning, end of beginning; beginning of middle…etc." Structure is independent of pacing—you can have a fast-paced beginning or a slow-paced beginning, for instance. And you can look at lots more complicated patterns than beginning-middle-end; the standard sawtooth plot skeleton, for instance, or spiral structures.

The trouble is that people often talk about pacing using the same kinds of up-and-down metaphors they use for structure because it is rare for a story to work if it's all cruising along at exactly the same speed. Cruise control is not a good idea for stories; you normally want variation. Fast bits and then a slower bit so the reader can catch his or her breath. Not only does this sound a lot like the sawtooth plot skeleton pattern, one of the easy ways to manipulate how fast something feels is to change the tension. Which means that the peaks of the sawtooth plot structure ("We are going to solve the problem this time, for sure!") quite often feel faster paced (because they tend to be more tense and there's a lot going on), and the valleys of the sawtooth plot structure ("That didn't work; *now* what do we do? Let's sit here for a while and eat worms") quite often feel slower.

So the two things can hum along pretty much in parallel a lot of the time, but they're not actually the same, and you can get into trouble if you start trying to fix the one when the real problem is with the other.

The Escalation Problem

One of the problems that plagues a lot of stories has to do with endings and the escalation of threat. It's a particular problem for long-running series, though it can turn up in trilogies and even stand-alone novels.

The first thing is that not all trilogies or series are the same. Some are accidental—the writer wrote a book that was supposed to be a stand-alone, and then everyone wanted more, more, more. Some are episodic—monster/murder/McGuffin-of-the-week. (The McGuffin is the thing that everyone in the story is after for some reason.) Some are closed (or potentially closed)—there is one central story, and when that's finished, the series is theoretically over (like *The Fugitive*, if anyone besides me still remembers that show). Some are completely open-ended.

Escalation is a problem for nearly any series that goes on long enough—the characters save the world, solve the murder, or catch the spy and get stronger and better during the process. Saving the world again (or solving a similar murder, or catching more spies) would be not only repetitive but too easy to be interesting. The writer has to come up with a newer and bigger challenge—saving the universe, maybe, or solving a much more difficult murder, or protecting a nuclear plant from a bigger, tougher terrorist group. And that can get ridiculous pretty fast.

The escalation problem occurs most often and most obviously when a writer does an accidental series. If the problem the characters faced in the original "stand-alone" book or trilogy was too large, it can be hard to find a new threat that doesn't seem anticlimactic. If you *know* you're doing a series, you can plan your challenges so that the characters aren't saving the kingdom or the police chief in book one and saving the universe or the president by book four.

The closed-ended series is subject to a slightly different kind of escalation problem. If you know that your characters are supposed to end the series by saving the world, you have to make sure that when they finally get to the climax of the series, it doesn't turn out to be an anti-climax. You have to either make sure that the characters don't get too powerful over the course of their previous adventures or else make sure that every time the characters get more powerful, the difficulty of saving the world (or whatever) increases, too. (Of course, in the series, one makes it look as if it was really going to be this difficult all along, only the characters didn't know it yet.) And there's always the danger of getting off track and never actually completing whatever the original master plot arc was supposed to be because one or more of the sub-arcs turns out to be more interesting (to the writer, at least).

Even the McGuffin-of-the-week type of series is vulnerable to the escalation problem. This is most obvious with TV series because for just one full year of shows, the writers have to come up with about 30 plots, each with its own McGuffin… and beating the monster, catching the murderer, or finding the McGuffin can't be too easy, or people get bored. So you start with the heroes beating random strange monsters, and by the end of a season or two, they're fighting in the war between Darkness and Light, with the fate of the universe on the line, or they're stopping Ragnarok at least once a season.

The open-ended series probably has the least trouble with escalation, because the author can switch to a new batch of characters if and when the first set gets too powerful. Worlds and universes are very large places; it isn't that hard to find new characters who are far enough away that the overpowered folks from the first story aren't going to find out about their problem in time to deal with it. And there's always the next generation.

Avoiding escalation completely is really hard if not impossible. The author is caught between a rock and a hard place: if the characters have become stronger as a result of their adventures, the threats and obstacles they face must also become stronger, or the stories get boring pretty quickly. But if the characters have adventures and do not change, do not become stronger and wiser (or do so only at the proverbial snail's pace), readers also get frustrated after a while. About all you can do is pay attention, think ahead, and try to hit a pace of development for both your characters and your threats that is neither too fast nor too slow. (What? Who said writing was going to be easy?)

The Opening

It has become a truism in writing that one should always open a story with a "hook." The problem with this is that what "hooks" one reader will annoy or repel another, and this is seldom acknowledged by the advice-givers.

So you get one set of folks advocating "start with action" because getting dumped *in medias res* is what hooks them. You get another set saying that one should always start with dialogue because it's active and brings the characters onstage right off, and that's what hooks them. You get how-to-write exercises like "write ten one-sentence hooks," on the theory that opening with one exciting or intriguing line (like "The elephants blocked the highway from nine until noon; after that, the ostriches took over") is enough to carry the reader through whatever comes next.

The truth is that the opening generally needs to fit the story more than it needs to be wildly intriguing. A false hook—an exciting swordfight opening on a contemplative political story;

witty, character-centered tea-party dialogue opening up a slam-bang horror/action novel; an intriguing incident or setting opening on any story in which it plays no other part—will alienate both those readers who don't like that sort of opening (but who might very well like the rest of the story as it actually plays out) and those readers who very much like that sort of opening but who are then disappointed by the rest of the book or story.

In the opening sentences, paragraphs, and pages of any book, the writer is making a series of implied promises to the reader: These are the people you will see more of. These are the kinds of problems they will have to solve. You can trust me to pose interesting questions, and you can trust me to answer them satisfactorily. This is the sort of story you are reading, and this is how I am writing it. Every time the writer breaks one of these promises, it pushes the reader away from the book. Push hard enough or too many times, and the reader puts the book down and never comes back.

This doesn't mean you can never, ever write a story with a misleading opening; it only means that doing so is harder to pull off than writing a story with an opening that fits. There needs to be a reason for the misdirection, some payoff to the reader that will make them chortle in glee rather than growl in outrage. And the bigger, longer, and more misleading something is, the bigger and more compelling the payoff has to be to justify it.

And I find the whole concept of the "hook" to be a little oversold anyway. Take a look at some first lines from real-life published novels:

> "The youthful gentleman in the scarlet coat with blue facings and gold lace, who was seated in the window of Lady Worth's drawing-room, idly looking down into the street, ceased for a moment to pay any attention to the conversation that was in progress."—*An Infamous Army*, Georgette Heyer

> "It is said that fifty-three years after his liberation he returned from the Golden Cloud, to take up once again the Gauntlet of Heaven, to oppose the Order of

Life and the gods who ordained it so."—*Lord of Light*, Roger Zelazny

"The queen waited."—*The King of Attolia*, Megan Whelan Turner

"The music room in the Governor's House at Port Mahon, a tall, handsome, pillared octagon, was filled with the triumphant first movement of Locatelli's C major quartet."—*Master and Commander*, Patrick O'Brian

"Miri woke to the sleepy bleating of a goat."—*Princess Academy*, Shannon Hale

Few to none of these examples would get a passing grade if they were turned in to a creative writing teacher as part of that "write ten hooks" assignment, yet the books were not only published but have lasted and/or been celebrated. They're interesting sentences but not exaggerated. Most of them provide at least a hint of a character or a place or both, and that's what's a bit intriguing. Which is all one really needs.

Chapter's End

Having just talked a bit about beginnings, I'm now going to talk about endings…sort of. Specifically, I'm going to talk about chapter endings because when you're writing a novel, you end up having to do quite a lot of these.

A good chapter ending, from the point of view of a writer, is one that draws the reader on to keep reading even though the chapter is over. (From a reader's point of view, this tends to end with finishing the novel at 3:00 a.m. and being grumpy at the office all the next day, but that's another matter. And really, most readers who say that sound kind of smug about it…) The question is, what draws a reader further in?

The common answer is the cliffhanger—leaving the protagonist in the middle of some dire situation so that the reader will have to keep reading in order to see how he or she gets out of trouble. This is the equivalent of the "hook" for starting a story, and it's just as misguided. "How does the hero get out of this situation?" is certainly one possible place to end a chapter, but if every chapter ends with crocodiles snapping at the hero's heels or a train bearing down on the kidnap victim who's tied to the tracks, the story starts to look like bad pulp fiction or a cheesy action serial from the 1920s. Which is fine if you want to write cheesy action serials or bad pulp fiction, but not so good if you have other ambitions.

So how do you end a chapter to make readers want to keep reading? All you really have to do to have a good chapter ending is lead the reader to expect that something is coming up soon that they'll really want to find out about. It can be a revelation ("I bet that in the next chapter George is finally going to tell Jack what Harriet has really been doing all this time!"); it can be action ("I bet the battle comes next!"); it can be the answer to a question ("Why is everyone being so sinister about that interview? Well, she's going in; I guess the next chapter is where we find out"); it can be the arrival of a much-anticipated character; or it can be an important discovery.

Somebody complained at me once about one of my books, claiming I'd ended every single chapter on a cliffhanger so that they couldn't put it down. While very gratified by the reaction, I couldn't remember doing any such thing, so I went back and looked. The first several chapters ended with: (1) the end of an interview and the POV being shown out of the building, (2) the end of a wait for another interview and the POV being shown into the office, (3) the end of another conversation and the main character exiting to the street, (4) the POV arriving at her rooms, (5) the main character getting dressed and leaving her rooms, (6) the POV and escort preparing to head off down the street, and (7) a secondary character asking a question.

Not very cliffhangerish sounding, any of them, I'd say… but that's looking at it from an action point of view. In each case, the most recent bit of action has ended; the interview is over, the wait is over, the character is leaving somewhere or arriving somewhere new. If you look back at what has just happened, there appears to be closure.

But that's only if you look very specifically at the action in each scene. I could equally well have described the first several chapter endings as: (1) the POV, having been given directions, sets off to do the job she came to do;(2) an interruption of a conversation that had unpleasant overtones and that insinuated that the coming interview will be unexpected in some way; (3) a verbal threat made against the character on her way out of the building, with more mysterious insinuations about what's really going on; (4) the character's safe arrival at her rooms, having successfully dodged a threatening stranger who was following her for reasons which remain both unknown and unresolved; (5) the character donning weapons in obvious preparation for trouble before leaving her rooms; (6) the character and her escort, having survived an unexpected attack, considering which direction to head to avoid further trouble; and (7) the cops demanding an explanation for various dead bodies and assorted mayhem.

In each case, the chapter ends both with closure and without closure. The incident is finished, but the POV character is left with new information to mull over…and that information is, quite frequently, obviously incomplete, which adds to the tension. Both the POV and the reader know that they are missing what is very likely to be important information and that without it, the POV is likely to make mistakes. Furthermore, each chapter ending looks "closed" if you look back at what just happened (which is what I did with the first set of descriptions), but if you look forward, the reader has been led to expect that something interesting or tense is likely to be coming up soon: a conversation, an encounter, an explanation, something. And each of those things will provide the reader with the answers they're looking for…but they'll also raise a bunch more questions that won't be answered for another chapter or two. So the reader has to keep on going, and going, all the way to the end.

If you set it up right, you can end a chapter with your POV character going to sleep and still have readers react as if it's a cliffhanger, because they're eagerly anticipating whatever they expect the POV to be dealing with once he or she wakes up in the next chapter.

From the Mailbag: Whose Turn Is It?

I know some people who feel quite strongly about keeping to the main character's POV except when it's absolutely necessary to go to someone else, but I've also seen that rule (like so many others!)broken successfully. It can be so useful to show someone else reacting to the MC.

Any guidelines on choosing? I keep having to write these scenes in more than one version to see which is the right way.

OK, first off, single-character-viewpoint, tight third-person is one kind of viewpoint. There are lots of others. It's a stylistic choice: does the writer want the focus and intimacy that comes with sticking to a single character's view for an entire novel, or does the writer want the flexibility that comes with using multiple viewpoints or omniscient third-person?

From the way the question is phrased, this particular writer is probably using a third-person multiple viewpoint structure. I call it a structure rather than a type of viewpoint because you can obviously do multiple first-person as well as multiple third-person or even do a mixed multiple viewpoint, with some of the viewpoint characters told in first-person and others in third-person. Or, I suppose, second-person, though that would be very unusual…and is getting a little off-topic.

Back to multiple viewpoint. I group this into several loose categories: (1) the ensemble cast, where the viewpoint characters all have their own storylines and importance; (2) a plot-centered book with a wide-ranging plot that really needs to be seen from multiple angles; (3) a character-centered story with a main character who needs to be seen from multiple angles; and (4) the braided novel, where three or four plotlines interweave and overlap a bit but may not come together until the end.

How the writer picks the viewpoint character for the next

scene depends on what kind of story he or she is telling.

A straightforward braided novel that has, say, one viewpoint character for each of three plotlines might go in strict rotation: a scene from A's viewpoint, then B's, then C's, then back to A, repeat until they all come together at the end. If one plotline is more central than the others, it will likely have more scenes (perhaps A-B-A-C-A-B-A-C), or the A scenes may just be longer than the B or C scenes. Not all writers like to be tied down to a mechanical rotation like this, but if it's right for the story, you can learn a lot from doing it…and it makes the question of whose viewpoint to use in the next scene really simple.

A plot-centered or character-centered book where there is a central thread that the writer wants to view from several directions is more complicated. A multiple-viewpoint, plot-centered story is a lot like a football game—the person who has the ball is the one who's important, the one who's moving the plot forward. So for each scene, the question is "who has the ball here?" Which character is moving the story forward? Who did the quarterback (your main character) pass or hand the ball off to this time—or are they still running with it? Or has the other team intercepted?

A character-centered book is similar, except that instead of moving a plot-football forward, the idea is to get ever more interesting and deeper understanding of the central character from different angles. The first question here is therefore "whose opinion of the main character changes the most during this scene?" Which character does the scene make the biggest difference to, in terms of their relationship with or opinion of the main character?

An ensemble cast is, for me, the hardest kind of book to keep balanced because you have all these people who are in the same place, who are supposed to be of equal (or nearly equal) importance. The one time I tried this, I found the balancing act very difficult. I had to look at it in all three ways—who's doing the next plot-important thing? who do these events matter to the most? who's had too many/not enough viewpoint scenes so far?—and then make a conscious decision each time as to which factor I was going to let have the most weight this time. (There is a reason why that story is lying mostly abandoned on my hard drive...)

When all else fails, trust your backbrain. Go with what feels right. If nothing does, do the best you can; maybe later it will become clear what the right choice should have been. And yeah, rewriting a scene several times from different viewpoints is a pain, but I know more than one pro who does exactly that. So if it's any comfort, you're in good company.

The Big Finish

Nearly every piece of fiction has one main character and one central problem. Even when the story is told from multiple viewpoints with an ensemble cast, each of whom has a different important plotline, there is almost always one plot problem that is *the* problem that the reader wants to see solved and one character for whom that problem is just a little more important, more life-changing, more critical in some way, than it is for any of the other characters. There's also one person—usually the same one—with whom most readers are expected to identify or sympathize with.

This doesn't mean that the other characters and plotlines are unimportant; on the contrary, the complexity is what draws a lot of readers to multiple-viewpoint-and-plotline stories. But one of the ways that complex stories can (and often do) go wrong is when the writer forgets or misidentifies the main character and the central problem, and as a result, the climax of the story falls flat. This can completely wreck an otherwise excellent novel.

Some writers try to give the finish of each plotline equal emphasis, which would be fine if the reader were reading the plots as a series of independent novellas, each starring a different character. In a novel where the plots have been braided together, though, going this route spreads out and flattens the "big finish." Instead of one peak moment and several lesser ones, there's a saw-edged row of similar points, one after another, until the reader loses track of when the novel is really over and ends up feeling vaguely dissatisfied, even though everything has been wrapped up point by point.

Instead, what generally works better is to give the greatest emphasis (the most tense, dramatic, emotional scene) to the solution of the central problem. The more other problems and plotlines that can be tied in to finish at exactly this same time, in this same scene, the better. For instance, if the central problem is defeating the Evil Overlord of Galaxy Prime, the battle may also rescue the hostage from plotline two, solve the romantic triangle of plotline three, and give the heroine of plotline four the chance to finally overcome her phobia about spiders when she shoots the Overlord's giant mutant spider pet, all in the same battle.

But the center of the battle is still defeating the evil overlord, and this is what determines the way most readers will see the book. If the evil overlord wins or dies but takes the main character with him, then even if the hostage rescue, happy romance, and psychological healing are all wildly successful, the book will still generally be considered a tragedy. If the main character beats the evil overlord and survives, then several unsuccessful subplot endings will only make the book "gritty" or maybe "dark" or "realistic," rather than a tragedy, because the central problem (the evil overlord) came out the way we wanted it to.

Sometimes, of course, there is no possible way for a subplot to be wound up during the grand finale. In a multiple-viewpoint book where one or more of the established point-of-view characters is not present at the big battle or great reveal, this is especially true. In this case, the question becomes what order the finishing-up scenes should happen in. If the writer is going for a big finish, the way he decides is based on what effect each scene and subplot wrap-up will have on *the* scene, the one that's the solution to the central problem.

Most of the time, subplots that can't finish up during the grand finale get wrapped up very quickly immediately after so that there is little or no release of tension until after the main problem has been solved. Occasionally, though, wrapping up a subplot just before the main finish will *add* tension to the grand finale, especially if the wrap-up folds two apparently independent subplots together. The hero's search for his long-lost sister finishes…with the discovery that she is the hostage who needs rescuing. The traitor has finally been discovered… but he's already given the Evil Overlord the security code to get through the shields.

The other mistake people sometimes make is giving the big finish scene to the wrong viewpoint character. This is really only of concern in a multiple-viewpoint novel, but it still happens more often than you'd think. The author gets so caught up in cycling through each character's experience of the battle in short action bits that when the main character finally offs the Evil Overlord, that bit is shown from the point of view of one of the other characters who's been watching, rather than from the main character's viewpoint. If the writer has been doing a Sherlock Holmes and Dr. Watson thing from the start (where Holmes is clearly the main character, but Watson is always the viewpoint), then it's fine, but if the main character has been a viewpoint, the writer needs a really powerful reason to deny him the POV in the big finish scene or it just won't work very well.

Fear

All writers are afraid of something at one point or another.

We are afraid of looking foolish; we are afraid of rejection; we are afraid of overreaching, of not knowing how, of getting it wrong, of not being good enough. We're afraid of being broke, being taken advantage of, being stuck with something that turns out to be a bad deal. We're afraid that the idea that seemed so brilliant a week or a month or a year ago is not brilliant at all, only nobody is quite willing to say so. We're afraid that in choosing to write *this* story, we're letting a much better one get away.

Fear is paralyzing. It affects everything: creativity, the mechanics of planning and working and sending things out, even the simple enjoyment of telling a story you really want to tell. Everything is suspended, like hitting a permanent "pause" button on life, because as long as you don't move, none of the things you're afraid of can possibly happen.

But fear is a natural part of doing anything new. Everybody is nervous the first time they exercise a new skill, and triply so if they're doing it in public. What a lot of folks don't take into consideration is that for writers, every book is a new thing. Yes, we develop skills over the years, but they're always being applied to a new story. "You're only as good as your latest book" is an industry truism, and it's just as scary a thought for bestselling veterans as it is for struggling midlist writers and beginners.

I think that a lot of the problem stems from the difficulty of the balancing act all writers face. On the one hand, you must believe in the value and quality of your work. On the other hand, you must believe that there is room for improvement or you will never try to get any better. It's a teeter-totter, and when it gets out of whack, it's all too easy to end up in a frozen panic.

The other problem is that writers have a difficult time trusting themselves. We know that the stuff we turn out isn't perfect; if we didn't realize that to begin with, our critique groups, friends, and editors would straighten us out in a big hurry. We have to know that it's not going to be perfect and do it anyway. And every so often, the teeter-totter tips, and the fear goes up, and we stop.

Getting past the fear happens in different ways for different writers at different times. I think the key is to recognize it and admit what's going on. It's a lot harder to make excuses about not writing when you've taken a long, hard look at yourself and admitted that really, you're just scared to mess up. Support from friends is vital—the sort of friends who won't simply dismiss the problem.

Experience helps, too. The first time I had to redo seven chapters of a manuscript, it took me a solid year (after I figured out that was what I needed to do) to sit down and start ripping the manuscript apart because I was afraid that whatever I came up with instead was going to be even worse than what I already had. The second time, it took me a bit over eight months. The third time, it took about two weeks, and the enormous reduction in elapsed time was due entirely to the fact that I recognized the situation and the feeling, so that I could roll my eyes at myself and decide that it would be silly to waste all that time when I knew what I had to do, and that I was eventually going to do it.

Taking small steps, or even just zooming in on the details, can make a big difference. Yes, I'm afraid my novel won't be any good, but right now, I just have to think about this one scene, this one paragraph, this one sentence. And then the next sentence—but not until I get to the next sentence.

Which is another part of the trick: setting the future aside. Because the future is what fear is all about—all the horrible things that might happen, that we might not be able to handle if and when they do. Some of them are inevitable—death, taxes, rejection—and there's no point in worrying about what you can't keep from happening. Other fears are phantoms. But the only thing any of us can actually do anything about is whatever we're doing right now this minute.

Not writing a sentence because I'm afraid my novel will end up being terrible, I'll look foolish, I'll be rejected…well, that seems like an awful lot to load on to one measly sentence. Sometimes, it really is better to look at the small picture for a little while.

Stressing Out

Sooner or later, everyone gets stressed, and stress affects everybody's writing, one way or another. There are a few folks whose writing is their escape from stress, who write more when they get more stressed and less when they get happy, but that doesn't seem to be all that common among published writers (probably because it's too hard to balance on the knife-edge of stressed-enough-to-write-but-not-so-stressed-that-there-really-isn't-time-to-write). Most writers hit a certain level of stress and find that it's using every bit of energy they have just to stay alive, and there's none left over for writing. (Which can add stress if writing is your main occupation and source of income.)

Everybody gets overstressed at some point, and the result can be quite dramatic in terms of productivity (and if it isn't, you frequently end up paying for it later). There are a bazillion books out there on how to manage stress, and they all say the same things and they're all right: exercise, eat right, take care of yourself, take a break, take a walk, meditate, talk to people about it, find ways to reduce it if possible (move, change jobs, change the locks on the house or the phone number), see a professional if it gets to be too much. The trouble is that they're all long-term solutions, and we're a quick-fix society…and most people don't even start trying to deal with stress until they're already in over their heads and sinking fast.

But it's like writing: nobody else is going to make you write, and nobody else is going to take all the stress out of your life for you. You have to work at it yourself. Some of it you can get rid of permanently; some, the only thing you can do is to change your attitude. And sometimes, it's a matter of remembering your priorities. Much as we all love it, writing a book is not the most important thing in the world. Not compared to, say, getting your kid to the emergency room when she's fallen out of a tree and broken her arm, or taking care of your elderly mother who has dementia, or calling the plumber about the flood that's happening in the basement *right now*. Sometimes it's OK not to write for a while.

It can be hard to admit that there's just no time for writing right now, especially when your backbrain is nagging you to Get This Story Down Immediately. You have to be honest with yourself about whether writing is part of your coping mechanism (in which case it may be worth it to make the time because it will help reduce the stress) or whether it isn't (in which case you need to not-write or you will just make the stress worse).

On the other hand, if your frontbrain is what's telling you that It Is Your Job/Duty To Do Revisions Today or that You Cannot Waste This Valuable Writing Time Just Because You're Stressed, tell it to go take a hike. You don't have to write when your mom is in the hospital or your kid is running a temperature or you're worried sick about layoffs or the roof just blew off in a tornado. You can if you want, but you don't *have* to.

Be warned that which hand you're using may well change with the circumstances. Most of the time, writing is part of my coping mechanism, but when my mother was dying and just after, I lost a good six months or more of writing time because even the thought of dealing with the plot was the very last straw that I couldn't cope with on top of dealing with the estate and everything else. And it took a while to realize that trying to make myself write "in order to cope" (which had always worked before) was the exact wrong thing *this* time.

People aren't machines—and even machines need down time for repairs and maintenance.

Frames

"Frame story" is a bit of a misnomer; it's actually short for "story with a frame," and it's a very specific story structure in which the opening (whether that's the prologue, chapter one, or the first scene) and closing (whether that's the epilogue, last chapter, or last scene) form a separate-but-related story or incident that "frames" the main story. Some stories have a double frame—the story-within-a-story-within-a-frame—and you can theoretically take it down as many levels as you want, as long as you can keep it all clear for the reader.

Frame stories used to be a lot more popular than they are now. The as-told-to frame, where two characters are talking (often in a bar) and one starts telling the other the story that is the main story, got used quite a bit—supposedly having an authority figure within the story tell a tall tale made it more believable or acceptable to the reader.

Personally I think that the reason frame stories fell out of fashion is that it's difficult to come up with a framing incident that is interesting enough to get the reader involved, memorable enough that when the reader gets to the end they'll recall what's supposed to be happening, but not such a tense cliffhanger that the reader will scream in frustration and flip straight to the end to find out what happens.

There are, however, two kinds of frame stories that you still see every so often. The first is the prologue-epilogue frame, in which the prologue and epilogue form a separate-but-related story or incident that brackets the main story. The prologue presents a character who is going to read, write, tell, be told, or set in motion the main story, and the epilogue returns to the character to give his or her reaction once the story is finished.

A frame prologue-epilogue usually takes place later in time than the main story, making the bulk of the novel a sort of mega flashback. Generally the prologue/first frame scene ends with someone leaning back and saying or thinking, "So why shouldn't I hang/court-martial/fire/exile you?" and the person in front of him saying "Well, sir, it's like this…" and we're on to the start of the real story, only coming back at the end to find out if sir really did hang/court-martial/fire/exile the tale-teller.

The main trouble with this one is that the main story needs to be very strong to compensate for the fact that we know the characters who've appeared in the prologue are going to survive. I've also seen a few of these in which the author appeared to think he or she needed an excuse to write in first-person. If that's all the frame is, it's probably scaffolding that can be taken down and dispensed with once the rest of the story is finished, as most of the readers I know don't need that kind of justification for a first-person story. (And I should probably add that a story within a frame does not have to be in first-person, even when the first frame scene ends "Well, sir, it happened like this…")

The second sort of frame story you see around a fair bit is more like one of those shadowbox frames that has multiple compartments, each containing a different picture. It's usually used to string together a bunch of closely related short stories. If the frame story is strong enough and does a good enough job of stitching the short stories into a coherent whole, you get what's commonly referred to as a "fix-up novel;" if it's not, you get something more like a short story collection with a series of introductions by the characters, like Poul Anderson's *Tales of the Flying Mountains*.

A good writer can use a frame structure to reinforce or undercut the events or the theme of the main story. You can give things an unexpected or humorous twist in the final segment of the frame, revealing information about motivations or manipulations or behind-the-scenes players that nobody in the main story had. Also, the frame story does not actually have to include the protagonist of the main story; maybe the frame is the sidekick or one of the villain's minions explaining what happened to his or her mother.

The main question to ask when considering whether to use a frame is: Does it add anything significant to the story besides word count? Does it make the overall story even cooler? If it doesn't pass the coolness test, you should probably pass on including it. On the other hand, if all the story coolness is in the frame, maybe the frame should be a story of its own. Frames are, after all, supposed to enhance what they surround, not draw all the attention to themselves.

The Structure of the End

Most novels have three parts: beginning, middle, and end. At least, that's what Aristotle said, and who am I to argue with a guy whose writing advice has been taken seriously by folks for the last two thousand years? I want to talk about the end.

First off, let me point out that the end part is a whole section of a story or novel, not just the big story climax or the final confrontation scene. The big climax or grand finale is the thing that gets the most attention in most how-to-write books, because it's clearly critical to the whole book—mess up the scene where the main problem gets solved, and everything else falls apart. But really, there's a lot more to it than that.

The first bit of the ending section is the transition from the middle part to the end part. Often it's a gradual transition, like heading for a mountain and not really being able to pinpoint the spot where the foothills end and the mountain range begins. Other times, there's a sharp demarcation—a character suddenly sits up straight and says, "I know how to steal the sword!" and we're clearly off into the endgame. Sometimes, it's even sharper, with the author dividing the story into sections or parts or books in a way that makes it obvious that the characters have reached the point of no return and, one way or another, are about to take their final swing at solving the central story problem.

The second part of the ending section is the specific setup for the big climax. The general setup, where the reader works out what the central story problem is and why it matters, usually takes place in the middle of the book; the specific setup is the point where they settle their affairs the night before the battle, or the hero agrees to marry the villainess as the last possible way of saving the family farm, or the prince announces he's going to be coming around tomorrow with this glass slipper for all the unmarried girls to try on.

Right before the big climax, the characters hit bottom in as many ways as the writer can make work at once. The heroine's True Love appears to have abandoned her just before the battle in which the army is outnumbered five to one; the villainess locks the church doors as the wedding march starts; Cinderella is locked in her room while the stepsisters try on the shoe.

And then comes the climax—the big scene in which the heroine's True Love shows up with reinforcements just in the nick of time; the organist reveals herself as the hero's mother who's brought the paid-off mortgage so her son won't have to marry the villainess after all; Cinderella escapes in the nick of time and not only can wear the shoe but has the other half of the pair.

In a straightforward story, the author has been promising and building up this particular conflict for chapters and chapters. The climax is the payoff—the point where the central story problem gets faced and solved once and for all, or where the problem overwhelms the characters for good. It's very difficult to pull a bait-and-switch in the climax scene—to have an entire novel in which the problem appears to be returning the rightful king to the throne, for instance, and then have the climax be the establishment of a parliamentary democracy. It can be done, but only by (1) carefully planting clues in the beginning and middle, and (2) having the "switch" (the unexpected solution) be a more satisfying solution to the problem than the one the readers thought they were going to get. Not a better solution, a more satisfying one in the context of the story.

Finally, there's the denouement or validation, where any remaining loose ends get tied up, awards and weddings and funerals take place, and the characters are poised to move off into the sunset and the rest of their lives, for good or ill. There are three common, closely related mistakes that writers make here: (1) trying to tie up every single subplot and loose end, (2) running on for too long, and (3) overwriting the ending in a desperate attempt to find a killer last sentence.

Mind you, a killer last sentence is an excellent thing if you can in fact find one. It is not, however, a necessity. (Given a choice, you're much better off spending all that time looking for a killer opening sentence.) Also, sometimes things that don't look like killer ending lines, like *He walked out and closed the door gently behind him* or *"Well, I'm home," he said* can become killer ending lines in context.

That whole last sentence thing is a lot harder to recognize than you'd think. When you've been immersed in a novel for months, it's hard to let go. Sometimes even with a short story. When I was writing "Stronger Than Time," an editor friend asked to see it. I sent a rough draft with the comment "I know it needs about another half page, but this is what I got," to which the editor wrote back, "Don't you dare add anything. It's perfect right where it is." And it is, and I can see that…now. Then, I was quite taken aback, as at the time I was really sure I needed to get my remaining characters actually out of the castle instead of just talking about it.

Really abrupt endings, where the validation or denouement is cut to a sentence or two, are not my favorite things, but on the whole I'd say they're better than the ones that go on and on, even after the main problem has been solved. There's a balance point that feels right—the longer the story, the longer the validation sequence. A short story may be fine with a few sentences or a paragraph; a novel may need anywhere from a paragraph to a chapter or so; a multi-book series may need several chapters of wrap-up to really feel finished.

THE BUSINESS SIDE

Essays on everything related to **the business end of the writing business**, from the specifics of record-keeping and query letters to more comprehensive matters of administration, publicity, production.

In Praise of Editors

Over the years, I have worked with a lot of editors. Some have been better than others; some have just been a better fit than others. But they all do pretty much the same thankless, undervalued, and misunderstood job—which is most especially misunderstood by people who have yet to get published.

It's not really surprising. For those who are not yet published, editors are the evil, unappreciative Dark Lords who reject writers' brilliant, deathless prose over and over and over. They are the gatekeepers whose job it is to sort through massive slush piles and find the diamonds therein—and each and every aspiring writer believes that his or her manuscript is one of the diamonds. You have to think like that, really, in order to persist in the soul-deadening process of submitting again and again after receiving rejection after rejection.

All too often, however, beginning writers can't shift gears once they get past the gate. They fail to realize that gatekeeping is the smallest part of an editor's job. They're convinced that every comma and period is perfect and golden as it is, and they continue to view editors as the enemy, and resent—or refuse outright—to even consider any of the editor's comments or suggestions. I've run into quite a few such people over the years, and I've seen the "works of genius" that they consider too perfect for any editor to improve. And frankly, they've all been terrible. You can practically use the attitude as a diagnostic for horrible prose.

Writing is a skill and a craft as well as being an art. And the art can be destroyed all too easily by insufficiencies of skill and craft. Art can also be improved by close attention to skill and craft. A good editor can point the way. They're not writing tutors, of course; the writer has to do the work him or herself. But a writer who has an editor has presumably acquired writing skills on his or her own already (enough, at least, to warrant the offer of a contract from said editor). It shouldn't be that hard to keep going with a few editorial pointers to help, especially with all the material that's available on the web these days.

An editor's primary job is to make each manuscript the most effective, most readable, most wonderful piece of work it can possibly be so that it will sell millions of copies and both the writer and the editor will look good. Editors don't always succeed (especially at the million copies part), but they have had lots of practice at seeing subtle flaws that may have escaped the author because the author is just too close to the project. They also have a lot of experience in judging what works and what doesn't work. That is their artistry.

Being human, editors also make the occasional mistake, which is why you can argue with them. But if you are going to argue, you really, really need to start by listening and thinking about what the editor is asking for first. There is very little that is more embarrassing than confronting one's editor in righteous indignation over some outrageous editorial demand, only to realize halfway through the argument that the editor was right all along.

Editors are not the enemy. Inadequate writing skills are the enemy.

The Business of Writing

Introduction

I have never met a would-be writer who has a business plan.

OK, I haven't met many professional writers who have a formal business plan, either. Nevertheless, every last professional writer I know, of whatever genre, pays a great deal of attention to the business of writing, one way or another. Unfortunately, for most writers, on-the-job training is all they ever get when it comes to the business end of things. (Quite a few don't even want that much, and reality tends to be a nasty shock for them, because if you are writing and selling your stories, or hope to do so, you're running a business whether you like it or not.)

I'm lucky. I grew up in a family of entrepreneurs who talked business over dinner and pretty much anywhere else they happened to be. I enjoy reading business books and magazines; I enjoy talking business (except when my Dad and my brother start going off into engineering specifications). I loved getting my MBA, and I really enjoyed being an accountant and financial analyst before I quit my day job twenty-five years ago to write full-time. I just liked writing more. Plus, I knew even then that as a full-time writer, I'd get plenty of chances to do business-type stuff, while as an accountant, I probably wouldn't get a lot of opportunities to write about dragons.

Back in business school, I learned the standard model for business organization, but I don't believe I've ever seen it applied to writing. So I've decided to do that now. There are seven basic areas, and I'm going to do one section per area after this overview and maybe a summing-up afterward, so if this is something you're totally uninterested in, you can skip the next chunk. (Though if you are hoping to get professionally published at all, let alone make a living at this, I'd really recommend at least skimming.)

The seven basic areas that every business has to cover, one way or another, are:

1. Operations—This includes primarily production, but also design, development, and fulfillment. For writers, that's everything from having the idea to delivering the first draft: research, developing/ prewriting, notes and outlining, and, of course, actually writing the book and shipping it off to the editor.

2. Sales and marketing—Sales is defined as "the act of selling a product in return for money or other compensation." For writers, sales can be split into direct (selling a book directly to the reader) and indirect (licensing production to a publisher, who produces and sells the book directly to readers). Marketing is the strategy that a business uses to get to the sales part.

3. Quality control—This is where products and processes are tested for defects. For writers, this obviously includes all of the editing and revision parts of the job, but it also includes less obvious things like motivation, confidence, and getting enough sleep.

4. Finance—All the monetary aspects of a business. For writers, this used to break down primarily into managing cash flow, recordkeeping, and tax preparation, but it's rapidly getting more complex as new options arise in the other areas, which need to be balanced and evaluated.

5. Administration—The overall organization of people and processes, including everything from office management to the human resources department. For writers, it covers the day-to-day tasks of making and tracking submissions, filing, and general office work, but also things like skills development.

6. Public Relations—This has to do with the relationship between a business and the public in general—both the business' current customers and all of the rest of the people who aren't customers

now but who may or may not become so at some future point. Writers usually lump it in with sales and marketing, but it's much more general.

7. Executive—This has to do with strategic planning and with overseeing everything else; for writers, that means keeping an eye on all the other categories to make sure nothing is left out and everything stays in balance (which can be quite a trick for a one-person business). This is also where long-range forward planning goes, as well as a whole set of choices that get lumped under "managing your writing career."

Generally speaking, the first two areas (Operations and Sales and Marketing) are considered "line" functions because they are the things that bring in the money. Everything else is a "staff" function—that is, tasks that support the money-making side of the business but that don't directly generate income. Staff functions are necessary (just try running a business without paying taxes!), but the fundamental difference between jobs that directly generate income and jobs that don't remains.

Juggling all this stuff is especially complicated for writers because we're trying to do most/all of it ourselves. Yes, the editor, agent, accountant, publicist, and housecleaner all count as help, but it is very rare for a writer to be able to hand the whole of any of these seven job areas off to any of these support people—and it's rarer still for a writer to be able to afford even one full-time employee. Also, even when you're just getting started, it is common for more than one of these areas to be active at the same time. Once you're fully launched into a writing career, they're pretty much all going on simultaneously and constantly—and not in any particularly logical order, either.

The kinds of things writers need to do in each area, and the degree of importance of each, varies somewhat depending on what stage the writer's career is at, too. Unpublished and just-published writers will have to put more of their Administration time into setting up tracking systems for the long haul, for instance, whereas a midlist writer might be spending that time networking and practicing writing skills, and a bestselling author might be keeping an eye on foreign editions and making travel arrangements for publicity gigs. It's all still Administration, though.

I could probably natter on about each of these areas for pages and pages at a time, but I'll talk mainly about the general kinds of things involved in each area rather than a specific set of how-to recommendations.

Operations

> This includes primarily production, but also design, development, and fulfillment.

The business of writing starts with Operations, the first, largest, and most important of the line function areas. It includes all of the aspects of production/manufacturing, but also such necessary elements as purchasing, order fulfillment, research, development, and design.

For writers, production means actually writing the first draft and delivering it to an editor. This is the one area of the seven that changes least, no matter what stage of your career you're at. Whether you're new at this or a veteran of twenty years and thirty published novels, you still have to produce new work.

Production is often hard to get your arms around because it doesn't have a lot of individual tasks that are clear and obvious and that build up to the end, like "buy envelopes," "address envelopes," "stuff envelopes," and "mail out query letters." "Write a page" and "write another page" don't provide quite the same sense of direction, especially when you aren't really sure how many pages there are going to be. Yet production is vital because it's the thing on which everything else depends. If you don't produce a first draft, all the way through to the end, then Sales and Marketing has nothing to sell, Quality Control has nothing to edit, Finance has no income to track, and there's no point to Publicity or Administration.

Since writing a novel takes a fairly long time for most of us, Production is where the majority of writers really need to spend the majority of their time. Breaking it up into one-half to two-hour chunks seems to work best for most of us, as the mental machinery tends to wear out after a few hours for a lot of us. (Yes, I know people who can sit down and write for ten to fifteen hours per day, but I'm not one of them, I don't know many of them, and unless you have already demonstrated your own ability to do this and have lots of ten to fifteen hour chunks of time available to do it in, you're probably better off not counting on being able to pull this off.)

For those who self-publish, production also includes producing the actual books (whether that means printing and hand-binding them in the basement, hiring a vanity press or print-on-demand place to produce the copies, or putting together a cover picture and formatting the files for an e-book). And let's not forget inventory management, for those who opt for the traditional basement full of books (whether self-published or purchased from publisher stock).

Operations also includes research and development, though R&D is sometimes broken out as an eighth important area. "Research" here means the stuff you have to do in order to make the story work; market research comes under "sales and marketing." Operations research includes finding out what kinds of clothes people wore in the thirteenth century, or doing the calculations to figure out how to make two orbiting spaceships collide, or looking up what species of spiders live in the South African jungle where your protagonist's plane is about to crash. Research is why writers who've been around for a while have huge libraries of nonfiction with titles like *Practical Blacksmithing, Alexander the Great and the Logistics of the Macedonian Army, The 1811 Dictionary of the Vulgar Tongue, Extraordinary Popular Delusions and the Madness of Crowds, Mad Princes of Renaissance Germany,* and *Rats, Lice, and History,* to pick a few random titles from my own shelves.

Writers are all intellectual pack rats, absorbing and squirreling away all sorts of interesting nuggets of information to use later. But stockpiling all the random items that come along is rarely enough to make a book work as well as it could.

Even if you're inventing the entire background, history, and all of the ecology, there are going to be things that you're better off looking up than trying to make up, if only so that they'll hang together or be reasonably plausible.

"Development and design" covers any prewriting that happens between getting the idea and sitting down to write the first scene. For a lot of writers, developing ideas is a seamless part of the whole writing process. For others, brainstorming, fitting things together, and outlining in advance of actually sitting down to write are an absolute necessity. Again, this is a place where each writer has to look at his or her own process and honestly evaluate what is working and what isn't, and then go for what is working, even if it is annoying and not at all the way one would like to be working.

Purchasing and order fulfillment are relatively minor matters for writers. Once you have a computer and software, you don't really need another one for the next book; notebooks and pens aren't horribly expensive or difficult to come by, and there really isn't much else a writer needs in order to write. Similarly, sending a finished book off to the publisher is usually not an everyday occurrence, nor is it particularly complicated: you check whether the editor wants hard copy or electronic, then send whichever it is off.

Sales and Marketing

Sales is defined as "the act of selling a product in return for money or other compensation." Marketing is the strategy that the business uses to get to the sales part.

Sales and marketing is generally considered the second of the two line functions in business because it generates income directly. The Sales part is pretty obvious: you give someone something—a proposal, a manuscript, a book or e-book—and they give you money. The Marketing part is all the various research, techniques, and strategies that you use to get the sales.

Sales, for writers, splits into two categories: licensing and direct, or selling to editors versus selling to readers. Early on, in the traditional publishing industry, it's all about licensing. The writer sells (licenses) his or her work to a publisher/editor, who handles the actual production of the physical book as well as a lot of the things that come under Quality Control. Selling to an editor involves the grunt work of sending the manuscript out over and over until you get an offer, followed by the contract negotiations over exactly what rights and subrights the author is licensing to the publisher. Eventually, most of us get an agent to handle this part, but that doesn't mean it goes away entirely. The author still has to OK the deal and then review and sign the contract, and there's often a lot of networking on the author's part that goes into getting the offer in the first place.

If you're self-publishing, the whole licensing area drops out (except possibly for subrights); instead, you have expanded the Operations area and vastly expanded the Marketing and Publicity areas in order to do all the things a traditional publisher would do.

Either way, direct sales to readers don't come into the picture until there's an actual physical book available to sell. For the traditional publishing industry, the publisher handles the vast majority of selling to readers, too, but there are at least some genre writers who generate direct sales themselves at personal appearances or by setting up their own sales tables at conventions and book fairs. Usually this kind of direct marketing to readers works best if one is in a genre such as science fiction (which has lots of conventions) or children's/Young Adult (school and library book fairs). For the self-published, there's all of that plus the getting-the-book-into-bookstores part, which takes considerable time, effort, and persuasive ability.

Direct sales are also something that you have to watch closely. While it can be very satisfying to talk to readers and watch them buy your books, you have to sell at least one hardcover or two to three paperbacks per hour just in order to make minimum wage for the time you're spending at the table. Add the same numbers for every hour you spend getting to the convention, hauling books in and out, setting up and tearing down, collecting and paying sales tax—for most writers, it's just not cost-effective.

For e-book publication, there's nowhere near as much time and effort involved in distribution and direct sales; you sign up with the big e-retailers, put a link on your website or blog, and you're pretty much set. On the sales and distribution part, anyway.

Which brings me to the marketing half of Sales and Marketing.

There are two basic types of marketing: push marketing, in which one tries to get the book prominently displayed in as many places as possible, so as to encourage potential readers who pass by to pick up the book and buy it, and pull marketing, in which one tries to get a lot of potential readers to go to bookstores and ask for the book, "pulling" it into the store. Most of the marketing publishers do has traditionally been push marketing to bookstores and wholesalers. Authors do both: push marketing to editors and pull marketing to readers.

Like Sales, Marketing splits into two parts: marketing a manuscript to editors/publishers/agents, and marketing the book to readers. For writers who don't yet have an agent, marketing a manuscript basically means doing a bunch of research to find out which publishers/editors/agents are most likely to be interested in their particular book and then polishing their query letter/proposal. Those of us who have agents are not exempt from this; there are always questions of strategy that only the writer can decide. Would a collector's edition be feasible or is it too early in the writer's career for anyone to be interested? Is it better to do a free podcast now as a promotion or try to sell audiobook rights later? Will that high-profile work-for-hire generate enough visibility to be worth the lost time working on one's own original series?

This part of marketing can also include choosing new products, which for writers means picking what to write next. Depending on your overall strategy for your writing career, that might mean working out what's "hot" in the current market, drumming up a work-for-hire contract, or settling down to whatever you're most longing to work on next. Whichever route you've chosen, it will require some thought.

The second part of Marketing—promoting books directly to readers—is where most writers focus their efforts once a book comes out, and it will eat your life (and every bit of cash you make on the books) if you let it. There are horror stories about writers who wrote their first book and then had their careers collapse because they spent three to five years after it came out doing nothing but promotions and answering fan mail.

Direct promotion covers everything from autographings to "author loot" (like bookmarks) to special website promotions to conventions to book launch parties. Most of the time, the author foots the bill for this themselves, and it can be quite high, especially for those determined to "do everything possible to make the book a success." They'd usually be better off thinking for a few minutes about how much bang they're getting for their bucks and then choosing only those promotional events/items that make for the largest explosions. Figuring out what's best to do is as important as actually doing it.

Promoting a book directly to readers is absolutely vital for the self-published, but it's more and more necessary even for those of us who are published by traditional publishers. In-house publicity departments are run ragged, and publishers expect their authors to step up and fill in the gap. The catch is that doing the wrong thing can blow you right out of the water, and it's not always obvious what "the wrong thing" is. Even experienced professional publicists mess up now and again.

Marketing a manuscript to editors means doing the research to find out if the book you have written fits their line. There is no point in sending a fluffy romantic comedy to a publisher that only does gritty action-adventure-thrillers, or a science fiction thriller to an academic press that only prints textbooks. Editor marketing also means not cornering the editor at her cousin's wedding, his sister's bat mitzvah, or their son's college graduation party and handing them a copy of the manuscript along with a demand that they look at it. (I am not making these examples up, only changing names and relationships to protect the innocent.) This is not networking; it's obnoxious, highly unprofessional, and pretty much guaranteed not to work anyway.

Marketing a book to readers is a lot harder because the market for fiction is so huge and diverse. Again, market research—but this time, look at what other writers are doing to promote their books, what other publishers are doing, and what's being done for completely different entertainment products. Talk to readers and bookstore clerks about what they like/don't like to see happen. Talk to your fellow pros and find out what they're doing and not doing and what they think has worked and what hasn't. Then consider your own time, energy, and abilities, and do some brainstorming.

The most difficult part of marketing a book to readers is getting attention in more than your local community. An ad in the church bulletin usually isn't costly, but it also doesn't reach a lot of people. Bookmarks passed out to local bookstores may raise awareness in your city or town, but they don't do much for the rest of your state, let alone the rest of the country. The Internet and social media have made it possible to reach people all over the world, of course, but doing so effectively takes a lot of time. If you're self-e-publishing, you're pretty much committed to it, though.

Quality Control

This is where products and processes are tested for defects.

For all writers, Quality Control (QC) obviously includes all of the editing and revision parts of the job; for the self-published, it includes packaging details as well—everything from design (page layout, font/typeface, cover design) to things like the choice of paper and cover materials.

QC isn't considered a line function, most places, because it doesn't directly generate sales, but it's still a vital support function. Even if your overall business strategy is to produce vast quantities of minimum-quality stuff, sell it cheap, and make money on volume, there's still a point below which customers just won't buy. This is as true of writing as it is of any other field.

A surprising number of beginners think they can neglect

quality control at some level—most often, the line I hear is that "it's the editor's job to fix my grammar, spelling, and punctuation." What these folks are forgetting is that editors are their customers, too. And as I said, all customers demand a minimum quality level in the manuscripts they buy.

That minimum applies to every aspect of the manuscript, from formatting and mechanics (grammar, spelling, punctuation, syntax) to the more subjective aspects like "is it a good read?" The format and mechanics stuff is easy enough to find out about—check the publishing house's submission guidelines and/or ask your editor, or get a copy of the Chicago Manual of Style. Fixing the mechanics, on the other hand, can be a long and tedious process, depending on the exact problem (if you don't know what a comma splice is, for instance, you're going to have a fairly hard time finding them, let alone fixing them).

This is one of the reasons why so many writers recommend learning grammar, punctuation, spelling, and syntax thoroughly, until getting it right is unconscious and effortless. It will save you enormous time and effort in the long run. If you haven't a clue about grammar, you can try finding a tame English major who is willing to go over your manuscript, trade proofreading with a writer friend, or you can hire your own copyeditor. Hiring your own copyeditor is relatively expensive and not recommended unless you are self-publishing, in which case it's part of the production costs that a traditional publisher would handle for you but that you have to do yourself as a self-publisher.

Many writers spend most of their QC time and effort on the subjective aspects of the story, which is fine as long as they're reasonably sure that the format and mechanics don't need attention. The subjective aspects are what most revisions are about, and they're also where first readers and critique groups come in. Since "is it a good read?" is a subjective question, it's generally a good idea to get other eyes on the manuscript at some point to double-check that what the writer thinks is "a good read" is coming out as "a good read" for other people, too. For many writers, getting those other eyes early in the process is better than getting them later. Those who don't possess a temperament that allows for taking critique/comments from others have to work much harder to compensate for the lack of alternate opinions.

In pretty much all cases, QC is a matter for more than one set of eyes. By this I mean that if you try to do it all yourself, you are highly likely to miss things, whether they're dangling participles or stylistic problems. The author does get to decide whether or not to take the advice of others to heart, but it is a really good idea to find someone to ask for help and think really, really hard about rejecting that help once it's been given.

Quality control is something that can (and probably should) be applied at every stage of the production process, so long as it doesn't interfere with production. For writers, that means that any early brainstorming sessions, redrafting and rearranging chapters, and major structural fixes are just as important as critique groups and final polish—and that editorial revision requests also count. The trick here is to remember that QC is not a line function; production is. That means that if the QC part (also known as the Internal Editor) is getting in the way of production, QC gets pulled back and put off until later, after the production part has been done but before the product goes out to potential customers (i.e., editors).

It is also common for writers to place too much emphasis on QC—to demand perfection (or at least a much higher standard of work) than is necessary or desirable. Perfection is not achievable; it is certainly not achievable in your very first story or novel. As long as you do your best, you can't expect more than that. This time. If you finish something and aren't satisfied—and I know very few writers who are—spend some of your time between books working on your skills in whatever ways you find useful. After all, QC also includes making sure the production people are capable of doing the jobs they've been assigned.

Oddly enough, in writing, quality has very little to do with the absolute speed of production. Every writer has a speed that can be considered "too fast"—i.e., if they write that rapidly, the quality of their work suffers—but how fast is "too fast" varies wildly. I know writers for whom one book every two years is "too fast," and others for whom a book in two weeks works fine, but twelve days is just too short a time period. It depends on the writer and sometimes on the story. This means you have to be hard-nosed about looking at the actual quality of whatever you've produced and not get distracted by how fast or slow you produced it. Sometimes this means not telling your critique group that you wrote the last six chapters in two days until after they've made their comments.

In addition to the editing and revising parts of the writing job, QC also includes less obvious things like motivation, confidence, getting enough sleep and exercise, working at your writing skills, eating properly, taking a break now and then—all things that make a surprisingly large difference in the overall quality of your writing output.

Exercise, food, breaks, and sleep are particularly important because they are things that aren't clearly part of the production process and that sometimes seem as if they're actively interfering with it. If you neglect them, however, both the quality and the quantity of your production tends to drop like a rock. This is also an area where you cannot make comparisons with other writers. Everyone has different biochemistry, and the fact that Joe Pro can get by on two hours of sleep a night, four gallons of coffee, and a diet composed exclusively of Twinkies and still crank out high-quality prose doesn't mean *you* can. Be realistic about what you need, and then make sure you get it.

Finance

This has to do with all the monetary aspects of a business.

The financial end of the writing business needs and deserves a lot more attention than many writers give it absent emergencies. Especially the taxes part. Editors don't do house-to-house searches, but the IRS does, and they're not nice about it, either. Finances include a lot of recordkeeping, starting with the must-do stuff for the IRS. They still like paper trails, so keeping receipts and printed records of income and expenses is vital.

However, Finance for writers isn't only about keeping good records for your taxes and making your estimated tax payments on time. This is easy for a lot of writers to overlook because writers don't need a lot of cash flow to maintain the business—paper and pens don't cost much, and once you've gotten over the initial outlay for a computer and software, you're set for years. Really, the main thing writers need money for is their own income, and most think of that as a personal thing, not a business matter.

The trouble is that if you don't pay attention to where the money is coming from—which titles and formats are selling, which publishers pay more and on time—you can easily end up missing opportunities or find yourself suddenly unable to pay your bills.

It is also perilously easy to live in the moment if you don't have a reality check. Publishing tends to have a much longer pipeline than most jobs, and if you aren't shoving stuff in now, you can easily run out of cash three or five years down the road and have to scramble—or start hunting for a day job—to cover day-to-day expenses. Paying attention to your projected future income lets you know that this was the last of the advance payments and you only have until it runs out to sell a new proposal to someone.

Expenses are another problem area. I cannot tell you how many people have said to me, "But you're a writer so that's tax-deductible; why aren't you buying it?" What they don't get is that "tax-deductible" does not mean "free." It means it's an offset to whatever I made; if I didn't make money (or if I've already accumulated enough expenses this year), the benefit is zero this year and maybe something I can carry into next year, if I make enough money next year to cover it. And you don't want to pile up too many losses in a row or the IRS gets interested and you may lose all your business deductions for several years.

The rule of thumb I use is "If I wouldn't buy it on sale for twenty percent off, I shouldn't buy it just because it's tax-deductible." This is a little conservative because as a self-employed person in the United States, I pay both halves of the FICA (that's Social Security tax), which adds up to fifteen percent, and on top of that goes whatever my marginal tax rate is likely to be that year. So really, the "buy it if it's on sale" rate should be a bit more than 20% off, but I prefer being conservative. Writers in countries other than the United States, of course, have to work out their own percentages based on their particular tax situations.

If you're self-publishing or hand-selling your own books, you have a lot more recordkeeping because you'll need to track inventory (unless you're only doing e-books) and sales. I know more than one writer who's gotten caught at tax time because they thought that as long as they spent all their sales income on more inventory, it wouldn't count as income. If you are one of these, run, do not walk, to a reliable accountant and get them to explain to you what you can and cannot do and how to do it, or you will end up paying a whole lot more than you have to in taxes.

There also seems to be an unfortunate tendency for writers to underestimate how much they're going to need to live on. They overlook things like insurance and emergency funds and retirement savings when they're figuring out how much income they need to generate. But if you only include the expenses that come around weekly or monthly, and you spend your entire advance on them, you're in for a nasty surprise when the car, homeowners', or health insurance bill arrives, or when you have to spring for Christmas presents, or when the car breaks down. If you aren't making enough from writing to cover this stuff, then you need a day job, and you're far better off admitting it than pretending that the car will never break, you'll never get sick or have an accident, and that Scrooge was right about the whole "bah, humbug" thing.

Cash flow is a particular concern for most writers because either you know how much money you're going to get (advance payments) but not when you're going to get it, or else you know pretty much when you're going to get it (semi-annual royalty payments) but not how much they're going to be. What this means is that (1) you shouldn't count on having money to spend unless it's actually in the bank (I know writers who've had trouble making rent or mortgage payments because they charged a large purchase, figuring the advance would come in time to pay for it, and then the advance took another three months to arrive), and (2) you need to budget what's in the bank to last for however many months it'll be until the next payment is likely to arrive. Getting a $5,000 advance check doesn't mean you can spend half of it on a new laptop if you aren't likely to get any more income for the next ten months (unless you really can live on $250/month—do the math).

To clarify things a bit, here's an example: Jane Q. Newwriter has finished her first novel, *The Best Thing Since Sliced Bread*, and joyfully signs a contract with a publisher for a hefty first-time advance of $10,000 and typical royalty rates. Delighted by her good fortune, she immediately quits her day job, figuring she can live on that $10,000 for quite a while if she's careful. A month later, her rent is due, and there's still no check from the publisher, so she takes an advance on her credit card and complains to her editor. The editor explains that they're still processing the paperwork.

Another month goes by; Jane is living on her credit cards and starting to rack up the debt. Finally, her copy of the signed contract arrives from her agent, along with a check for $2,125— barely enough to pay off the debt she's already got and nowhere near enough to keep living on. What happened?

Well, Jane's contract divided the advance up into four payments of $2,500 each, and her agent gets fifteen percent of every check. That $2,125 is Jane's "on signing" payment, minus her agent's fifteen percent, and it got paid fairly promptly (Jane's signed contract has to also be signed by someone at the publishing house, reviewed by legal, and then the check has to be cut. This generally takes six weeks minimum, and as I said, up to three or four months if anybody is on vacation). Jane won't get her "on delivery" part of the advance until she delivers an acceptable manuscript (and it'll take another three to six weeks for that check to get cut, too); then she'll get one-fourth when the book is actually published (one to two years after she delivered it), and the final one-fourth will come when the paperback comes out (generally at least one year after the hardback is published).

So that $10,000 that Jane was counting on to live on for her first year as a full-time writer is actually getting spread out over a minimum of three years, probably longer. Since the book is already finished, she may be able to get the editorial revisions done fast and get her second $2,125 this year, but the "on hardcover publication" chunk isn't going to come until the book is published, and that will take one to two years after she turns in the finished manuscript. One year after that, when the paperback comes out, she'll get the final "on mass market paperback" part of the advance. Assuming, of course, that the publisher doesn't delay publication of either hardcover or paperback for any of a dozen reasons.

Add a zero to every number above, and you'll realize that even a $100,000 advance doesn't seem so large when it's spread over four payments and three to five years, and you've taken out your agent's fifteen percent and another thirty percent or so for the IRS.

Basically, what I'm saying is that when you're a writer, you either know exactly how much money you will get (the advance) but not exactly when it will arrive, or you know when it will arrive (the royalties) but not how much they will be. This makes long-term budgeting and cash flow management a critical skill for writers.

An especially vital aspect of cash flow management is putting aside enough to pay the taxes. I generally dump half my incoming checks straight into the tax account (which I keep in a separate bank from my regular checking account, to make extra-sure that I'm not likely to tap it for day-to-day expenses and then end up owing the IRS hundreds or, in a good year, thousands of dollars, and being caught short). It's hard to do, but boy, does it make quarterly estimated tax payments less painful. If I'm going to have to live on beans and rice for three months in order to make those payments, I know it right away, instead of having it come as a nasty surprise.

And then there's the other stuff: checking royalty statements, keeping track of advances and subrights sales so you can bug the publisher if the payments are taking too long, watching sales trends so you can tell which of your publicity efforts are having an effect and/or figure out when it's time to ask for new covers, a reprint, or a new push for a title (or do some of that yourself). A lot of writers consider this optional, mainly because they don't want to bother with all the recordkeeping and reviewing.

I don't consider any of this optional. Especially checking royalty statements; over the years, I've found something like $5,000 worth of errors (all of which the various publishers corrected promptly and without argument when they were pointed out). And the unexplained discrepancy that looked at first glance as if I owed the publisher $300 turned out to be a more complicated error that meant they actually owed me $1,000, so yes, I report everything I find, whether it looks as if it's good for me or for them. Computerization has eliminated errors in addition and subtraction, but it has resulted in a lot more data entry problems, so the checking still needs to be done.

Keeping good records allows you to know how your business is doing financially—and quite often why, which can give you an idea what to do about it. It also provides essential input into lots of decisions, from whether to attend a bookstore event/autographing, to whether to change publishers or agents, to which of two equally tempting ideas might be better to work on next.

Note that I didn't imply that all of these decisions should be made strictly on financial grounds. You may be well aware that the autographing at a local bookstore will take three hours (what with driving time), and you're only likely to sell two hardcovers to folks who wouldn't have bought them anyway (meaning you're working for around $1.30 per hour, less gas money), so financially it would be a dead loss. But you may want to do it anyway for the publicity, or for contact with your fans/readers, or for goodwill with the bookstore and its employees (who may be more willing to hand-sell your book once they've met you), or just because you get such a lift out of doing this kind of thing that you always come home and write six times as much for the next three days.

On the other hand, if you're paying $300 to fly to another city for a similar autographing, the expense is so much greater than any goodwill generated that it's probably not worth doing. On the third hand, if you're going to be in some other town anyway, it may well be worth the good publicity to set up a couple of local autographings or unpaid library appearances (especially if you can do enough of them to justify deducting some of the travel expenses).

Crunching the numbers is something many would-be writers think of as boring and uninteresting, but it is surprising how fascinating all those figures can be when it's your book, your sales, and your money.

Administration

This is the overall organization of people and processes, including everything from office management to the human resources department.

For writers, Administration covers most of the day-to-day tasks of making and tracking submissions, answering mail, returning email and phone calls, filing, organizing manuscripts, maintaining the website and blog, and that's just off the top of my head. This is where the famous Secretary Hat goes—the job of logging submissions and rejections and then getting the manuscript back in the mail.

Administration, like Finance, is often considered dull, unglamorous, and downright boring. It generally involves a lot of paperwork and organization, which puts a lot of folks off. But like Finance, Administration is something no business can do without. The most obvious part is the aforementioned getting the manuscript in the mail—as I've said before, editors do not do house-to-house searches for publishable manuscripts. If Administration doesn't get the manuscript out, the story won't get published.

There are, however, a lot more ways in which Administration

is important. Keeping track of submissions, for instance—you probably don't want six novels all sitting at the same publishing house at the same time, even if it is your first choice of publisher. You certainly don't want to forget that this story was rejected by Editor A at Publisher A three years ago and send it back as a "new" submission. You may want to keep track of which markets respond promptly and which take years or which places have bought more (or paid more for) particular types of stories.

You also don't want to lose track of how long things have been under submission—there's a point at which you really ought to query the publishing house to find out if the manuscript got lost somewhere in the process, and that point is neither six days nor six years after you mailed it off. You don't want the email from the agent or the prospective editor to sit unanswered in your "in" basket for a week. You want your files and data entry up to date in whatever system you have so that if and when somebody asks whether you own the Portuguese language e-book rights for a story you published twenty years ago, you can look it up without spending hours and hours digging through old piles of paper, only to discover that the contract you're after seems to have vanished.

Administration can also cover a lot of miscellaneous and occasional jobs, like travel agent, monitoring and reordering office supplies, correspondence, keeping the library in order, finding research materials, keeping the web page current, and scheduling and coordinating whatever meetings or interviews or events need to be scheduled and coordinated.

In a large company or corporation, pretty much every department has its own Administration section because every department has paperwork, phone calls, and organizing necessities. For writers (and any small business), Administration doesn't have such hard edges. Deciding what to write next is Operations; but is keeping track of the story notes and supporting research Administration or part of Operations? Deciding on a list of publishers to query is Marketing, but composing and printing the letters is probably Administration. Doing the taxes is Finance; filing the receipts and entering income and expenses into Quicken all year could be considered either Administration or Finance.

It isn't particularly important that this area be broken out from all the others. What is important is that the work gets done—submissions get tracked, manuscripts get mailed, contracts get filed, the web page gets maintained, e-mails and letters get answered, and so on.

However you choose to keep all the various records and processes, it is generally easiest to set up a good system right from the beginning. The longer you wait, the more likely it is that your early work will never get properly entered when you finally get around to it. The problem is that the earlier you are in your writing career, the more all this tracking and recordkeeping seems like overkill or, at the very least, over-optimism. And besides, it's boring and it takes time and it's boring and it takes energy and it's *boring*. Nevertheless, if you stay in the writing business, your future self will thank you for doing it all right from the start. Trust me on this one.

Administration also includes the Human Resources department. Since few writers have any actual employees, this covers stuff like dealing with your agent, accountant, and any other professional services you have contracted for, plus whatever skills development you decide to invest in for yourself. "Skills development" here refers to anything that's going to help the business. Writing skills are one obvious area; you can work on them deliberately in lots of ways, from doing informal experimental bits and pieces, to critique groups, to attending a seminar or workshop, to taking classes in grammar or whatever other area you may feel weak in.

There are, however, lots of other business-related skills that are good for a writer to develop. Basic financial management is a fairly obvious weak point for way too many people; checking the latest marketing and publicity techniques never hurts; website management changes so rapidly that it's certainly worth reading up on every year or so, and maybe even taking a brush-up class periodically. Publicity and Marketing are areas where writers tend to be at one extreme or the other: either they're naturals or they're floundering. There are books and classes on all these things, frequently in community education centers (which are usually cheaper and less time-intensive than college-level night school).

If you're starting to feel overwhelmed, I'm not surprised. I started feeling overwhelmed about two sections ago, and all I'm really doing here is describing, in categories and a bit more detail than usual, the stuff I have to do to make a living writing. Seeing it all laid out in print makes me realize just how much I and all the other pros I know are juggling all the time, and there are still two areas to go.

Public Relations

This has to do with the relationship between a business and the public in general—both the business' current customers and all of the rest of the people who aren't customers now but who may or may not become so at some future point.

Public Relations (PR) is subtly different from Marketing, in that PR is about the business as a whole, while Marketing is about one specific product. Obviously, there's a lot of overlap because both of them involve the way customers and potential customers see the business.

Full disclosure: PR/Publicity is probably my least favorite aspect of running a business, right up there with Sales and Marketing. So if you're looking for good tips and tricks, this is not the best place for them. This is just a basic overview; if you want to get really into this stuff, find somebody who's a natural and/or who really likes it, and ask them for advice.

For writers, PR is a lot more personal than it is for most businesses. The closest thing a writer has to a brand name is their own name on the book cover; this means that "self-promotion" (which many people are uncomfortable with and which some other folks frown upon as "showing off" or "not being about the books") happens to some extent, whether you want it to or not.

Being aware of this is half the battle because PR becomes

more and more relevant the more books you have out, the larger your readership, and the longer you write—and until they invent practical time travel, you can't go back and fix any minor mistakes you made early in your career that snowballed into large problems as time went on.

For the unpublished and newly published, PR is usually indistinguishable from Marketing. When you only have one or two books out, everything you do in public tends to be targeted at selling those titles, and larger implications seldom get considered. Also, when an author only has one book out, he or she doesn't usually get invited to do the sorts of things that would fall under general PR as opposed to marketing a specific book. This gives the writer a chance to ease into the PR stuff, attending conventions as a pro and getting used to doing panels before having to worry about being Guest of Honor at a Worldcon or giving TV interviews on one of the major networks (unless of course your first book is a megahit bestseller, in which case you'd better learn fast. We should all have such problems.).

As with Sales and Marketing, there are two levels to consider when you're thinking about PR—professional (that is, the reputation/relationship the writer has with editors, agents, reviewers, other writers, and industry professionals), and the general reputation the writer has with fans and readers at large. There's a lot of overlap, of course, but sometimes it's useful to stop and consider for a moment. Dressing up in a clown suit and walking the streets wearing a billboard advertising your new book may get you some attention from local readers, but perhaps you'd be better off coming up with a PR gimmick that looks a little more professional from the editor/agent point of view.

A lot of early PR is basic courtesy and common sense: when you're out in public, don't be obnoxious; don't insult people; don't demand to be treated like a star; find the right balance between talking about your new book all the time and never mentioning it at all. "Out in public" most definitely includes Facebook, Twitter, blogs, comments on other people's blogs, and any other Internet venues, even if they're supposedly locked or private. This is especially important because the Internet is so very public—whatever you say can be easily seen by publishers, critics, agents, major authors, and important book buyers, none of whom, thirty years back, would have been likely to have much contact with a newbie author. It's a lot easier to shoot yourself in the foot nowadays.

There are writers who've made a point of creating an obnoxious public persona for themselves and succeeded anyway, but there aren't many. If you are considering something like this, you need to bear in mind that the way you present yourself in public, right from the start, will be with you for the rest of your writing career. If you get tired of acting that way, or decide that it isn't serving you well, it'll take an enormous amount of time and effort to change perceptions of you. There are possibly apocryphal tales of authors who had to change their names and start over because they couldn't stand the public persona they'd constructed, but couldn't persuade people to see them any other way. It's much easier to be yourself.

You can, of course, go whole hog on the marketing/ publicity for your early books—hitting the convention circuit hard, coming up with ways to get you (and your books) talked about on social media, throwing big book bashes in unusual places for potential readers. The problems with this are (1) it takes a lot of time and energy, (2) it takes money (in varying amounts, but very little of it is totally free), and (3) if you don't know what you are doing, or don't have the personality/ experience for it, this kind of thing can backfire horribly. Some writers are naturals at this kind of thing, but for those who aren't, it's usually better to start small and learn it gradually, rather than jumping in with both feet and ending up with two muddy shoes stuck in your mouth.

As a writer's career develops and their audience expands, the scope of PR gets larger. Rightly or wrongly, people associate writers closely with their books and assume that if they like/ dislike the author, they will like/dislike the books (and vice versa). The kinds of things you get asked to do (or that you can persuade people to let you get in on) get gradually larger and more significant as you publish more titles—instead of a talk to the six English and Language Arts teachers at your local high school, you're giving a talk to three hundred librarians from every school in your state or to the fifty folks who make major buying decisions for all the schools in the state.

Some writers (me included) find being "on" in public very tiring; other writers find it energizing. If you're one of the latter, you may need to remind yourself periodically that PR is not a line function, and you need to apply that energy to Operations. If you're one of the former, you need to know that actively doing publicity is not obligatory. You can become a writing hermit who is never seen in public—but that, too, is a publicity choice. In other words, you can minimize this area, but you can't get away from it entirely.

Executive

> This has to do with strategic planning
> and overseeing everything else.

For writers, the Executive area means keeping an eye on all the other categories to make sure nothing is left out and everything stays in balance (which can be quite a trick for a one-person business). This is also where long-range forward planning goes, which is a whole set of choices that usually get lumped under "managing your writing career."

Exactly what is an Executive decision and what falls into one of the other areas of business is a slippery thing to determine—and generally unnecessary as well. As long as you decide whether to let the publisher have e-book rights or whether to hang on to them and publish the e-books yourself, it doesn't matter whether you call it Operations, Finance, or Executive. The important thing is that the decision gets made.

Larger decisions fall squarely within the Executive category, especially those "managing your career" decisions. There are a lot more options than many would-be writers think of, ranging from basic and fairly obvious decisions (Self-publish or traditional publishing? Large, regional, small, or micropress? E-books or paper? Short stories or novels?), to things that affect specific areas like Finance (go for the highest possible advance or trade high advances for a better royalty rate or even a royalties-only deal?) or Publicity (Push early and often or wait until there are more books to push?), to career development (strictly original fiction or work-for-hire? Under your name, a pseudonym, or multiple pseudonyms? In one genre or several?)

All these decisions can and do get revisited periodically, and sometimes they change as circumstances change. You may decide initially that you're going to stick strictly to novels, and five years later unexpectedly get asked to participate in a prestigious short story anthology with some of the most prominent writers in your field. You might still end up turning the opportunity down, but I guarantee you'll want to think really hard about it first.

This is also where I'd put managing the backlist, which is a key element in making a living for any writer who's been at it for a while. Your backlist is all of your older titles; it of course includes the stuff that's out of print, but it also includes stuff that's been in print for a couple of years and maybe even some of those "trunk stories" that never sold at all. Older titles can be resold to new publishers once they go out of print; if you or your agent put some elbow grease into it, subrights like audiobooks and foreign translations can provide a surprising amount of income. And then there are e-books and print-on-demand, which have opened up a lot of options for the backlist. But again, you need to put some effort into getting things out there and maintaining them.

One of the most important aspects of the Executive area is keeping everything else in balance—making sure that Publicity isn't taking over the time that needs to be spent on Operations, that the Finance and Administration paperwork is kept up to date, that Sales is covering the backlist as well as the current work. This is especially tricky because in writing, all of this stuff comes in waves: Finance is pretty dead for most of the year, bar an hour or two a month for recordkeeping, but it suddenly becomes a critical activity in April when taxes are due. Quality Control has a big surge right before a new book comes out (with the copyedit and galleys to go over); Publicity and Marketing usually have their surge right after. So you can't assign X hours per week to each area, week in and week out. You have to put a lot of hours into whatever is "hot" at the moment, while keeping an eye out to make sure the stuff that isn't currently swamping you gets enough attention that it won't blow up into some other kind of crisis.

Long-range planning is a major component of the Executive area. What do you want your eventual writing career to look like? Some writers make as much or more from giving workshops, speaking engagements, writer-in-residence gigs, and teaching as they do from the books they write; others make their money cranking out titles in multiple genres under multiple pseudonyms; still others work in multiple areas, writing screenplays or comics or role-playing game scenarios as well as short stories and novels; some stick to one much-loved series or set of characters.

There isn't a one-size-fits-all way of managing your career because there are many different possible goals and many different paths to reaching each one. Also, no two writers I know have ever been faced with the exact same set of opportunities and challenges coming out of the blue, nor have they made the exact same set of choices when faced with similar opportunities.

In the past thirty years, I've accepted or turned down various opportunities ranging from editing anthologies, to writing a work-for-hire, to helping a friend launch a small press, to teaching classes in writing, to writing a book specifically for a packager or a new line being developed by a friend/editor. Sometimes my friends and colleagues thought I was crazy to take the risk I took; sometimes, they thought I was crazy for not taking advantage of whatever it was. At present, I don't regret any of the choices I've made; I think that's because I had a clear idea of what I wanted to do in the long run and where I wanted to end up and why (if not always how to get there).

Another major component of the Executive area is keeping an eye on what the market is doing and educating yourself about what it has done in the past and what possible directions it may be going in the future. Over my career, there's been a major, market-changing event about every ten years—the Thor Power Tool tax decision in the 1980s, the collapse of the independent distributors in the 1990s, the explosion in e-books in the 2000s. Some were predictable, some weren't—but all of them affected the way I handle my business (whether that means the kind of publicity I do, the way my agent negotiates various contract provisions, or which publishers I put at the top of my "I want them to publish my books" list).

Pulling It All Together

So there you have it: all seven areas of business—operations, sales and marketing, quality control, finance, administration, public relations, and executive—laid out for writers. Looking at them all at once like this is rather daunting, but not looking at them at all is a recipe for messing up.

If you are a professional writer—or hope to be one—you are running a small business. It's kind of a peculiar small business, but it's still a business. Even if the main thing you are interested in is the art of writing, the business aspects deserve careful consideration and attention because they affect both the time and energy you have for creating your work (if you're spending twelve hours a day putting out fires because you neglected one area or another, there's not much time or energy left for writing). How you manage your business also affects the availability and distribution of your finished work. This doesn't matter much if you want to sell one hundred copies to your family and friends, but it makes a big difference if you're hoping to make a living at this.

If you're just getting started or have yet to sell, most of your time will be doing Production (writing), Quality Control (editing and revising), Sales and Marketing (researching publishers and sending the manuscript out), and Administration (tracking your submissions). Finance will kick in as soon as you have either income or expenses to track; Publicity usually shows up a few years down the road.

Midlist writers tend to be juggling a lot faster, as they typically have several projects somewhere in the pipeline, meaning that they may be in the process of writing one book (Production), editing another (QC), while a third is just hitting the bookstores and needs a Marketing or Publicity push; two backlist titles are going up as e-books and those files need reviewing (more QC and Administration); meanwhile, Croatian subrights on half the backlist have sold and need to be tracked until the checks arrive (Administration and Finance), and maybe the writer should see if his or her agent can get them interested in the other half (Administration and Marketing); and an unexpected opportunity to edit an anthology has come up, which could take the writing career in a whole new direction and which the publisher needs a "yes" or "no" on by the end of the month (Executive/strategy). And, of course, writers who've achieved "lead title" or bestseller status have even more complications in all areas.

In other words, the farther along in your career you get, the more work has to be done in each of the business areas and the more complex that work becomes. This means that no matter what sort of planning you do in regard to your writing business, you'll probably need to revisit it periodically and make adjustments according to where you currently are in your business, what the market is doing, and how your goals, skills, resources, and opportunities have changed.

As I said to begin with, most writers don't have a formal business plan. This is because most formal business plans are designed for small businesses that are trying to get a loan from a bank or for giant corporations that are trying to project their future business. They're heavy on the financial stuff—sales projections, breakeven analysis, three-year projected P&L, and other monetary concerns. That doesn't work particularly well for writers because (1) they're hardly ever going to need a loan to support the business, and (2) the timeline for developing a writing business is usually a lot longer than three years, which makes financial projections really difficult unless you have several contracts already in hand.

For writers, planning the business is about managing their own resources (time, money, energy) in order to have their writing job/career/business go in whatever way they want it to. This obviously means that you have to start by figuring out which way you want things to go. Are you looking for the validation of professionally publishing a few stories? Are you hoping to make a living? Will you be happy writing one gigantic forty-volume popular series about the same people and places, or do you want to do something different with every book? Would you be happy doing some high-paying ghostwriting or working under several pseudonyms, or do you want all your work to be your original stuff with your name on it? What does "being a writer" mean to you?

Once you've done that, think about what you are willing and able to do to get there. I've talked to folks who weren't willing to give up one hour of television per week in order to work at their writing yet who were supposedly desperate to become bestselling writers. You can't run a decent hobby business on one hour per week, let alone a writing business. Be honest with yourself about what you want, how much time and energy you're willing to put into getting it, and how well those two things match up.

Also think about the kind of time and energy you are willing to put into each of the seven business areas, which ones you think you're good at (or can be), and which ones you're pretty sure you'll hate. Then think a bit about how best to design your career in order to minimize the need to do stuff you hate and get maximum benefit out of the stuff you like doing and/ or are good at. (Hint: if you hate doing the Production part of Operations, i.e., the writing itself, this is probably not the career for you.)

Writing is a job, a career, and a business, as well as an art. If you don't think about the business end before you actually start selling, you'll have to play catch-up later, and the longer you wait, the harder it gets to figure it all out.

A final caution: Always keep in mind that there are only two line areas: Operations and Sales/Marketing. The Executive area, under which "making a business plan" falls, is not one of these. In other words, thinking about how you're going to handle all this is worthwhile, even necessary, but it won't do you any good at all unless you have a product (a manuscript, story, or book) to sell and can sell what you've produced. The first thing is always, always the writing: doing it and improving it and getting it out in front of editors and/or readers.

Addendum (Retirement)

The very first question is: what does retirement mean to you as a writer? Writing isn't quite the same as other jobs; most of us can't imagine retiring in the traditional sense (leaving a day job and not doing it any more). Writers also have more of an option to continue working than people in normal jobs—as long as our brains and our fingers continue to work properly, so can we. I've known a good many older professional writers who've worked into their eighties, right up to the last minute.

So what does "being retired" mean for a writer?

For me, the main thing it means is having a choice. The majority of professional writers have historically worked on portion-and-outline, meaning that we write an outline and fifty to one hundred pages of a book, sell it, then have to write the rest to a deadline set in the contract. At some point, this gets more than a little old. "Being retired," for most of the writers I know, means not having to work to deadline—being able to write what we want, when we want, and then sell it. Some still choose to sell on portion-and-outline, but even then, having a choice makes a difference.

Choice also means the ability to experiment more—to write in other genres, for instance, without needing to consider the potential financial downside of trying to build a whole new readership. It means not needing to feel guilty for skipping your writing time for a few days in a row. It means being able to slack off on some (though not all) of the less enjoyable tasks involved in running a business (the ones I've been droning on about for eight or nine sections now).

In order to have those choices, a writer, like everyone else, needs retirement savings. How much you need will depend on the lifestyle to which you would like to become accustomed and on how you have managed (and will continue to manage) your writing career. Because there are so many different paths for a writing career to take, planning for retirement has to be a bit more active than for most people.

On the one hand, writing income is irregular, which means Social Security payments (which are based on average annual income) may not be as large as you might have expected (that's assuming you think that there will still be Social Security payments by the time you retire, whenever that is). On the other hand, if you have managed your writing so as to generate royalty income and keep your backlist available and productive (as opposed to concentrating on big money advances), your existing work can continue to generate income for a long time even if you aren't putting out anything new.

What this means is that your preference for your career changes how you handle your retirement planning. If you've been getting irregular big-money advances and not worrying so much about your books earning out or about the backlist, then your income will drop as soon as you stop writing. You'll also want to keep an eye on how much Social Security thinks it's going to pay out when you start getting it. As with most people, you want enough of a retirement fund plus Social Security to live on; there are plenty of financial counselors and online websites to help you figure out what that will be. On the plus side, if you're not writing new stuff and don't need to manage the backlist, you're pretty much done with your writing business.

If you've managed your career with a vast quantity of work-for-hire or low-to-medium advance originals that come and go and never come back again, you're in the same shape as the big-money advances people, except that your annual income is likely to be more regular and therefore your Social Security payments will be larger and you may not need to sock away quite as much in your retirement plan. Once you stop writing, you're done with the business.

If your books are the sort that earn out their advances and continue to sell for a long time, or that can be resold after the first publisher loses interest, you likely won't need quite as large a bundle in your retirement savings because your backlist will continue to bring in income. However, you will need to continue managing your backlist, making sure that things stay in print and get resold and reissued over and over. In other words, you have to keep running the business to some extent, even if you aren't writing anything new.

And if you absolutely intend to keep writing at full speed until the day you drop, you still need a cash cushion, albeit a smaller one, to deal with everything from medical emergencies to unanticipated changes in the writing market that affect your ability to generate adequate income. The older you get, the greater the likelihood that you will lose a year or two of writing time to illness or unexpected surgery. Medicare and health insurance may pay your doctor and hospital bills, but they won't replace the income you lose, and illness is a huge drain on creativity.

How much you sock away into a retirement plan under each of these circumstances depends on how much you make and how much you want to be able to spend once you decide to declare yourself retired. The calculation is pretty straightforward: you decide how much income per year you want to have, figure out how many years you expect to live after you retire, and plug the numbers into one of the many retirement-planning calculators online (be sure you pick one that adjusts for inflation and that has a reasonable rate of expected return on your investments).

Once you have determined what you think you need in your retirement account, it is wise to consider it a minimum, not your whole goal. The more money you have in the bank (or investment account), the more options you have. Options are good.

As a self-employed person, there are several kinds of tax-advantaged retirement accounts that you can use to accumulate your savings: a traditional IRA, a Roth IRA, a SEP (Simplified Employee Pension), a solo 401K. You probably want to educate yourself about these and then consult with your accountant or a financial planner because they all have different rules, advantages, and disadvantages. Or you can ignore the tax benefits of these and just stick money in a bank or a normal investment account. In my experience, you'll be far better off going with one of the tax-deferred plans that works for you. Myself, I have a Roth IRA, an SEP, and a normal investment account, and I max out my contributions to the first two every year and try to add to the third as well.

The main trick to retirement savings is to start early. The power of compound interest is amazing. When I was in business school, they made us do the actual calculations, comparing the amount of money at retirement generated by two strategies: one person who put $2,000 in an IRA starting at age 20 but who stopped at age 30 and one person who did the same thing, only starting at age 30 and going on for the next 30 years. The one who only saved for 10 years but who started early *always* came out significantly ahead of the one who got a late clue. In other words, the sooner you start, the less you are likely to have to contribute out-of-pocket over the years.

Different Strokes

I talk a lot about differences in the writing process and the way every writer thinks differently and therefore has to work differently. All those differences apply to a lot more than the writing process, though, and it is just as destructive when folks don't understand that.

Take the heady days following the publication of one's novel. A sizeable number of writers seem to become obsessed with numbers for those first few weeks. They check their Amazon rankings and Bookscan numbers. They pester their editors for orders-shipped figures and their local booksellers for sales numbers. They do complicated mathematical extrapolations that they would never have considered even thinking about two weeks earlier.

The obsession doesn't go away even after they've become relatively successful; they just start checking whether they're number seven or eight on the bestseller lists (and trying to decide whether number seven on the *New York Times* bestseller list is better than number five on the *Washington Post* bestseller list) or comparing how long their new book stayed in the number X spot compared to their last one or to some other writer's.

There's nothing really wrong with this (unless the writer is one of those who goes a little crazy trying to process all this data), but it's not obligatory, either. I mean, once the book hits the shelves, there really isn't much the writer can do to influence those numbers directly, but if they like looking at them, why not? The trouble comes when people who don't really care about this stuff start feeling as if there's something wrong with them because they feel no particular urge to look at their numbers every hour or so.

Similarly, there are different approaches to managing your career—and advocates of each sometimes get passionate about their preferences. For instance, there's the take-the-money-and-run school of thought (which includes most of the agents I know) that advocates pushing for the largest advance on the theory that a known advance means a predictable (and to some extent controllable) income stream and that a publisher who hands out a large advance is more likely to work hard at distributing and promoting the book than one who's only given out four figures ahead of publication.

At the other end of the spectrum are the folks who advocate taking a tiny advance (ideally in exchange for a better royalty rate), on the theory that this spreads the writer's income out over time (resulting in lower taxes) and avoids the problem faced by writers who got such huge advances on their last book that it couldn't meet expectations, and now no one will make an offer on their new one.

Again, neither choice is generally wrong, and either choice may be wrong for a particular writer, given that particular writer's financial circumstances and production rate.

In the same way, some writers choose to focus on trying to establish a series or on settling into a particular market niche, while others focus on spreading out into as many different areas as possible. Some writers advocate writing as much as possible, as fast as possible; others think that they get better results from working more slowly and carefully. Some take six months off from writing to publicize each book as it hits the shelves; others find their time is better spent working on their next title. Some change agents every five years or so; some stick with the same one for twenty years or more.

None of these choices are right in general, or wrong in general. Just as there is no one-size-fits-all method of writing, there is also no single best way of managing your writing career. It's a good idea to check out what other people are doing, but you have to decide for yourself whether what they are doing is something that is likely to work for you and whether you think it will work well enough that it's worth trying for yourself.

And it is always, always your own responsibility to decide whether something is not working and when it's time to change it…whether that's something that's not working in your writing style or whether something in your career seems to need rethinking.

Query Letter Principles

Lately I've been getting a lot of queries about, well, queries.

The first thing I'm going to say is that I am explicitly talking here about queries for novels. You do not query for short stories; short fiction is a quick enough read that it's as much work for the editor to answer a query letter as it is for her to read a submission, and reading the submission on the first go-around means the editor doesn't have to deal with it twice, so that's what they prefer.

The second thing is that a cover letter is not a query letter. If you're submitting a manuscript, whether it's short or long, the cover letter should basically say "Dear Editor: Here is my story of XXX,XXX words. I hope you like it. If you don't want to buy it, here is a SASE. Yours truly, The Author." You can fiddle with the phrasing, and if you have relevant credentials, you can put in a line or two about them (but not a four-inch list of semiprozines or every creative writing class you ever took), but that's basically it.

A cover letter does not include a story synopsis. It does not need one; the actual story is attached. It also does not include warnings about your lawyer or rave reviews from your friends and relatives (unless one of your friends or relatives is somebody like Stephen King, J.K. Rowling, or the owner of the publishing company). This ought to be obvious, but from the rant I heard recently from an editor, apparently it is a much more obscure and difficult concept than I thought.

Query letters are just that: a one-page letter containing a summary of your story and any other relevant information that you send to editors/agents in hopes that one of them will ask to see the manuscript. Query letters also should not contain warnings about your lawyer or rave reviews from friends, though they do generally contain a paragraph or two of story summary.

A query letter is a sales document. This is where most of the people who have trouble with query letters get off on the wrong foot. The first common problem is that the author does not think of the query as a sales document at all or does not think much about what that actually means. Instead of telling the editor the things the editor needs to know, the writer talks about what he or she found exciting about writing the book.

Sometimes, this is fine—if you've written an action-adventure, and what got you interested and excited and happy about writing it was the exciting face-off at the end between Darth Vader and Dr. Demento, describing what you're excited about is exactly what you want to do. If, however, what got you interested was the really neat backstory and/or worldbuilding that you did, or the nifty looped-and-braided structure you came up with, this is the equivalent of going up to someone who has a bad headache and saying, "I have these really pretty red pills—they're cubes, very unusual, and you just don't get this nice, shiny red color in pills" when what the person you're talking to wants to know is, "Will they get rid of my headache and how fast?"

The other really common mistake would-be authors make is to make the query letter sound like the back blurb on a book.

This is understandable; the goal of both the query letter and the back blurb is to get someone to read the book, right?

Not quite. The goal of a back blurb is to get the reader to buy the book for himself so that the reader can spend an enjoyable couple of hours reading it. The editor isn't going to be reading the manuscript for personal enjoyment. What the editor wants to know is not "Is this something I might enjoy reading, to the tune of twenty or so bucks?" but "Does this look enough like something other people will buy from my company that I'm willing to spend my precious time evaluating it?"

You may have written the greatest domestic comedy of manners since Jane Austen, and it won't sell if you send it to a line of action-adventure novels. You can, of course, write a query letter that makes your domestic comedy of manners sound like a clone of *The Hunt for Red October*, but as soon as the acquiring editor gets a look at the actual manuscript, she'll bounce it.

Therefore, the first principle of writing query letters is that the summary you give needs to reflect the actual book you have written. Also, notice that I keep saying "story summary" rather than "plot summary." A good many writers see "plot" and automatically think "action plot," even if the central, A-level plot is a political, intellectual, or emotional one. They end up describing the B-level kidnappings and car chases (which are really maybe ten percent of the story and not the center of the book) because that's "the plot," when the story is about two brothers trying to reconnect after not seeing each other for twenty years.

A corollary of this is to start where the book starts and end where it ends. If the protagonist is a starship captain with an interesting background, you don't start the query with two paragraphs about the interesting background that all happened before chapter one, nor do you waste valuable words explaining how many children the protagonist has after the book ends, nor do you describe the further adventures that might make great sequels when/if you get them written.

The second principle is to be as specific as possible (given that you have, at most, two or three paragraphs to fit everything into). "After many adventures" is not specific. "After being kidnapped, taming a dragon, and rediscovering the Library of Alexandria, among other things" contains specifics without going into so much detail that the mid-book adventures crowd out the other important stuff. Do not be coy. "In a shocking twist, Joe Hero must face his greatest fear to overcome his nemesis" is neither shocking, nor specific, nor even interesting… and could apply to about nine million slush pile manuscripts, all but about three of which aren't worth the editor's time. The synopsis should describe your specific book, clearly enough that the editor can tell that it isn't one of those other nine million.

Boiling ninety to one hundred fifty thousand or more words down into two or three paragraphs is, of course, hard. I'm going to provide some examples, so you can see how it works.

Here is a bad example of a query letter story synopsis:

"Having been tragically orphaned at the age of ten, Dorothy Gale has been sent to live with her only relatives on a farm in Kansas. She has great difficulty in adjusting to her new life and to her dour new guardians. As her aunt and uncle have no children and the farm is miles from the nearest house, Dorothy is lonely and friendless, a situation that will be familiar and appeal to many of the children who are the intended readers of this book.

A year after arriving at the farm, a freak storm separates Dorothy from her aunt and uncle and she has to make her way back to the farm on her own through many strange and startling adventures. My nieces love this book, and it is their favorite bedtime reading. My wife and her book club think it would make a great movie! I'm sure you'll want to see the manuscript and find out just how Dorothy gets home again!"

The book in question is *The Wonderful Wizard of Oz*, and all of the problems with it are things I've seen multiple times in real-life query letters: spending the first paragraph on backstory that is not even mentioned anywhere in the book (I made almost all of the details up), leaving out all the specifics the editor would really want to know about the actual book (Oz, the wicked witches, the Scarecrow, Tin Woodman, and Cowardly Lion), offering the opinions of relatives, attempting to tease the editor into finding out "just how Dorothy gets home." This query makes the book sound like a modern "problem novel" about grief and adjusting to a new situation, and the "freak storm" sounds as if it's the beginning of the climax of the book instead of happening on page four (which is where it is in my copy).

A somewhat different wrongheaded query letter might look like this:

"It's the middle of the Napoleonic Wars, and the British army is raising militia to combat a possible invasion. One such regiment is quartered in the sleepy village of Meryton, where officer George Wickham makes the acquaintance of the Bennet sisters. Both Elizabeth and Lydia are drawn to him, but it is Lydia who follows when the regiment is moved to Brighton. While older sisters Elizabeth and Jane struggle with their own romantic problems back home, Lydia and George must choose between duty and their hearts, and more lives than their own will be affected by their decision."

The problem with this query is, again, what it leaves out. None of the facts in it are wrong; they're all in the book. It's just really misleading—it makes *Pride and Prejudice* sound as if it's focused on the military angle, with George Wickham as the main character. And it's being coy about the ending again, but since the whole "plot summary" is about a subplot, it hardly matters. You could actually get a decent novel out of this summary, but it wouldn't be the one Jane Austen wrote.

What you want in a query is specifics:

"When a cyclone carries Dorothy off to the magical Land of Oz, her one desire is to return home. On the advice of a good witch, she embarks on a journey to the Emerald City to find the wizard who may be powerful enough to send her back to Kansas. Along the way, she rescues a Scarecrow and a Tin Woodman, befriends the Cowardly Lion, is attacked by wolves, and barely escapes from a deadly field of poppies.

Finding the wizard sends Dorothy and her friends on a new quest—to retrieve the broom of the powerful Wicked Witch of the West. Even when she is captured, Dorothy remains determined. In the end, she defeats the witch and returns triumphant to the wizard, only to discover that he is a fraud. Dorothy must embark on a third journey, to find the good witch who can tell her the secret of the magic slippers that will take her home to her aunt and uncle at last."

This is not, perhaps, the very best possible example of a story summary suitable for a query letter, but I'm a novelist—if I could say it in less than one hundred thousand words, I wouldn't have written the book in the first place.

Oh, and one other basic principle of query letter story summaries: boiling down fifty or a hundred thousand words or more into two paragraphs is going to sound stupid and thin no matter what you do. Accept it. Your query letter isn't competing against other people's rich, deep, fascinating novels; it's competing against other query letters. All of which also have to boil their rich, deep, fascinating novels down to two or three stupid paragraphs. So don't worry about it.

On Agents

Let's talk about agents. Actually, let's start *before* agents: Do you have a novel-length manuscript to market? If not, don't bother trying to attract an agent. Skip reading this section and go finish your book.

If you have nothing to sell, an agent can do nothing for you, and they aren't going to use up a spot on their client list on the off chance that you'll someday produce something worth their time. Also, if you are writing short stories, you won't be able to get an agent to handle them. Period, the end. Even when I was starting off back in the early 1980s, the only writers I knew whose agents handled their short stories were people who were still with the same agent they'd had since the 1960s or early 70s—and that was only because they were grandfathered in.

So you have a novel-length manuscript to market and you want not just an agent but the *right* agent. What do you do next?

Well, the very first thing you have to do is decide what you want in an agent and why. This means (1) finding out a little about what agents normally do and don't do for their clients and (2) thinking about why you write, what you want out of your writing, and which of the things you found out about under (1) are things you want/need.

(2) is something you have to do for yourself; nobody's list is going to be quite like anyone else's. (More on that in a minute.) So we begin with (1)—what agents normally do.

There are three main things that you can expect a legitimate, reliable agent to do: (1) submit novel-length manuscripts to markets, (2) negotiate contracts on your behalf, and (3) collect your payments from your publisher(s) and send them to you, less the agent's cut. Your primary agent (or their office) will handle these three things him or herself for the domestic market; for subrights (foreign language translations, movies, merchandising), the primary agent often uses subagents specializing in those areas.

To the best of my knowledge, current rates as of this writing are fifteen percent for first rights and twenty-five-plus percent for subrights (varying depending on why kind of subrights and what the subagent's percentage is). In other words, the primary agent takes fifteen percent of whatever the publisher pays you, when the publisher pays you. Under no circumstances do legitimate agents charge a reading fee or ask for an up-front payment (though some agents do ask for expense reimbursement for things like overseas postage, phone calls, and photocopying. These expenses should be minimal—even before email and Skype, I don't recall ever paying more than about fifty dollars for that in any given year—and they should be clearly itemized). This stuff should all be laid out in the agency contract.

In addition to the three basics (submission, negotiation, collection), agents can and do perform a variety of other functions, depending on their temperament and inclination. Some provide various levels of editing for their clients, ranging from a quick wash-and-brush copyedit to agents who act almost as co-authors or packagers starting from the first glimmer of the developing idea. Some provide in-depth career advice. Some are well-known in the business for their foreign contacts or for their ties in Hollywood. Some are really good at hand-holding nervous writers (and most of us get nervous at some point in the process). There are also different approaches to managing an author's career: some agents make it a policy to ask publishers for big advances; others, for retaining the maximum number of subrights; still others, for publicity packages or author promotion opportunities.

Everything mentioned above, beyond the three basics, is optional *at the discretion of the agent*. I'm emphasizing this because a lot of folks go into their agent hunt with really unrealistic expectations, which can end up with bad feelings on all sides. Know what you must have, what would be nice to have, and what you absolutely don't want an agent to do for you, ever.

Finally, there's the question of ethics. I'm not talking here about the problem of scam agents who are out to soak authors for all they are worth; if you do part two of the agent hunt right, you'll discard most of the scammers right off. I'm talking here about the author/agent relationship with publishers. This is, in my opinion, an area where it is vital to have a match between author and agent. Whether it's the agent who's willing to push the envelope and the author who's determined to be a goody two-shoes, or vice versa, the fact remains: if you aren't in agreement with your agent about which moves are ethical and which ones aren't, you're probably going to be very unhappy, very quickly.

These extra questions are where (b), above, comes in. For instance, speaking for myself, I don't want my agent editing my work. I don't expect a lot of career advice, either, certainly not of the "XYZ is hot now; you should drop everything and write that" variety. I do welcome input when I'm trying to decide what to write next (of the "which of these six ideas do you think you can sell right now?" sort). I don't expect financial advice. I do like a certain amount of reassurance when I'm worried and especially when I'm late on a deadline. I do want to have the occasional in-depth discussion about what the best next move would be—hold the rights for the backlist and try to resell them or start marketing them as e-books on our own? Concentrate on increasing foreign translation sales or put more effort into publicity for initial publication and hope the foreign rights sales follow? And I'm not interested in pushing the boundaries of what I consider fair and reasonable in my business dealings.

Other writers have different lists; you likely will, too. The point is to know what, if anything, you need/want, over and above someone to submit, negotiate, and collect for you. Once you have that, you're finally ready to start agent hunting.

On Agents, part the second

So you have your FINISHED novel-length manuscript and you've done some thinking about what you'd like your agent to do for you in addition to submissions, negotiations, and collecting from your publishers. Now it's time to actually start looking for an agent.

And the first thing you do is, you check around and make a list. If you have writer friends, ask who their agents are, whether they'd recommend their agents, what their agents do for them, and whether they've heard of any agents who're looking for new clients. Check *Literary Marketplace* to find out who is agenting your favorite authors. Make friends with your local indie bookstore owner (especially if the store specializes in your field)—they often hear a lot of industry gossip, including stuff about agents.

If there's a writer's organization in your field, check their website for information (the Science Fiction Writers of America have a number of excellent articles on the subject of agents and the etiquette of agenting, for instance; some other sites have lists of reputable agents). Some writer's organizations accept serious-but-as-yet-unpublished writers as affiliates (the Romance Writers of America and the Society of Children's Book Writers and Illustrators, for instance); the memberships can seem pricey to a cash-strapped beginner, but if you're in this for the long haul, you'll probably be joining something eventually anyway, and they can be an invaluable source of inside information. If there's an active local chapter, you'll have a place to meet other folks who are actively working in your field, many of them professionals. (Do remember that they are not there *just* to give you advice and answer questions for you, though. People are a lot more willing to talk to folks who've shown up at a few meetings and offered to help with organizing the refreshments than to someone who shows up out of nowhere with a list of fifty important questions that they *need* answered *right now*, and never mind that discussion about e-book contracts you were trying to have with someone else.)

The Association of Authors Representatives is another place to check; not only do they have a nice, informative FAQ, but their members are required to subscribe to a code of ethics that they have published on their website.

Once you have your list of named agents, check them out on the *Writer Beware* and *Preditors and Editors* websites to eliminate scam agents and as many other problem types as you can. Google the remaining names. Agents who are taking new clients often mention this on their websites; also, in this day and market, you want an agent who is web-savvy enough to at least have their own website (you'll want to decide for yourself whether a particular agent is or isn't putting enough/too much time into maintaining a web presence). You also want to check whether the agents on your list are familiar with the field(s) you're writing in; if you are trying to write hard action-adventure science fiction, for instance, you probably don't want an agent who sells mostly children's fantasy and paranormal romance. If you can, find out one or two of the agent's current clients and talk to them; if you can find one of the agent's ex-clients, talk to them, too. In both cases, try to consider what you're told objectively, bearing in mind that current clients are likely to be happy and ex-clients are likely to be unhappy and sometimes it's about personalities and not actually about service.

Yes, this is a lot of work. Yes, this will take a lot of time. Yes, you do all this before you ever write or email an agent. Why? Take another look at number three under "what you can expect a legitimate agent to do" in the previous section. Your agent is going to be collecting your *pay*. *ALL* of your pay, and then sending your share along to you. Do you really want to put that kind of trust in someone you haven't thoroughly checked out?

So you have a short list of possible agents. Now what?

Ideally, you've been sending that novel-length manuscript around (or at least querying) while you've been doing all this research. Ideally some editor will have offered to buy your book while you've been busy making up your list. Ideally you had the sense to tell said editor, "That sounds really great, but give me a day or two to think" and then immediately called the first agent on your short list to ask if he or she will negotiate this contract with a view to taking you on as a client.

If your life is that ideal, it is very likely that you'll get an agent to bite within two or three tries. Having an offer on the table is not a guarantee that you will get your first-choice agent; an ethical agent with a completely full client list won't take on another client even if they really, really would like to because they doesn't have the time—and trying to make the time will mean shortchanging not only you but all their existing clients. But if you've done your homework as outlined above, you have several possible agencies to try.

If your life is not ideal…well, the process is pretty much identical to getting an editor: you query the agent, submit the manuscript, and wait; repeat as necessary. The only difference is that the cover letter says "…and I hope you will consider taking me on as a client" instead of "…I hope you will consider publishing my book."

And just as with editors and publishers, there aren't any reliable shortcuts. If you have a friend who is a published writer, they *may* be willing to recommend you to their agent, which will probably get you put on top of the agent's slush pile. It will NOT get you an automatic acceptance; in some cases, it may not even get you to the top of the slush, depending on what the agent thinks of that particular author's judgment. And if you don't know the author (and I mean know them really well, not just as a casual acquaintance), don't ask for a recommendation. I personally find it annoying to have someone I've seen twice in the hall at a convention come up and demand a recommendation for a book I haven't even read (and probably don't have time to read right now even if that sort of approach didn't automatically make me disinclined to even look at the first page, which it does). I've been known to recommend people to my agent, and she's taken a few of them on, but in most cases I was the one who offered, based on what I'd seen of someone's work. The one time I recall being asked, it was (1) someone I'd known for several years, (2) someone whose work I loved (and she knew it), and (3) a request for a general letter of recommendation, not a specific referral to my agent (who, sadly, wasn't taking clients at the time).

A few last points: even in this day of the Internet, most agents live within a short driving distance from New York/Boston (if they're book agents) or Los Angeles (if they're screenplay agents). This doesn't mean you should ignore the perfect person who lives in backwoods Montana, but it does mean you should be a little more careful to ask around before you sign on with such a person, to make sure they are legit and have the experience they need to run an literary agency at a distance from their primary customers. If you can arrange to meet with a prospective agent at a convention or some other place you're going to be, by all means do so; if not, a phone call once you're at the negotiation stage is definitely indicated. A lot of writer/agent agreements fall apart because of personality clashes that might have been dodged if the two people involved had actually talked to one another for a few minutes before entering an agreement.

Hurry Up and Wait

The first thing you need to know about getting published is that the process is best described as interminably long stretches of boredom and anxiety, punctuated by moments of panic and frantic activity. And this applies to the whole process, not just the submission part.

Most people who want to be professionally published figure out pretty quickly that the submission process is the poster child for hurry up and wait. You get your submission package together (meaning whatever the publisher says they want, in whatever format they say they want it—portion-and-outline, full manuscript, hard copy, electronic, carved onto the back side of a replica of the Rosetta Stone, whatever). You run around getting packaging and postage together, collecting publishers' addresses and editors' names. You send it out.

And you wait.

Weeks. Months, sometimes. Years, even—it took more than a year for my very first rejection letter to arrive, and I found out later that at that time, that was a really fast response for that particular publisher. (They were three years behind on their slush reading. They've caught up since then.)

The thing is, everything else in publishing is like that, too. You get your acceptance letter, and there's maybe a flurry of email with the editor, and some tearing around to get an agent before the contract comes (if it's your first sale and you don't have an agent yet), and then you wait to get the contract. Once you get the contract, there's a flurry of negotiations (most of which happens between your agent and your editor, but since it's your book, you have to make the final decision about any compromises), and then you sign the thing and send it back.

And you wait.

Weeks, sometimes months, later, the check arrives. Some time after that (weeks or months again), you get a revision letter from the editor. There's another little flurry of activity—emails, usually—while you try to figure out how much of it you're willing to do and which bits are deal-breakers for either side, and then you sit down for a couple of months of revising.

At least this time you have something to do.

You send off the revisions and, you guessed it, you wait. If you are lucky, this time you actually find out how long you are going to be waiting because the editor tells you when the book is scheduled, and you can back up the next set of hurry-ups from that.

Eventually, about six to nine months before the book is due to hit the shelves, the copyedited manuscript arrives. You then have somewhere between two days and two weeks to hurry up and review all the changes, corrections, and queries the copyeditor made, and accept, reject, and answer them. Invariably, a really good copyedit job that you can just sail through, nodding your head, will arrive with the maximum two-week deadline for returning it to the publisher, while the hatchet job where the copyeditor decided to change "Yellowstone National Park" to "yellow stone national park" will arrive with a two-day deadline (usually just as you are leaving the house for a weeklong business trip).

You go over the copyedit, send it back, exchange a few emails with your editor about any additional clarification that's needed.

And you wait.

One to two months later, roughly, the page proofs or galleys arrive, and once again, you have between two days and two weeks to turn them around. This time, you're checking for typos and places where the copyedit changes didn't make it through to the final print version. Again, the proofs invariably arrive at the worst possible time. If you've really been humming along (or if your publisher is very slow), you may get proofs for one book and editorial revisions for a different one both at the same time, or even galleys for one and copyedit for a different one (which is a real nightmare because they both have similar, very short, not-very-flexible turnaround deadlines).

And then you wait for the book to hit the bookstores, wait for the reviews, wait to find out if they'll buy your next book. And the cycle continues.

Publishing is not for the impatient.

Day Jobs

People make time for the things they love. That is why I am always a bit skeptical at first when people tell me that they can't write because they have a day job, especially when their day job is a relatively non-demanding 40 hours per week.

People have to make time for the things they love because otherwise they never have time to do them. This is as true for full-time writers as it is for everyone else.

Up until 1985, I had a traditional day job, as a Senior Financial Analyst at a major corporation. I wrote five novels during my last five years at that job, on lunch hours and coffee breaks and weekends (when I got coffee breaks and weekends—it was a more-than-40-hours-a-week job for quite a few months out of the year). Since then, I have had a nontraditional day job: managing my writing career. As I have said with considerable redundancy, writing professionally is a business, and running a business, even a very small one, takes time.

From answering fan mail to data entry for my tax records, I have to do dozens of writing-related things that are not actual writing. By far the biggest chunk of time goes to the cluster of activities I lump under "publicity," which encompasses everything from the aforementioned answering of fan mail to updating my web page to scheduling appearances like autographing. And I do relatively little in this regard, compared to a lot of more socially ept and publicity-aware writers, because I basically hate this part of my job. (Most of it; blogging comes in here, and I like that.)

The second big chunk of time goes to selling. Not to the public—to editors. Yes, I have an agent, and she takes care of most of it, but she still has to come to me with ideas and suggestions and expressions of interest and the very occasional actual offer. Movie deals that fall through (I'm not sure there is any other kind, rumors to the contrary notwithstanding) can eat months. And there is a sporadic low-level stream of little things—notifications of anthology openings, requests to write the introduction to this book, requests to do a blurb for that one (which is several hours gone right there since I never blurb without reading the manuscript first), requests for blog interviews or newsletter articles, requests to donate copies of my books to this or that charity auction—all of which take time to read and answer even if the answer is "No, I'm sorry, I don't have time right now."

And then there's the financial stuff—mainly just tax records and royalty statements, in my case. I gave up on actually selling my own books years ago because even just the paperwork for collecting and paying sales tax was too much, and on top of that there was tracking for cost of goods sold. It wasn't worth the effort. But a lot of writers do sell copies of their own books at events or when they're on the road or just out of the trunk of their cars to random people they meet.

Then we finally get to things that are more directly related to actual writing, like research (of which a lot more is necessary than many people believe). Research falls into two categories: stuff that is related to current work in progress (currently the journals of Lewis and Clark), and stuff that is not related to anything…yet. (I just bought a book on the history of pirates that falls into this category, as did *Mad Princes of Renaissance Germany*. I mean, what fantasy writer could resist that title?)

The deceptive part of all this is that it rarely all shows up at once, which means it is easy to discount or overlook just how much time it all takes. If you don't allow for it, though, you can end up with less time to write after quitting a traditional day job than you had beforehand.

I'm not actually complaining…well, no, OK, I am. I'm on my third deadline overrun, and I really need to make this one or else, so yeah, I am complaining. But I still love my job, warts and all. I just don't actually have all that much more time to do the production part of it than I had back when I had a day job.

Keeping the Pipeline Full

Writing is a profession with a very long lead time. For the majority of writers, writing a novel takes somewhere between six months and two years. Then you have a wait for editorial revisions, and then it's usually one to two years before the book is published. And, as I mentioned earlier, the advance money is spread out in irregular chunks over all that time.

Essentially it's like a long, long pipeline, with the writer standing at one end pouring manuscripts in. No matter how fast you pour, it takes quite a while for the money to start coming out the other end. This can be intensely frustrating, especially at the start of one's career. One works for years for a payoff that never seems to arrive or that looks inadequate when it does finally start trickling out.

A lot of people get discouraged during that initial start-up period. It's hard not to. It takes a long time to fill up the pipe. Eventually, though, money does start arriving.

And that's where things get even trickier. Because that pipeline is long enough that a lot of the time, there isn't much correlation between how productive a writer is being and how much money is coming in. As your career builds up, there are occasional bursts of subrights money—which covers everything from foreign editions to audiobooks to movie options and merchandising—as well as money for reselling books that have gone out of print and had their rights reverted (though as e-books become a larger part of the market, I expect "out of print" will become a quaint notion and rights reversion will get a lot more complex). About half my income in any given year derives from books I wrote more than ten years ago.

So money does not end up being good positive reinforcement for continuing to work hard at producing stories. Which is the next place where a lot of writers get into trouble. Since that pipeline is really long, it is quite easy to let up and coast for a while because once you have filled up that long pipeline with work, the money will keep coming out for a good long while, even if you stop putting things in at the other end.

The trouble, of course, is that if you stop putting things in, eventually the flow at the other end dries up, too, and then it's another long, long haul to try to fill the pipeline up again. If I finish the current novel within the next month, I could sit back and not write another word for two solid years, and I'd still have a new book coming out each year. Three years, if you count the paperback versions. Of course, at the end of that time, I would have at least a three-year drought before any more books came out because that's how long it would take to refill the publishing pipeline, and if it takes me a year or two to write and sell a book, that gets added on top, so call it four or five years.

This is why I keep saying that discipline and persistence are the two most important characteristics a writer can have—because it takes discipline and persistence to keep writing when it gets hard or when it doesn't seem as if you need to (because the far end of the pipeline is spitting out enough money to meet your bills now, and three years from now is a long way off). Also because discipline and persistence are much rarer qualities than the talent that so many want to depend on instead.

Talent doesn't pay the bills.

A Few Things Not to Do

In the last couple of months, I've had the opportunity to observe a number of new writers doing things that…well, to say they don't work is a serious understatement. I'm not talking about the writing itself at the moment. I'm talking about the business end.

There are oodles of lists of what not to do in the submission process, and I'm not going to repeat them here—besides, you folks know all that stuff already, right? Unfortunately, a bunch of just-published-for-the-first-time writers have come up with a whole lot of brand new ways to sabotage themselves—and not just with industry professionals, like editors and agents, but with reviewers, publicity people, booksellers, readers—people who either are their ultimate audience or who have a whole lot to say about how and when and whether readers can look at the book.

A lot of it comes out of the facts that (1) publicity for a newly published title is more and more being pushed off on to the authors, and (2) authors are not publicists and often really, really don't know what they're doing. Even so, some of this should be common sense.

Take the matter of getting reviews. Usually the publisher prints up a couple of hundred ARCs (Advanced Reading Copies) and sends them to big review magazines like *Kirkus* and the *New*

York Times book review section and then sends the author ten or twenty with instructions to "send them out to places we won't think of." By this, they mean specialty bloggers, local papers that have book review sections that might be particularly interested in a local writer, local radio stations that do book stuff, library newsletters, already published authors who might give a blurb or a mention on their blog—anywhere that the author thinks might have a shot at getting some attention for the book but that isn't the sort of national-level, distributor-level publicity that the publisher is sending the ARCs to.

In other words, most of the people the author will be approaching are professionals, working in a professional capacity, from whom the writer is asking for free publicity. It is therefore not a good idea to tell them how to do their job—yet I have seen more than one letter explaining to a prospective reviewer just how important reviews are (they know) or saying that the reviewer's response will be considered inadequate if all the writer gets is a good review on their blog. No, the reviewers are supposed to go to Amazon.com, Barnes & Noble, Goodreads, and various other review websites and rate the book five stars in each and every venue. (Yes, more than one person did this. I didn't believe it, either, until I went and tracked down where I'd seen it before.)

When you're asking for a review, you're not doing the reviewer a favor by offering them a free ARC. They're doing you a favor. Don't demand extra work (which is what "don't forget to review this favorably on six review websites" is doing). If you've read their column/blog/whatever and you don't think they do a good job, don't waste your breath/paper/electrons telling them how you think they should do it right. Just don't send them the ARC. There are always more places you could send the things than you have copies.

Don't explain to the reviewer or publicity person that reviews are really, really, really important and you're trying to generate buzz so could they post/print their review on the first Monday in August so that the publicity will all hit at the same time. Not even if you say "please." It's their column/blog and they presumably know what they're doing; saying "The book will be released in the first week in August" is the most you need (and that's probably printed in the ARC, so you probably don't need it in the cover letter).

And speaking of Amazon reviews and other online reactions, arguing with reviews and reviewers is an extraordinarily bad idea. Arguing with people in comments is worse, if that's possible. Some people will hate what you wrote. Deal with it. Telling them that they're wrong makes you look like an idiot—they know better than you do whether they like the book or not. It doesn't really matter that they're having a knee-jerk reaction to something that reminded them of that horrible thing that happened in second grade that has nothing to do with what you wrote. The author yelling at a reader or getting defensive about his or her writing always looks bad, no matter how much of an idiot the reader is being. Yell in the privacy of your home, not in public—and remember, everything online is public to some degree.

Printing up your own bookplates and bookmarks as giveaways is fairly common these days, but if you're going to do it, consult someone who actually knows something about graphic design. Once you have them, do not, not, not go into bookstores and demand that they put your giveaways up by the cash register. That is premium space that large corporations pay actual money—lots of it—to get their items into; the store is not going to put your stuff there for free, and it is ridiculous to get mad at the overworked clerk who tries to politely tell you this (or who accepts your freebies without comment because they don't want to argue and then doesn't put them out, which you discover a week later when you pop around to check whether the store needs more).

Basically, don't act as if you're entitled to free space, free publicity, free comments, free reviews, free anything. And if you have no idea what professional behavior looks like, don't jump into the publicity game because under those circumstances it will only end badly.

Long Range Thinking

Back when I was getting started, I had the privilege of talking to a number of long-established science fiction/fantasy writers and writer/editors—Ben Bova, Gordon R. Dickson, L. Sprague de Camp, et al. One of the things I noticed sort of vaguely at the time but really didn't think about all that much was the emphasis all of them placed on managing the backlist.

Part of the reason I didn't think about it much was because at that point I didn't *have* a backlist; I had one novel just barely in print, another in production, and a third under submission. I didn't think any of that advice could possibly apply to me.

Fast forward thirty years, and I am now the hoary old pro with a much greater appreciation for what "managing the backlist" means, why it's important, and why I should have been thinking about it a lot more carefully all those years ago. It's my turn to pass the advice along for the latest generation of writers to ignore for a while. Hopefully a few folks will remember at one or more critical points in their careers.

First, a definition: for our purposes here, the backlist is all of a writer's published work that's more than two years old, whether it's still in print or not. Two years is kind of an arbitrary cut-off point; I picked it because if you have a hardcover/softcover deal, the book usually gets some sort of sales push on its initial publication in hardcover, then another push when the paperback comes out a year later. By two years in, it's definitely no longer "frontlist." If the book is a paperback original, it probably ends up being part of the backlist by one year after publication.

For a career writer, the backlist is important because it's a potential source of free money or almost-free money. You or your agent have to do some work to track it and to resell it, but compared to the amount of work it takes to write and sell a book in the first place, this is minimal. And these days, the backlist is even more important than it used to be, because of all the interesting new avenues for selling that the Internet has opened up, podcasts and e-books being only two of the most obvious.

One of the things this means is that an awareness of the importance of one's eventual backlist is highly desirable from very early in one's career. Everything that gets published will eventually be part of the backlist. If all you think about up front is the current part of the deal, figuring you'll worry about managing the backlist when the title becomes backlist, you're moderately likely to miss things that affect what you can do with a backlist title until it's too late to fix them.

Example one: Years back, a friend of mine wrote a trilogy that was canceled after book two. Annoyed, the author took the third book to a small press publisher so that the current fans of the trilogy could finish it. The small press did a bang-up job, and everyone was happy…then. Ten years later, the author had to turn down a lucrative offer from a major publisher for the whole trilogy because the small press publisher still had the rights to book three and was perfectly happy selling ten copies per year and so wouldn't revert the rights. If the author had been thinking about long-term possibilities, he could have made sure that the small press contract contained a reversion clause that would have made things simple—after ten years, or upon notification by the author if sales are less than 50 copies per year, or whatever.

Sorcery and Cecelia was originally published in 1988 as an "orphaned" book—the editor who bought the manuscript had left the company and there was no one at the publisher who wanted to push the book. It didn't do well and went out of print fairly quickly. My co-author and I got the rights reverted right away, as a matter of principle, even though there seemed to be no likelihood whatever that we could ever resell the title (lousy sales of the first edition tend to make other publishers less than eager to acquire a title).

Ten years later, things had changed and we not only sold *Sorcery and Cecelia* to a new publisher, we also sold two sequels, *The Grand Tour* and *The Mislaid Magician*. Ten years after that (i.e., now), we were able to get them all issued as e-books by Open Road Integrated Media.

The point about all this is that one never really knows

what is going to happen in the future. The market is constantly changing; so are the readers. People whose books were once wildly popular are now completely unknown (quick! Who was number one on the *New York Times* Bestseller list for the week of June 21, 1953? Annamarie Selinko's *Desiree*, number one for twenty-one weeks, that's who. Google is a wonderful thing), and books that died when they first came out become sneak hits months or years or decades later.

A writer who keeps this in mind will aim for long-run flexibility so as to keep as many options open as possible, for as long as possible. There's no guarantee that you won't make mistakes; it is practically certain that you will. If you think about the long-range possibilities, though, you can at least make conscious decisions: "I would rather have a small but steady stream of e-book sales now than hold off e-publication on the chance that I'll get a better deal in five years" works, for me, much better than "I want an e-book NOW!" and then, five years later, "Wah! If I'd only known there was a chance of this, I'd never have put out that e-book!" or "I'm holding out for a big deal" and then, five years later "Wah! Nobody's interested in buying this; I could have had five years' worth of e-book sales if I'd only done an e-book back then."

Deadlines

So I was asked about deadlines, specifically whether they're good or bad and whether they interfere with the process or enrich it.

The answer is "it depends on the writer." I know writers who freeze up at the mere thought of a deadline and writers who can't seem to write anything without one.

It also depends on what else is going on in the writer's life at the time. A writer who is under a lot of pressure in other areas of her life (unexpected illness, serious financial problems, a death in the family) may suddenly find that having a deadline is one thing too many to handle, even though it's never been a problem in the past. I've also known writers for whom the existence of a deadline was the only thing that kept them going during times of illness or financial crisis. Mileage varies.

So first comes the old "know thyself" part. Which sort of writer are you?

If you can't write (or can't write much or steadily) without a deadline, and you don't yet have one, you'll have to figure out some way to persuade your backbrain that you have to get chapter three finished by next Saturday. Some folks take writing classes because it gives them a time and place at which they have to have some amount written. Others join writing groups for the same reason (though for this to work, the writer has to really take it seriously, and I've seen too many critique groups where eighty to ninety percent of the participants just didn't have anything at all for any given session, which makes it hard to take it seriously as a deadline). Still others make a solemn promise to someone that they'll see pages every Sunday, with the recipient given the right to impose penalties. (I know one writer who missed this sort of deadline and was forced to buy the recipient a hot fudge sundae…and watch her eat it.)

The more common problem, though, seems to be people who freeze in the face of a deadline.

If you're this kind of person, the first thing I recommend is that you stop for a few minutes and think about why this happens to you. And be brutally honest. At least half the people I meet who have this "problem" only have it with their writing. They don't freeze up when faced with a deadline at the office, and when they had papers due in college, they just buckled down and did them (OK, sometimes at 4:00 a.m. the day they were due, but the papers got done).

For folks like this, the problem is not so much the deadline as it is the fact that it's a fiction writing deadline, which says to me that a good part of the difficulty is in the way they think about writing fiction—as something scary and special and not subject to the normal rules of work. Fixing this is a matter of attitude adjustment, which is never easy and which may involve lots of poking around in your childhood and your backbrain in order to figure out what you really think, why you have these reactions, and how to change them to something more productive.

But that still leaves the other half of people who have problems meeting deadlines. There's still a lot of variation in this group: some people are convinced that no one can do creative writing to deadline (this is not true; many people can. The question is whether this particular writer is one of them or not); some chronically underestimate how long it's going to take them to write ten pages (or how many pages it will take to cover X amount of material); some simply have bad time management skills; some procrastinate out of habit; and some go into such a panic at the thought of missing a deadline that it becomes a self-fulfilling prophecy—their brains start running around in circles and screaming about the deadline instead of making up the stuff that will allow them to actually meet the deadline.

Again, diagnosis is key. If you're having trouble meeting the deadline because it is one thing too many on top of your child's cancer, dealing with your soon-to-be-ex-husband's lawyer, taking care of your elderly parent, and worrying about layoffs at your job, what you do will be very different from what you'd choose if the problem is habitual procrastination or underestimating how long it'll take to get ten pages done.

Once you know why you're having problems meeting deadlines, most of the solutions are common sense. There are a gazillion books on time management and beating procrastination out there; if one of those is your problem, it's fairly easy to figure out what to do. (Actually doing it is another story, but no one can really help you with that part.) If it's lack of discipline, the solution is likewise both obvious and not something anyone else can help with.

If you're one of the folks who panics and/or freezes… well, if your brain and/or your backbrain is busy worrying or panicking about when something is due, it doesn't have a lot of room left for actual work. Basically, you have to find some way to take the pressure off. In extreme cases, this may mean writing everything on spec (you aren't required to sell on portion-and-outline after you've started publishing professionally, and of course if you haven't sold anything yet, you pretty much have to work this way, as I don't know any publishers who buy uncompleted first novels).

In less extreme cases, negotiating a deadline that's much longer than you need can help and so can an understanding editor, agent, and/or spouse/partner. The main thing that seems to work, though, is forgetting about the deadline and refocusing on getting the writing done. For some, this means putting the deadline out of their minds and logging lots of concentrated time writing on a regular basis. Having a writing buddy to check in with (or to go for a "writing date" with—one of my friends and I have taken to hauling our laptops to a café once a week to spend an hour or two working) can help. If you're of a more methodical/analytical mind, figuring out how many words per day you have to write to meet deadline and then making sure you meet that minimum every single day can work, as long as you only think about today's word count and not that looming, panic-inducing deadline.

And of course, asking other writers for their methods of beating deadline anxiety can be useful, as long as you don't take any of them for the One True Method. Every writer develops his or her own tricks as they need them.

Collaborating

People go into collaborations for different reasons, and each project and co-author is a different situation. Sometimes two or more writers collaborate because they came up with a brilliant idea in the bar at three in the morning, and it still looks brilliant and fun the next day. Sometimes the collaboration springs out of something that began as a mutual writing exercise. Sometimes two friends discover they're working on very similar projects and decide to share. Sometimes one of the writers is trying to cheer up the other or help them out of a hole. Sometimes two writers find that they work much, much more effectively when they toss ideas back and forth between them and then dash to the computer to get something down than they do trying to crank stuff out on their own.

Similarly, there lots of different methods for collaborating. One that works well for a lot of people is "I write my characters; you write your characters," in which each writer comes up with some characters, they decide mutually on which ones will be the central viewpoints, and then they work out (in advance or as they go along) which scenes will be from which viewpoint. The writer who has that character writes the scene.

Another one is to have one viewpoint character and switch writers at the end of every scene or chapter. I heard once that this is how Fred Pohl and C.M. Kornbluth worked, with one writer spending his chapter getting the hero into a terrible fix and leaving him on a cliffhanger and the other writer then having to write him out of the mess. I don't know if that's true, but it would certainly explain the plot pattern in some of their collaborations.

I've also known collaborations where one writer does one type of writing—all the dialogue, say—and the other puts in all the action or the narrative. This works really, really well when each writer is playing to a particularly strong point, but it requires a whole lot of trust in each other.

Yet another collaboration style is the one where one writer does the prep work and a detailed outline, the second writer comes up with a first draft, and the first writer does the rewrite and polish. This is especially common in the sort of commercial collaboration wherein a publisher matches up a new, up-and-coming writer with one who's more experienced and who has a large following, in hopes of boosting the newer writer's audience, but there are other collaborative partnerships that just naturally fall into this pattern.

And there's the one where both writers are in the same room, with one looking over the other's shoulder, switching places whenever the one at the computer gets stuck or the one watching can't stand it anymore. It doesn't seem to be common (since it requires both writers to be in the same place), but I know at least one set of roommates who work this way, and I've seen several folks do this to produce short stories while both were attending a convention.

There is no one right way to collaborate with someone; there is only what works for a given pair of collaborators. I've worked on several, and each of them was different. For the Kate and Cecy books, Caroline Stevermer wrote Kate (and later Thomas), and I wrote Cecy (and later James); we didn't talk much about plot, and the only editing of each other's writing we did was for typos and consistency. Because they were in letter format, we were essentially doing the "you write your characters, I'll write mine" method, plus the switch-writers/viewpoints-at-the-end-of-each-chapter method. The big advantage of working like this was that there was never any problem with the characters all sounding alike, or with one of us not really "getting" the other's characters well enough to write them from the inside.

For two other collaborations (each with a different author), we picked a viewpoint character, one of us wrote until we got stuck (which was sometimes in mid-sentence), and then we handed it off to the other person. The next writer would go over the previous writer's work, editing and making changes, then go on until they got stuck, whereupon they'd hand it back. The editing-and-revision pass kept the viewpoint character's characterization and the overall style remarkably consistent, even though, as I said, sometimes we switched writers in mid-chapter, mid-scene, or mid-sentence.

Another collaboration I worked on involved you-write-your-characters-I'll-write-mine, but with lots and lots of joint plot planning and a lot more editing of each other's chapters than Caroline and I did.

In each case, I don't think the results would have been nearly as good if we hadn't worked the way we did. Trying to write Kate and Cecy with lots of plot planning and each of us editing the other would have (1) killed the books dead (Caroline is the sort of writer who cannot discuss her work in advance of writing it without killing it), and (2) probably smoothed out the voice and style more than was appropriate for an epistolary novel. Trying to write a single-viewpoint collaboration without editing each other would likely have made it lumpy and inconsistent in style, voice, and quite possibly stuff-that-happens (also, in both cases, there really wasn't anybody else either of us wanted to write. It was that character's story and nobody else's).

All of the successful collaborations I'm familiar with have been ones in which both of the writers were having a tremendously good time. The fun quotient isn't a guarantee that the project will get finished, much less reach professional publication—I've had loads of fun working on each and every collaboration, but the three Kate and Cecy books are the only ones that ended up published, and only one of the others made it to any sort of ending.

One of the great things about collaborating is that if you pick the right collaborator (and the right method), you can write until you get to a sticky spot, then hand it off to your collaborator and let them deal with it. In most cases, what is sticky for you will not be sticky for your collaborator (and vice versa), which minimizes "stuck time."

Another big advantage is that whatever you've just written has an immediate audience—your collaborator—who is just as excited about the material as you are. There is nothing quite so motivating as wanting to show off for someone you know is going to giggle and squeak and gasp in all the right places.

If you're considering collaborating with someone, there are a number of things to remember:

1. If both of you don't feel as if you're doing eighty percent of the work, something's probably off. If you're the sort of person who's going to track time, effort, and word count in some misguided attempt to make sure each of you contributes the same amount to the project, you are probably not well-suited to collaborating, and if feeling as if you're doing eighty percent of the work is going to make you grumpy, you probably shouldn't try it, either. Collaborations are not usually twice as much work as a solo novel, but they do involve more total work than a single-author book. This means that if you

divide the total work of a collaboration in half, each author will be doing less work than if they wrote a solo book, but not fifty percent less. If you're not prepared to feel as if you're doing more than your share (and unwilling to recognize that your collaborator also feels this way and that both of you are, in fact, doing more than you expected), you may wreck the project and possibly the friendship.

2. Collaborations are a meshing of two different processes as well as two different writing styles. A number of the folks I know who have done successful collaborations do not work the same way on their collaborations as they do on their solo stuff. Sometimes both writers end up with a sort of half-and-half compromise style of working that they can both live with; sometimes they do it one person's way rather than the other's; and sometimes, the collaboration gets done in a way that neither person uses when writing on their own. Be prepared to be flexible.

When you're collaborating, you have to be willing to adapt to your collaborator (and vice versa) in terms of working methods as well as stuff like plot and characters. If one writer normally works in huge bursts of activity with long fallow gaps between, and the other is a three-pages-a-day plodder, they may want to think twice about a collaboration method that means they have to switch off every time a scene, chapter, or POV character changes. If one writer is a "can't talk about it in advance" sort and the other isn't, you'll have to experiment to figure out whether the one who usually can talk isn't allowed to do it at all (which can kill the project if they're a must-talk sort of writer), or whether the two of you can talk to each other but not to anyone else, or whether the must-talk writer can talk to anyone but their collaborator.

3. The whole point of a collaboration is that it's something both of you are doing. I've known several promising collaborations that collapsed because one of the writers got so invested in his or her characters or plot twists that they absolutely refused to let the other writer change or invent anything. In a collaboration, no matter how much you love a character, plot twist, idea, style, chapter, prologue, or background detail, you are not the one in charge. You can argue, beg, plead, whine, and blackmail to get your collaborator to agree to take the story where you want it to go, but in the end, you both have to agree. There's no point in winning the argument if it results in your collaborator being totally blocked because they just don't think it would happen that way. If you can't agree, you may need to take your lovely, shiny plot/character/idea/whatever and turn it into your own solo book.

4. Collaborations are jointly owned. This means that unless you have a written agreement that spells out contingencies, each of you owns half the project, and neither of you can legally do anything with it (or with the characters, setting, elements of background) without the other's permission. Much of the time, this is not important, but when it does become important, it is absolutely vital. And if you can't manage to work out a basic agreement that says either of you can/can't write about the world/characters without the other's permission, and that if one of you dies, the other one gets full ownership/gets to make artistic and business decisions/can't touch it again, then you probably aren't going to manage a successful collaboration. This is not about not trusting your collaborator. It's about protecting both of you. People die; they get Alzheimer's; they lose interest; they go haring off after possibly brilliant but incompatible alternatives

("Why don't we change everything to stream-of-consciousness and make this into a pastiche of *Ulysses*?"). I've known several authors who've had to abandon months or even years of work because they didn't bother making a written agreement and others who've avoided serious potential problems because they had it all spelled out in advance.

Most of the failed collaborations I've observed or been involved in have failed for artistic, rather than monetary, reasons. One writer lost interest, or discovered that she couldn't slow down/speed up to the other writer's working speed, or got so fascinated by a character or plot twist that he wanted to make it the center of the story (and in at least one case, went off and did so, with the erstwhile collaborator's blessing). Or one writer was so invested in her vision of the story or characters or background that she couldn't let the collaborator contribute or make changes.

5. Not all collaborations go to completion. Based on my experience, most of them don't. It's OK to start one that's supposed to be strictly for fun. (That's how Kate and Cecy got going, after all. We didn't know it was a book until after we finished; we thought we were just having a whale of a good time.)

Which brings me to the last point: if you are not having big fun, collaborating may not be worth the aggravation. And it will be aggravating at times—when your partner is late with their next draft, when he doesn't have time to meet and work out that little plot problem you need to settle, when she wants you to meet at an inconvenient time, when he or she is excited and you're feeling worn down (or vice versa). It can be fun anyway. If it isn't, it's OK to talk it over with your partner and agree to stop.

IN SUMMARY:
THERE IS NO ONE TRUE WAY

One of the things you find a lot in writing books and classes are prescriptions: This is THE (only right and workable best) way to write/develop a career as a writer.

And they're wrong. Or so I think, anyway.

There is no One True Way to write. (This is practically my motto and has been for years.) I know professional writers who outline, who don't outline, who start at the beginning, in the middle, at the end, who start with characters, with plot, with setting, with theme, with idea, who develop whatever bits they're missing in every order imaginable. And they all write books that sell, and many of them win awards.

But I don't know any writers at all who wouldn't really like to make the writing process easier for themselves. And I have often seen individuals who have had very little contact with other writers fall into the trap of thinking that the way they have found that is natural for them is automatically the one and only way that will work for everybody.

It's understandable. When you have struggled and labored for years, and suddenly you stumble across a method that makes things (relatively) easy, it's like the sun coming out, or winning the lottery, or any other revelation. It often doesn't occur to people that that other way of doing it, the one that was soooo difficult and sooo laborious for them, might really work well for some other people. Or that their shiny, wonderful, perfect method might not be nearly so perfect for other writers.

Even very experienced writers and editors fall into this trap.

It took me several years to cure one of my friends of telling me encouragingly, "It doesn't have to be long, you know." For her, short is easy and long is hard; I'm the exact opposite. She has finally accepted that I can do it fast or I can do it short, but not both. She doesn't understand it, but she accepts it. And she's had far more experience with other writers of various types and temperaments than I have.

What all this means is that first, it is worth trying out even the most ridiculous-sounding recommendations for how to write because you never know when one of them might turn out to work for you. And second, if whatever method you are using *isn't* working for you, it is not only OK to move on and try something else, it is a really, really good idea to do so.

Writing is a product-oriented business. Editors want a good story; they don't really care how you get to it. Worry less about how you are going about doing it and more about whether what you are doing works. Or better yet, don't worry about it at all.

Just write.